MODEL BUILDERS' MANUAL

First published in July 2019
Reprinted February 2021, October 2022, February 2024 and January 2025

A catalogue record for this book is available from the British Library.

ISBN 978 1 78521 555 1

Library of Congress control no. 2019934644

Published by Haynes Group Limited,
Sparkford, Yeovil,
Somerset BA22 7JJ, UK.
Tel: 01963 440635
Int. tel: +44 1963 440635
Website: www.haynes.com

Haynes North America Inc.,
2801 Townsgate Road, Suite 340,
Thousand Oaks, CA 91361

Printed in the UK.

Acknowledgements

Over the years, many people and companies have assisted with information and advice – too many to name individually. However, particular thanks go to:

Dr David Baker for the introduction
Paul Fitzmaurice at Modelling Tools for loans of tools and equipment
David Jefferis at Scale Model News
Dean Milano for access to his collection
Mark Mattei for access to his collection
Andy Yanchus for access to his collection
Volker Vahle at Revell Germany
Jean-Christophe Carbonel at Model Stories
Darrell Burge at Airfix
Jamie Hood and John Greczula at Round 2
Frank Winspur, Dave Metzner and Bob Plant at Moebius Models
Larry Thompson at Pegasus Hobbies
Nick Argento at Glencoe Models for injection moulding advice
Dr Mike Ivacavage for 3D printing advice
James Gilbert at Giblets Creations for 3D printing advice
Ed Sexton and the late Bill Lastovich at Revell-Monogram
Pete Vetri and Rick Delfavero at Atlantis Models
Tony James at Comet Miniatures/Timeless Hobbies
Vince Brown at modelsforsale.com
Nigel and the late David Hannant at Hannants Ltd.
Neil Fraser, at Pocketbond/Bachmann UK
Tony Radoservic, at Horizon Models
Cris Simmons, for advice on millimeter scales
Members of the New City Scale Model Club

MODEL BUILDERS' MANUAL

A practical introduction to building plastic model construction kits

MAT IRVINE

Contents

OPPOSITE **Examples of some of the author's model collection on display at a Model Engineer Exhibition.**

Foreword

By Dr David Baker

Modelling goes back a very long way – at least to the earliest of organised human societies. The representation in miniature of objects in the natural world and those made by humans populate museums in every major city. There seems never to have been a time when people tired of representing what they saw around them through the honed skills that define humans themselves – the manipulation of hand and fingers to create out of natural and artificial materials objects which they admire, find of interest or fear. It is almost a hallmark of civilisation and the connection between tactile skill and the human imagination.

Models duplicate in miniature all of real and full-scale life including fascinating objects, instruments of peace and war and mechanical devices of all kinds. This connection between the full-scale world and that reproduced in miniature is a two-way street: it can educate and inform and it can display the way complex machines work; but it can also provide a three-dimensional understanding of basic principles and show how they can be made better, stimulating improvement in the real-world object.

As a young schoolboy I excelled in art (apparently!) but found great satisfaction in expressing that by building models of my favourite subjects: aircraft, armour, rockets, racing cars and sailing ships. To me it was a 3D world of imaginative and creative expression and it taught me a lot about the real world around me. It allowed me to physically assemble in ways not altogether different from the real thing, machines that fascinated me. It unified my desire to create something by building it in miniature and it brought together my other two loves: science and engineering.

Quite soon I connected all three and while I dived into an obsessive fascination with science, I maintained my love of model-making and continued to pursue this to the point where it became a conduit to another life. Why? Because through modelling I was drawn to the world of engineering and I realised that only by being closely involved with machines, how they worked and how they were operated, could I realistically unify all three pursuits.

At first, I was able to absorb the operating principles of aircraft, rockets and spacecraft by building scale models of them. And then, when I became professionally involved with the emerging space programme – the unifying catalyst for everything in my life – did I recognise the great value that I placed on creating duplicates in miniature. I am profoundly convinced that it was this base of creative building that unified my love of science, technology, engineering and mathematics – STEM subjects which are essential for stimulating, fulfilling and expressing the aspirations of a new generation of young people today.

When Mat asked me to write a few words for this commendable book I was at first unsure – I am not a good model-maker and I have no right to be recognised as competent in this activity. However, I was convinced when I read here that Alec Issigonis may have used Meccano for prototyping. He did.

When I was a boy, my father took me to meet Sir Alec (I must have been only 15 at the time) and this precocious youth promptly regaled the great man with talk of models. He patted me on the shoulder and said something to the effect that if I built models I could understand the inner workings of the machine in a way no other designer would. I never forgot that.

This book is to me a joy, itself crafted by a Master Modeller with enviable skills and a keen mind, identifying the nuances of accuracy versus compromise and with the ability to work quickly. This book is a compendium of crafts vital for honing skills and understanding the background to what is still a thriving, growing and important activity for young and old, a melting pot for future careers through engaging with a fascinating and relaxing hobby – and for some, like me, from youth to manhood, a great pursuit on the path to a connected career with real-world machines and objects of infinite curiosity.

David Baker
East Sussex, April 2019

Chapter One

In the beginning

Although here we are dealing with a subject that began in the 20th century, the idea of creating models, miniatures or replicas of objects around us is hardly new – it goes back centuries, likely aeons.

Models of ships, as well as figures, have been discovered in Egyptian tombs; Leonardo da Vinci built models of his ideas (even if, due to the engineering limitations of the time, he could not build them for real); theatre designers in Shakespearean times would have created miniatures of production sets to ensure The Bard would approve. Dolls house miniatures have been a mainstay of the hobbyist since the 19th century and children of all ages would have built cardboard castles to accompany their toy soldiers and carved model boats to float down the local river.

What is a 'scale model'?

As this book aims to mainly concentrate on the hobby side of building 'scale models', it's probably a good idea to define what exactly a 'scale model' is in the first place.

By definition, a 'model' is a representation of a 'real' object. Hence the use is not restricted to an Airfix Spitfire, but can include catwalk models wearing clothes that are the 'representations' of what the fashion industry will be producing for the coming season. (And can lead to confusion when it comes to typing into an Internet search engine: 'looking for models'!)

Models need not necessarily be 'to scale' – constructions sets by the likes of Meccano (originally in the UK) and Erector Sets (in the US) built excellent and intriguing models, but they were not 'to scale' in the general sense. Compromises were made because the parts themselves were not built 'to scale'. Meccano

and Erector Set strips and panels were laid out in set sizes, with holes in set places, while cogs and wheels were a predetermined size. Yes, you could build models – and very good models, too – but they were not to true 'scale'. However, they were useful for prototyping many new items that were mechanical in nature.

There is the story, almost certainly true, that the designer and engineer Sir Alec Issigonis used Meccano sets for prototyping. Although best known worldwide for designing the Mini, and turning the engine sideways to save space, he had worked for British Motor Corporation (BMC) for many years previously and also designed the more traditional Morris Minor. Apparently, the gear ratios of the Minor match the Meccano gears, which had been used to prototype the gearbox!

RIGHT Lego makes amazing creations – here is London at LEGOLAND®, Windsor, UK. But they are not 'scale models' as such; get closer and the 'edges' start to show!

BELOW Models built for wind tunnel testing. This is the X-20 Dyna-Soar at the United States Air Force (USAF) Museum, Dayton, Ohio, USA.

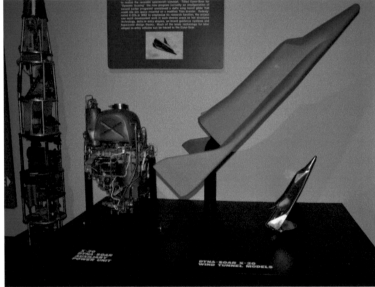

In more recent years, this 'semi-scale model' aspect has been dominated by Lego and its many imitators. Here, again, although the parts abound, with new ones seemingly coming onto the market every week, the builder is still limited to the overall restriction that they are all 'Lego parts'. Models can be built, but they will not be 'scale models'. From a distance, many Lego models can look very realistic and almost to scale, but as you get closer the surface begins to break up and takes on – to use computer terminology – the appearance of a bitmap. It is almost as if building with Lego is 'digital' model making, while true scale models are 'analogue'!

Consequently, a scale model has to far more closely resemble what it is a model of. If the real object has a curve, the model has to have a similar curve in the same position and with the same graduation.

What are models used for?

Although this book concentrates on the hobby side of model making, the subject crosses many other disciplines, and is well grounded in many professional careers.

The use of models runs across the board

LEFT A classic model of an airliner, a Boeing 747 in TWA markings. This would likely have started life in a travel agent's. It now resides in the Air Line Museum in Kansas City, Missouri, USA.

of engineering and product design. Models are used in prototyping anything from a new kettle to a complete aircraft. They are used in engineering for wind tunnels testing of new aeronautical shapes; they form architectural designs for new buildings and layouts for new estates or complete towns; they are widely used in museums, displays and exhibitions. Then, of course, there is the well-known use in the special effects departments of entertainments industries.

Many aspects of the above have indeed now been augmented and some may have been completely taken over by Computer Aided Design and Computer Aided Manufacture (CAD-CAM). A new house can be completely designed using a computer, and computers are used to control the manufacture of parts. But the building association putting up a new estate of houses will likely also have a traditional model of what the whole structure will look like when completed. Potential purchasers still like to look at something that is tangible, even if it is in miniature form and not just an image on a computer screen.

Cars can be completely designed 'in the computer' these days, but 'clays' (1:10 scale models) and even full-size vehicles modelled using clay as a top layer are still produced. Subtle changes can be made by sculpting the clay, almost quicker than changing the computer program, and the result can be immediately viewed full size. The eye can invariably immediately tell if something 'looks right', more so than a computer saying 'yes' (or maybe 'no').

Computers have also, of course, taken over a vast expanse of the entertainment industry – primarily film and television but, of course, there is a larger market that includes advertising and even corporate videos. Here, the introduction of CGI (Computer Generated Images/Imaging) has replaced a lot of traditional model making. Besides irritating a lot of traditional model makers (especially when early results were inferior), as with anything involving computers the results have got much better as the technology and program writing has improved. But it is still thought that traditional three-dimensional models are better as some things – the 'dirt' is invariably better when done 'for real', although CGI can do many things faster and easier than some traditional techniques. Most special effects supervisors will use

ABOVE Architectural models are still made – this one intriguingly shows the plans for the Space Shuttle Endeavour's new home at the Californian Science Center in Los Angeles, USA.

LEFT Clay models are still made for cars. This is a design exercise at the California Science Center.

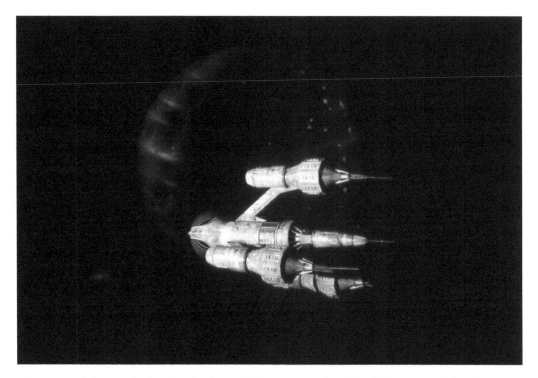

whatever technique suits the storyline best: CGI when it is better, traditional models when they are better.

Materials for model making

Model making can and does use a very wide variety of materials, but this book deals primarily with the 'plastic scale model construction kit', which we can define here as a miniature representation of a full-size object, made to a scale, intended to be put together from a number of parts and manufactured from some type of plastic.

The first models that fulfilled all the criteria of a 'plastic scale model construction kit' appeared in Britain in the 1930s with the famous Frog Penguin kits. The subject was primarily aircraft, with a smattering of ships and vehicles for good measure. These were the very first kits that fulfilled all the requirements of a 'plastic scale model construction kit', although the 'plastic' here was not polystyrene, but cellulose acetate.

Polystyrene

These days, the vast majority of 'plastic model kits' are made from polystyrene. Polystyrene is a very stable hydrocarbon polymer with the formula $(C_8H_8)_n$, first invented almost by chance (as many chemical materials are) in Germany in 1839. It's a very stable material when 'cold' and retains its rigidity through a wide temperature range. However, as it is a thermoplastic it will melt if it gets too hot (it starts to soften at around 90°C).

The actual burning of polystyrene is not recommended; it gives off a thick, black, highly unpleasant smoke. But when it is correctly heated into liquid form, it can be melted, injected and moulded, and is capable of being melted down and moulded again numerous times (as opposed to a thermosetting plastic such as Bakelite, which when 'cured' retains that structure and cannot be melted down to be used again). Polystyrene was initially thought of as a replacement for aluminium and, in fact, polystyrene is as strong as aluminium in the latter's basic form.

Cellulose acetate

Polystyrene didn't come into general use until after the Second World War. Up until that time, any plastic model kits (and these were really only the Frog Penguin kits) had to be moulded in cellulose acetate – this is manufactured from wood pulp but is also a thermoplastic (formula: $C_{76}H_{114}O_{49}$). Although cellulose acetate is visually similar to polystyrene, it is far less stable and far more prone to warping, which occurred with many Frog Penguin kits, making them – in effect – unbuildable.

Even after the general introduction of polystyrene in the later 1940s/early 1950s, many manufacturers continued to use cellulose acetate as a moulding material for model kits for a few years, as it was still easily – and cheaply – available. These include companies that are now obsolete, such as Gowland & Gowland and Varney, but also names that still survive (some to a lesser degree than others) including Airfix, Revell, Monogram, AMT, Hawk and Jo-Han. Virtually all of these early cellulose acetate models suffered from warping, even when built, hence the almost universal move in the early to mid-1950s to the far more stable polystyrene. Even then, one manufacturer – Gowland & Gowland – hung on to cellulose acetate for longer than most as its founder, Jack Gowland, was reputed to like the 'bright colours' that cellulose acetate was available in, as opposed to the dull, translucent raw state of polystyrene.

Expanded polystyrene

Polystyrene can be 'foamed' to make expanded polystyrene (EPS), which generically tends to

BELOW Universities are increasingly offering courses for model making, both traditional and CGI. This is the model making department at Bolton University, UK.

go under the trade name 'Styrofoam' (although this should really only refer to products of its inventor, Dow Chemical). As it is very light, it has been used in the structure for flying model aircraft, but is not usually a part of static model kits. It is, however, extremely useful for building dioramas (see Chapter 9, pages 126–139).

Acrylonitrile butadiene styrene

There is one other styrene variety that is found in the static model industry: acrylonitrile butadiene styrene (ABS). This tougher form of styrene is used particularly by the commercial plastic parts manufacturer, EMA. It is also intriguingly used for many of the kits made by one of the newer American model producers, Pegasus Hobbies – about the only mainstream manufacture to do so. ABS is a prime material for 3D printing (see Chapter 10, pages 150–153).

Enter the computer

The manufacture of new model kits has not been immune to recent developments in technology. CAD-CAM has sidestepped many aspects of traditional model kit design and manufacture, and the images can even be used when it comes to laying out the instruction sheets. CGI has not solely been used by the entertainment industry, as box art can be generated using very similar methods.

3D printing

3D printing – or rapid prototyping, as previously called – is currently in its very early stages but is growing at an exponential rate, already starting to replace some traditional methods of producing small parts for models – and even whole kits. This technique is likely to have the greatest influence on model making – and, almost certainly, all manufacturing. As 3D printers get cheaper, working processes become faster, quality improves and the resulting parts being produced become larger and more complex. This is likely to be the biggest change of all for modellers, although it could still take some time before we literally get the Star Trek Replicator in the home and with the press of a button (or these days, a voice command) get it to produce a complete

model kit (or 'tea, earl grey, hot', for that matter). See Chapter 10 (pages 150–153) for more on 3D Printing.

Traditional methods

Even with all these technological changes, there is still plenty of room for traditional techniques. Model-making design courses at universities and colleges are increasing, not decreasing; movie makers are returning to traditional model-building techniques, instead of insisting everything is 'computers', to create miniature special effects sequences; and the range of hobby model kits, even with the loss of many original names, has never been wider.

Using modern techniques has also meant that complexity has increased. Although some kits still have the number of parts you can count on two hands, these are increasingly very much in the minority, and kits with a hundred, several hundred and even a few over the thousand are, if not that common, certainly making up an increasing percentage.

Mind you, this has brought about a steep

ABOVE An intriguing variation on a 'model-making theme' – a model of a 'full size runner' built for a General Motors display in New York. The 'kit parts' are from an actual Chevrolet Corvette, and kit historian Andy Yanchus, right, is attempting to remove them, watched by model writer Jean-Christophe 'J.C'. Carbonel, left.

BELOW Models and the one construction kit used in conjunction with the full-size object, here the Taylor Aerocar at the Seattle Museum of Flight.

RIGHT Museums are the logical place for many models to end up – though here in the 'model shed' at the Pima Aerospace Museum in Tuscon, Arizona, USA, they can be a bit of a mix.

BELOW Three full-size 1:1 scale fibreglass YF-23s guard the gate at the Pima Aerospace Museum, in Tucson, Arizona, USA.

increase in price! Long gone are the days when a model kit could be bought for 2/- (2 shillings in British predecimal currency – these days make that 10 pence) or 49 cents in the US. Most kits will cost a minimum of £15 (18 Euros/$20) and many are considerably more expensive. But at least they're still available.

The intention

This book aims to be a 'starter' manual for any potential model maker. It's also hoped that it can be a good read about all associated aspects of model making that could interest the more experienced model builder, possibly even enlightening them with a few nuggets of information they were not aware of!

The book will cover the following:

- The history of how the modern kit industry developed, the instigators of the hobby and the names forever associated with it;
- How a model kit is decided upon and is then designed;

LEFT HMS Victory as a model galleon (one of 200 or so!) at The House on the Rock, located in Spring Green, Wisconsin, USA.

ABOVE Mixing your modelling: here, one of the original 'Motherships' from the movie *Close Encounters of the Third Kind* is on display at the Udvar-Hazy section of the National Air and Space Museum, in Chantilly, Virginia, USA.

- What sort of tools, paints and materials you will need to build model kits;
- Scales – the variety of such, and why they are so important;
- Basic builds of a conventional injection styrene model kit;
- Other associated techniques that may not be styrene but are long associated with the hobby kit, such as white metal, photo-etch and resin;
- The ideas and techniques behind dioramas – putting your models into some setting.
- Joining model clubs, attending shows and entering competitions;
- The odd and relatively new phenomenon of collecting – as opposed to building – model kits;

What this book doesn't do is demonstrate intricate individual builds of models – but that will be left to future volumes.

A WORD ON PLASTIC

In a world concerned with the overuse of plastic, and particularly its disposal, producing a book primarily concerned with this material may seem slightly obtuse. But plastic cannot be 'uninvented' – it is here to stay – and without plastic we would not have many of the products that make life more straightforward.

Although plastic has to be produced in the first place – and that involves industrial processes that have their own detractors – it is mainly with the casual disposal of plastics that the current situation rests. Does this affect the amateur model maker? Overall it has to be a 'no', as anyone buying a plastic model kit presumably has the intention of building it and keeping it, so 'disposal' doesn't really come into it.

Even if you don't keep the box and plans (as many modellers do), being made of paper and card these are straightforward to recycle. You may have more of a problem with the polythene bags the runners are packed in these days, but recycle these yourself as storage or for masking when you are painting. The only materials you will otherwise have left over are the runners for the kit parts. These actually could be recycled as they are made of polystyrene, one of the easiest types of plastic to recycle. Whether your local council does take polystyrene for recycling is another matter, but if you can find somewhere that does – and the amount is worthwhile – polystyrene can be recycled. The recycling plastic code for polystyrene is 6.

Chapter Two

The manufacture of a model kit

When a model kit company decides to produce a new subject, the first decision has to be just what that subject is! In the earliest days of the modern model kit – the last few years of the 1940s and into the 1950s – the fledgling model kit industry probably had it fairly easy as all subjects would have been new! The industry, with a few exceptions, was an Anglo-American invention. At that time, both countries had many aircraft manufacturing companies, which led to the subject that became, and remains, a worldwide favourite: aircraft.

Aircraft modelling had existed for decades before then, since there had been real full-size aircraft, but early models would have been built out of wood, invariably using balsa for its lightness, with tissue paper covering the wings. Many were built to fly, powered by rubber bands.

Then kits were introduced that could be called, in modern terminology, hybrid kits. These were mainly wood, but had a growing percentage of plastic parts. The aircraft fuselage would still be balsa and the wings possibly still covered with tissue paper, but the wheels, propeller and maybe a few other parts started to appear moulded in plastic. These models were not intended to fly, but would be static display items.

Soon after came the all-plastic kit. The very first were indeed the Frog Penguins of the 1930s, but they are almost a separate subject in their own right. For all intents and purposes, the 'modern' plastic model construction kit began, post-war, in the late 1940s and certainly was in full swing by the 1950s.

In the UK, Airfix was predominant but there were also smaller, and now-obsolete companies such as Eagle (later renamed Eaglewall, Kleeware and Merit – the last actually still exists as a company but long ago gave up the production of model kits) and the later incarnation of Frog, which had continued from before the Second World War. In the US, there were considerably more names, including Hawk, Strombecker, Pyro, Renwal, Aurora, Adams, ITC, Comet, Lindberg,

Jo-Han, Monogram, Varney and Revell – many names that still survive today, at least in one form or another.

All produced model kits of aircraft, initially favouring their own country, so Airfix's first aircraft kit in 1953 was the Supermarine Spitfire. In the US, the first 'all-plastic' aircraft model probably came from Hawk with its Curtiss R3C, although Varney with a 1:48 Boeing PT-17 Kaydet is also a contender, as is Renwal with

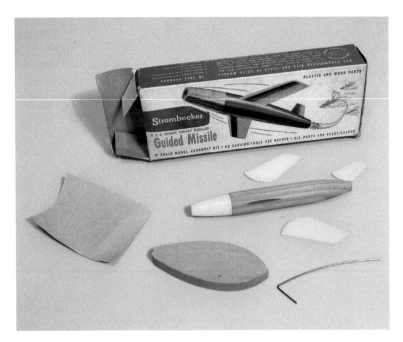

ABOVE The Strombecker Matador Missile: an example of an early hybrid kit using wood and plastic, in this case cellulose acetate.

a small-scale Martin Mars. (Though the last wavers between being an 'unassembled toy' and a 'true model kit'.)

The Hawk kit would have dated back to as early as 1948, though still using cellulose acetate as a material (it switched very early to polystyrene in the following year). First aircraft kits from Revell appeared in the US in 1953 and were all then-current US military planes: Lockheed F-94, Vought F7U-1 and Grumman F9F-6.

For both Airfix and Revell (and all the others) these first examples were, to put it kindly, simple in the extreme. The Revell releases, for example, had no undercarriage (though they were later retooled to include these), and pilot figures – assuming they were even there – were invariably one piece or even built-in crude representations as part of the fuselage halves, and were laughingly simplistic. But the industry had to start somewhere, and this was the very beginning.

Obviously, since the 1950s the catalogues of all the model companies around the world grew and grew. These early aircraft examples from Airfix and Revell were replaced with more up-to-date kits – Airfix has retooled the Spitfire, including other marks and in other scales, a number of times.

Of course, it wasn't all aircraft. Ships and cars also found their way into these early lists. One of the original American companies, Monogram had dabbled in hybrid kits, primarily wood but with some plastic parts, from 1952. These were aircraft, but its first 'all-plastic' kit was actually a car: a Midget Racer, a small one-seater racing car manufactured at around 1:16 scale in 1954. As with other examples, the first issue was moulded in acetate, only later moving to styrene.

Around the same time, Strombecker – another early US name – made hybrids kits of

RIGHT Monogram's first complete plastic kit. Here it is still moulded in cellulose acetate, but it was later moulded in polystyrene.

Regulus 1 and Matador missiles using wood and plastic. Issued in the early 1950s, these were never turned into all-plastic versions, but Strombecker had moved into making all-styrene kits around 1955.

The 1960s were the real heyday of hobby model making, with many of the model companies growing their catalogues, including kits that are now – half a century on – still available, and despite all the modern tooling techniques since introduced, still make up into excellent models.

Select your subject

So a subject has been selected. These days, it may even have come from a modeller. Contrary to popular urban myth, model companies actually do listen to suggestions from their customers, though this has to be balanced against practicalities: will this new kit sell in sufficient numbers to a) get production costs back and b) make a profit? All companies can likely quote examples of some modeller contacting them, requesting some obscure variant of an equally obscure aircraft, saying, 'I'm sure it will sell, I'd buy at least two…'. Unfortunately, kit companies cannot survive producing a model kit that will only ever sell two.

PHANTOM FRUITBAT

Top of the mythical requests from British modellers was for a kit to be made of the 'Fairey Fruitbat' (or, sometimes, the 'Farley Fruit Bat'). This has gone down in modelling annals as being an actual request for an actual aircraft which didn't actually exist!

Research, research, research

When a subject has been decided upon, the next task is to gather as much information about the subject as possible. You would locate photographs of the original, plus if the subject still exists for real it would be photographed anew. Then the engineering plans – if they existed – would be all gathered

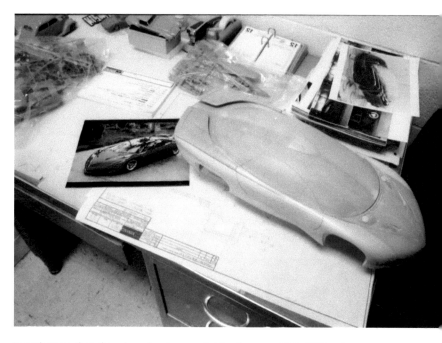

together so that the plans for the model itself can be created. This process has happened over the years and, as a starting point, still happens today – the initial research still has to be done. The next stages can now vary because of the differences in modern techniques that have been introduced.

The type of kit has to be decided. Is it going to be a simple kit intended for beginners or a far more complex kit to tax even the most experienced of modellers, or something in-between? The breakdown of the parts also has to be decided: is this aircraft fuselage going to be split vertically (as would be usual)? Some cases may dictate that a horizontal spilt would be better. How detailed are the wheel wells and the cockpit? Does it include pilot figures? Is it carrying weapons?

Making the parts

In an earlier time, these parts would actually be made to a larger scale than the finished object using wood, carved by hand, or resin. Some manufacturers, Aurora being one, made models in parts and to actual size from carved cellulose acetate. These parts could then be used to cut tooling using the pantograph method. Pantographs can reproduce the parts either at actual size or using a reduction method.

For injection moulding, two types of mould are common: one was cut directly into steel,

ABOVE Wood can still be used to make original patterns. Here is the Pontiac Banshee show car from Revell. Photos showing the original car are being used for reference.

almost certainly using the pantograph method; the other uses the copper-based beryllium compound to cast the original same-size parts, ending up as the female cavity. The former is cheaper and more hard-wearing, the latter is more expensive and wears faster, but the beryllium can be reused.

Beryllium is also highly suitable for 'non-regularly shaped parts' such as figures, and companies that specialised in figure kits, especially Aurora, used a lot of beryllium tooling. Unfortunately this meant that once the sales of that particular model had dropped off and modellers wanted a new kit, the tooling was scrapped and the tool frame and beryllium reused, hence the kit could not be reissued as the tooling did not exist. Remember that in earlier times the idea of collectability had yet

to surface and there was no compunction in destroying original tooling. This, however, has not stopped new tooling being made by a number of new companies that have emerged in recent years, either by retooling the kit completely or by using a set of original parts and copying them to make new moulds.

Sprue or runner?

With the tooling cavities for the individual parts created, the flow channels are cut. The main channels run round the cavities in the best possible pattern to maximise flow. These are called the runners – NOT sprues – though the latter term has gone into the modelling lexicon to such an extent it is likely impossible to dissuade its use these days. There actually is a 'sprue' in the whole moulding process,

BELOW Close up of the part that makes up the vent chamber, here on the fan belt assembly from the engine of a car kit.

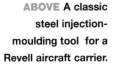

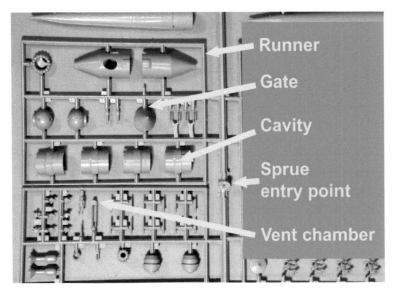

Runner

Gate

Cavity

Sprue entry point

Vent chamber

but this is the main core of molten styrene that flows into the mould and would not be found in a kit. The only exception could be a small stub in the centre of the runners.

From the runner and for where the molten plastic enters the cavities, a small opening is cut out called the gate. Ideally this has to be a compromise between keeping it as small as possible, so the amount of area to be cut and trimmed on the kit part when being assembled will not be too large, and making it large enough to allow the molten styrene to flow quickly enough – injection moulding is extremely fast! Manufacturers try to make the position of the gates as inconspicuous as possible and limit their number per part. But the styrene has to flow as fast as possible, so some parts will end up with a number of gates.

In older kits, there may have also been small tags added, mainly to the smaller parts, containing the part number; this number could be engraved on the inside of the larger parts themselves. These days, this has mainly been abandoned, replaced instead by notated diagrams in the instruction sheet.

The final task in creating a standard type of mould is to add ejector pins. These will push the moulded parts from the cavities. For a new tool, they will be flush with the parts, so as not to produce a mark, but they can start to show up as either small circular bumps or depressions when the tooling wears. To avoid this potential situation, they are usually situated on the inner surfaces of parts, so they ideally would not be seen in a finished kit.

Test shot

The mould will then be test shot to ensure that the cavities fill quickly enough and there are no 'short runs' – where the styrene hasn't flowed completely into the cavity. This can usually be corrected by cutting a 'venting chamber' somewhere on the opposite side to the gate, into which extra styrene can flow, ensuring the cavity is filled. It will mean an extra gate in the part and a small bit of extra styrene runner to remove. The parts will then be test assembled to ensure everything does, in fact, fit as it should and any modifications to the tooling can be done at this stage, before it

ABOVE **Test shots are examined to make sure the fit is perfect and there are no short runs.**

ABOVE **Test shots are often used at model shows if the final version is not available. Here is Grandpa and Herman Munster from Moebius Models.**

LEFT **Aurora used to make patterns from carved acetate, such as this example for a proposed, but never released, Wacky Races model from the Andy Yanchus Collection.**

ABOVE The Airfix Mosquito is an example of a completely CAD-CAM produced kit.

goes into production. Occasionally, kits have appeared in totally the wrong colour styrene – a bright red Spitfire, for example. These are usually test shots, as they have been run in whatever colour plastic was sitting in the hopper at that time, and their appearance on the market was almost certainly unofficial!

Small kits may only use one such tool, but many modern kits in larger scales could involve several. This is particularly the case if parts are to be moulded in several colours, or one runner will need to be chrome plated, especially common in model car kits. Some older tooling could in effect be two or more moulds within one frame, each fed with a different colour of styrene. This was common in earlier days when the overall painting of models was not exactly unknown, but far less common than it would be today. These days, kits are usually moulded in a single colour – white or light grey being the favourites – allowing for easier application of paint. However, there are some models, mainly intended for the 'junior' or 'beginners' end

of the market, which can still be moulded in several colours 'for play value'.

One aspect that won't be immediately apparent from opening the box of a kit is that the parts could have very well been from tooling made with 'inserts'. These are, more or less, what they sound like: individual removable sections – inserts – of the tool where different kit parts can be made. This is especially common in recent years where costs have risen exponentially, and so the maximum possible usage has to be got from any particular tool. If several different marks of an aircraft can be produced, which can increase sales as you can sell the same basic kit several times over, the overall costs will be proportionally reduced. The parts for the basic version are cut into the steel, but areas where a different version could be made are initially left empty. Perhaps one version of the plane has a different nose section with a radome, or a waterborne version that needs floats not wheels, or a different set of weapons under the wings. All these options can be covered by using inserts, which will be cut separately and fitted into the blank area of the main tooling.

Colour moulding

Regarding moulding in several different colours, there are techniques, primarily developed by Japanese companies, to inject multicoloured plastic into one mould so you can have different coloured parts on a single runner! This involves special insert techniques, becomes highly complex and was never that common – frankly, it can really be regarded as a gimmick. If different colours are required, it's far easier to have separate tooling for each colour.

Separate tooling will especially apply where there are clear parts, such as the classic windows for a car or truck and aircraft cockpit canopies. Here a separate tool has to be used to receive what is actually raw styrene, which is clear in nature. As many of these parts will be small, if the company has several similar kits with clear parts, these could very well end up in what is called a 'family tool', where the parts for several kits are moulded simultaneously.

Separate tooling also applies with cars, trucks and motorcycles that have 'rubber tyres'

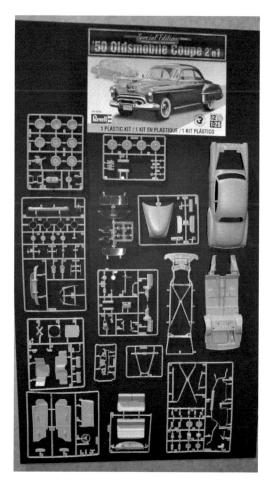

LEFT What you get: this is a display example of runners from Revell-Monogram of the 1950 Oldsmobile Coupe. Here, all is moulded in light grey as is common these days with most kits, plus clear windows and lights.

BELOW Usually there will be separate moulds for each colour, though they could very well be in the one tool.

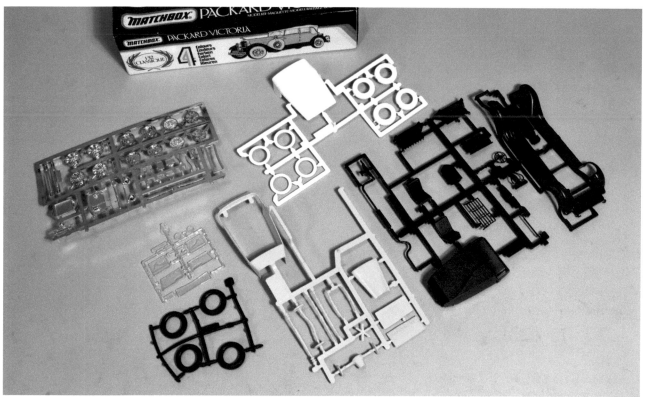

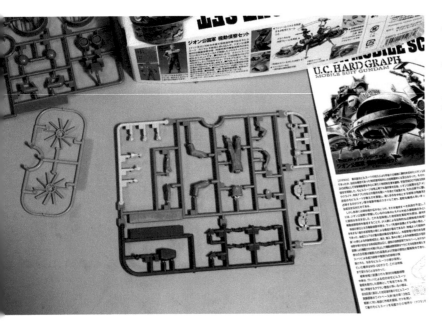

else besides) is termed 'high impact'. This is because the clear raw styrene is very brittle, and besides the actual colour pigment for the parts, rubber in the form of polybutadiene is added to make the parts less inclined to snap. The exact proportions of styrene to colour can vary tremendously, but an average ratio ranges from between 50:1 to 100:1. Incidentally, this brittleness of clear 'raw' styrene will be apparent when it comes to cutting the clear aircraft canopy or car window glass. Far more care has to be taken, as it will shatter much more easily than with the coloured parts that have a certain amount of rubber added.

Some already-used styrene can be recycled and added (to save cost). This can come from kit parts that have not moulded correctly and remains of runners, sprues and similar. It is usually not common to add much reused styrene, as it already contains colour, rubber and lubricant, so will affect the whole percentage balance.

The styrene itself comes as pellets with the colour and rubber already incorporated. Reused styrene will have to be ground up to a similar size if it's to be added. Hoppers above the injection-moulding machine then feed it through heating elements to make the styrene molten at around 200–230°C (400–450°F), then the tooling halves are pushed together in the machine by hydraulic rams and held by high-pressure clamps at around 300lb/in^2, or even greater, while the

ABOVE Multiple colours can be moulded into the same runner. This is from a Bandai 'robot' kit, but it is really a gimmick.

and military vehicles with flexible tank tracks. In the vast majority of cases, the tyres and tracks are not produced from actual 'rubber' (though there have been exceptions to the rule), but a vinyl compound that mimics actual rubber. These will be produced from their own separate tooling, and again could be a 'family mould' that is shared between several kits.

Ready to run

If the tooling moulds correctly, the kit run can be started and actual kit parts can be produced. Most styrene used for kits (and much

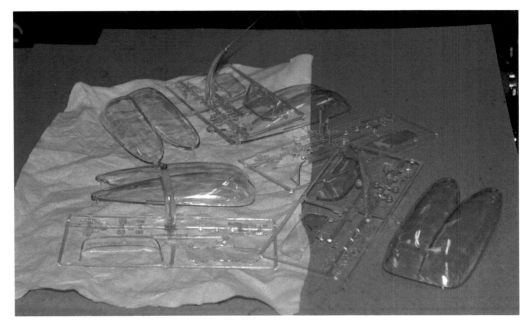

RIGHT Clear parts are made using a separate tool. These are for the custom top of the Monogram 1958 Thunderbird.

RIGHT **The hopper that feeds the styrene pellets into the injection machine below. This is one of the machines Revell-Monogram used in Illinois, USA.**

molten styrene is injected. The tooling has built into cooling cavities (much like a car engine block) where water rapidly cools the parts. The mould is then separated and the parts are ejected by the pins built into the tooling. This whole process works extremely quickly – most modern injection machines will recycle in 30 seconds, so you can see the amount of wear and tear on both the tooling and the machine is tremendous.

The emerging runners are then examined to ensure all parts have moulded correctly so they can be passed on to the next stage. For most practical purposes, only a percentage of the emerging runners are examined, though if a fault is discovered the whole previous batch will likely be recycled.

In earlier times much of this process was labour-intensive. People had to remove and collect the runners by hand, maybe even cutting them along predesignated divisions, so they would fit a particular box size. These days, the process is far more automated, with only inspection being left to the human eye. The usual procedure is to have an example of the runner alongside each machine, just to ensure the correct parts are being moulded!

PLASTICS
- 36 injection mold machines
- 4.5 million pounds of plastic used each year
- largest machine, 500 ton injection mold
- 165 plastic colorants used

LEFT A notice in the Ertl shop that indicated – at that time (1980s) – the amount of machines and materials that were in use.

LEFT Close up of the tooling – centre with the green pipe – in place in the injection machine.

RIGHT The layout of parts that should come out of that particular tool. These are parts from the Monogram 'Three Fighting Men', (more correctly 'The Three Soldiers'), a model of the Vietnam War Memorial in Washington DC.

Injection machine operators are not expected to intimately know the layout of each runner they are moulding!

Boxing clever

Although these are the main components of any model construction kit, they are not the only parts to any kit. There is, after all, the box itself. Almost universally gone is the idea of building the kit to fit the box, which resulted in some very odd 'box scales' (see Chapter 3, pages 35 and 39); instead kits are built to a constant scale so boxes are manufactured to fit

a general subject. A 1:25 scale car kit will fit a certain size of box, while a 1:32 car will need a smaller box. A larger box is logically required for a 1:48 scale P-51 Mustang than a 1:72 scale equivalent. Similar-sized boxes also have an advantage for packing and shipping, and even shop shelves, where boxes of the same size are more convenient to store and display. (Some American chain stores are known to have made standardised box sizes and shapes a stipulation when ordering model kits!)

In earlier days, some manufacturers were known for packing smaller kits in polythene bags – Airfix being the best known in Europe – though several American companies also used this bagged method. The advantages of this format were that they used less material, the instructions were printed within the header cards and they were lighter to transport. However, they couldn't be stacked on shelves, they needed special stands, and the idea lost favour, with Airfix and the rest eventually moving on to traditional boxes.

The artwork used in the boxes has become a collectable subdivision of model kits. The most famous example goes back many years to when Revell changed from moulding its kits in cellulose acetate, which consequently required one type of cement, to moulding in this 'new-fangled' polystyrene, which required a totally different type of glue. To this end, Revell had previously printed an A (for acetate)

BELOW Storage of the tooling: pallets are required, so they can be moved with a forklift truck – injection-moulding tooling is extremely heavy.

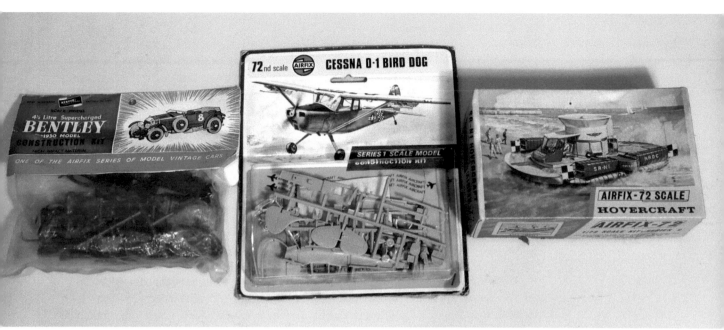

on the boxes. Now it uses an 'S' (logically for styrene). This was a purely practical warning to the modeller, as styrene will not stick with glue designed for acetate. In more recent times, when collecting became 'the thing', this whole subsection of S-type kits suddenly became collectable. It didn't matter what the subject matter was – after all, Revell made a very wide range of construction kits – it was just the fact that they were moulded in styrene and needed the 'S' on the boxes! (See Chapter 5, page 75.)

Art work

The box also needs a design and image to indicate what is inside. Over the years, box art has ranged from the extremely good to the, frankly, abysmal. But in the most part, box art has averaged out as being pretty good, interesting and artistic in its own right. The vast majority of early box art – and, in fact, this is still the case – uses specially commissioned paintings of the subject, the vast majority being from well-known artists in their field. Over the

years Airfix commissioned, among others, Roy Cross; Revell, Jack Leynnwood; Monogram, Richard Locher; Hasegawa, Shigeo Koike; Tamiya, Masami Onishi; and Aurora a whole range, including John Amendola, James Bama and Harry Schaare.

In recent years, some companies have made an effort to reuse the original artists, or similar, when reissuing old kits. Glencoe Models used John Amendola to recreate similar artwork for rockets that he had done decades before for some of its reissues, and also commissioned specialist space artist, Ron Miller, to recreate the style of Cal Smith who had done some

ABOVE Packaging changes over the years. Airfix moved from polythene bags, through short-lived blister packs, to proper boxes.

RIGHT New packaging (bottom) for the Glencoe Models' reissue of the classic Strombecker Convair Manned Observational Satellite Vehicle, top. (Glencoe shortened the name somewhat). Box art for the original was by space artist of the time, Cal Smith. Current space artist, Ron Miller, did the new artwork with homage to the original.

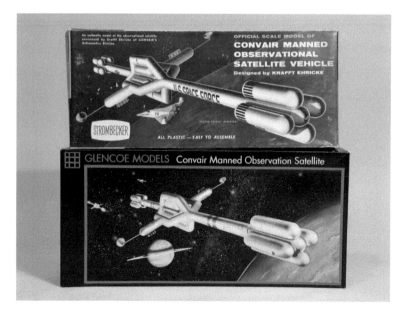

original Strombecker spacecraft artwork in the 1950s.

Original art work, especially from the American companies, specialised in being printed on semi-gloss paper, which was then glued to plain boxes. The boxes tended to be more substantial and the semi-gloss approach gave a certain quality 'look' to the finished result. Later issues, even using the same artwork, are almost always printed directly onto the card of the boxes, but the 'look' was different and never quite had the same appeal. It consequently meant original issues of kits – well, certain kits – became more valuable with these particular boxes.

Later, the styles of boxes changed, and there was a time when legislation required that the box artwork should depict what was inside the box, so the appearance of built-up models, built to varying degrees of professionalism, started to appear. To everyone's relief this didn't last long, probably as they didn't depict what you actually got in the box – only what you could do with what was contained. Legislation never actually insisted that you had to put a photo of the various runners, a set of decals and plans on the box, though that was actually inside the box! These days, the idea of a good piece of artwork being used for the box art has fortunately reappeared in the vast majority of cases. However, in recent years, the use of the whole box for artwork has become more common. Revell Germany, Round 2 and Glencoe Models do this in many cases, and more details have appeared, even images of the runners, so in a roundabout way these do show what you actually get in the box!

BELOW Contemporary artwork for the 1950s by Richard Locher. His signature can be seen just below the nose of the Tri-Motor.

Cement part 1 to part 2…

A set of instructions or plans also has to be devised to show how the kit should be assembled. With a small number of parts, plans could be kept very simple, with the classic 'cement part 1 to part 2…'. Initially, with the modern kit industry being almost entirely Anglo-American, the plans for such from Airfix and Revell were universally in English, as they would be sold exclusively in English-speaking countries. The plans gave precise details about the assembly order and tips were invariably added throughout the text. Renwal was extremely good at this, with full details as to the actual names of the parts, where to avoid getting cement if parts were moveable and painting instructions. It was very proud of its 'no show cementing technique', where cement could be placed precisely so as not to be prominently visible on the finished model.

This was fine for a kit going to an English-speaking market. If a kit was reissued for a market where English was not the predominant language, the plans – and, in many cases, the box art – were modified. However, there was also a growth of non-Anglo-American model companies, such as Heller in France or Tamiya in Japan, which would use their own primary languages.

In more recent years, with kits being distributed universally, legislation has required more languages to be included in any particular kit. North America was fortunate in that it could be covered with three: English, Spanish and French. However, European Union legislation required all 21 official languages of the Union to be used. This meant that writing the classic 'cement part 1 to part 2…' became somewhat impractical, therefore keyed diagrams became the norm to indicate all the processes. Some of the more obvious ones range from 'cement', 'don't cement', 'do the same the other side' and 'apply decals'. Others are far more obscure and you invariably have to delve into the small print to find out what they are actually intended to mean.

Markings in the form of water-slide decals are found in the majority of kits. With the subject matter of the kit having been decided, then comes the decision of which variant, version

LEFT Modern instructions need to take into account their worldwide distribution. Here is the same Revell kit for two markets: the US issue (left) only requires three languages; the European version (right) needs most official languages of the European Union!

and form it will be depicted in. Perhaps mainly associated with aircraft and either national military marking or airline company schemes for airliners, most kits will have lettering, panel lines or other forms that can only really be depicted with a decal. This also applied to cars, which could have wild custom flames, or armour with unit markings. All of these would have to be researched thoroughly, a decal sheet layout designed and then finally printed. Initially, most model companies did their own decal design and printing in-house, but recent developments and the splitting up of effort has seen that special decal companies have now been subcontracted to produce decal sheets for many mainstream companies. Cartograph in Italy is perhaps the most well-known maker of decal sheets, which it does both for itself and for model companies around the world.

What you get

In the majority of kits, this is what you get in the box: the parts, the plans, the decals. But there could be more. With model vehicle kits, you'll almost certainly get the vinyl tyres. With tracked AFVs, you could find the tracks themselves, made from a similar material.

In earlier times, original compounds of the vinyl had the unfortunate side effect of reacting with standard polystyrene and melting it! This meant the parts had to be packed in such a way that they were away from one another, otherwise you would get tyre marks on styrene parts – and it always seemed to be on the clear parts! They also had to be kept clear of the decal sheet, as the vinyl chemical compound could affect these as well. Packed in the box was one thing, but this problem was exacerbated when the kit was assembled, as you then couldn't avoid having the vinyl tyre in direct contact with the styrene wheel, or the tank track around the idler. There were many examples of the wheels for early car kits being melted! It didn't help that this fault wasn't discovered for some years – it took this length of time for the chemical reaction to take place, but by then it was almost certainly too late.

Later experimentation with newer compounds of vinyl got around this, but it meant for a time that some companies such as AMT supplied injection-moulded styrene tyres, rather than vinyl, which never looked quite right. The new vinyl compounds solved the problem and meant a return to what is, after all, a more detailed and authentic approach. With older kits, there are options for avoiding direct contact with the vinyl, such as ensuring the styrene parts are well sealed with, for example, a clear varnish.

You may also get metal axles or pins to hold wheels and in some cases, especially in military kits, real chains and tracks made from metal components. Some modern kits also contain other non-styrene parts, such as those made from resin, white metal or photo-etch, but these are dealt with in far more detail in Chapter 10 (see page 140).

Getting the news out there

Publicity for the new kit also has to be contemplated. There's no point in producing the best model kit the world has seen if no one knows about it. Consequently, model catalogues started to appear early on, when forward planning seemed to be more organised than could be said of more recent years. Modellers would be anxious to get their hands on the latest yearly catalogue to see just what they could expect over the next 12 months. And at that point, the announcements were almost always followed through. If a kit was announced as being issued in, say, 1965, you could be pretty sure it would be arriving in 1965. There were a few famous (infamous) 'non-arrivals' – kits that were announced but subsequently not issued – but these can be almost counted on the fingers of both hands. These days, it is more common for announcements to be given far closer to any potential release date – and even then, many rumours of 'potential kit releases' are still not followed through.

As it was long before the home computer became commonplace, and before the World Wide Web had been invented, the only other way to advertise was in the model magazines, a number of which had been running from the early days of kit production. (The original, *The Airfix Magazine*, in its original school blazer pocket format, started in June 1960.) These had long lead-up times so could easily be three months behind with the news, if not more.

Trade shows had also started, and many had days set aside for the amateur modeller. They could run on Thursday and Friday for the trade, then set aside the weekend for the general public. Here the model companies could display their wares and show off preproduction models or test shots, or at least the box artwork.

The buying

The final stage of this sequence was to await the arrival of the kit in the local model shop or hobby store, where you could spend your hard-earned pocket money. (Or in the olden days, and in the case of the UK and Airfix, you'd go to Woolworths, which due to a specific deal always had the new kits a month before the actual model shops got them in. This was a deal that may have been beneficial for the modeller but, on the face of it, didn't exactly do the model shops any favours.)

Over the years, things have changed – much of it, drastically. This primarily, and not surprisingly, was due to the growth of the Internet, which had introduced the joys (or otherwise…) of online shopping. This must have been the reason why many local stores have gone out of business and closed, though this, of course, is general across all shopping categories and not restricted to the model world. However, it has been beneficial for modellers living in outlying areas of countries where model shops (assuming they still existed) were not to be found, or even whole countries where model making was not a widespread hobby, having access to all modelling items from around the globe.

Trade shows do still exist, though with the growth of the Internet for both advertising and shopping and the severe diminishing of the local shop, they themselves have become smaller than in their heyday a few decades

LEFT Most new announcements, if not done via the Web, are given at model shows. This is Airfix at the IPMS National, in Telford, UK.

ago. In fact, the major American model and hobby show, variously termed RCHTA (Radio Control Hobby Trade Association) and later revived as the iHobby Expo, has gone. Much is now advertised via the Internet, though the main German show in Nuremberg and the main Japanese show in Shizuoko currently still exist. Other shows now tend to revolve around model clubs, with the IPMS (the International Plastic Modellers' Society, see Chapter 12, pages 166–175) being the main club worldwide, and many model companies chose to take trade stands at these shows to show off their new kits. Airfix and Revell both take large stands at the UK Nationals in Telford each year to advertise new products.

So the modeller has their new kit – the tools to build it come in Chapter 5 (see pages 66–79).

BELOW But you may find you still have a local hobby store....

Chapter Three

Scale

Model construction kits are almost always referred to as 'scale models', but that scale can differ vastly, depending on the subject matter.

Knowledge of scale is vitally important as firstly one needs some indication as to how large the full-size object is, but also if one is making a collection of similar objects – say a line-up of how the modern car has changed over the years or a collection of fighter aircraft from the Second World War – they have to all be in the same scale, otherwise comparisons become meaningless. Consequently, this has led to any scale that has developed over the years as the 'traditional' scale used throughout one particular subject, as 'constant scale'.

'Scale' is purely the indication of how the object differs in size from the original. These days, it is usually written down as a ratio, for example 1:72, 1:48, 1:25 or 1:16, however, it can also be written as a fraction, for example $\frac{1}{72}$, $\frac{1}{48}$, $\frac{1}{25}$ or $\frac{1}{16}$. Both ways, it means exactly the same thing: in both examples the model would be, respectively, 72 times smaller, 48 times smaller, 25 times smaller or 16 times smaller. Note that the diminutive of the ordinal number is not usually added – so '1:48' is just that. Taking it literally as 'one forty-eighth', the 'th' is not used, so no '1:48th'.

In the vast majority of cases, the scale model will be smaller than the original, and so scale will indeed follow this pattern, with the numerator being '1' and the denominator being some larger number, consequently the '1:X' form. However, there are some cases where the model could be larger than the original, such as models of insects, very small creatures or biological cells, in which case the scale could very well be written the other way round with the denominator being the '1', for example 6:1. Here this indicates that the model is six times larger than the size of the original.

OPPOSITE Here two Revell icons of London, the Routemaster Bus and London Taxi, are the same scale: 1:24.

RIGHT This line-up of model cars from the Dean Milano Collection all need to be to the same scale (in this case 1:25) otherwise comparisons become meaningless.

BELOW Northrop's two Flying Wings. Both are 1:72 scale, so they can show that the wing span, four decades apart, is the same. The B-2 Stealth Bomber from Italeri-Testors (top); AMT's YB-35 (bottom).

ABOVE RIGHT Gowland & Gowland set 1:32 as the first model car scale with its Highway Pioneers. It was later issued by Revell, though it retained the Highway Pioneers name.

RIGHT The range of car scales: from 1:12 through 1:16, 1:24, 1:32, 1:43 and 1:72.

LEFT Comparing Monogram's Corvette Stingrays: large in 1:8 scale, small in 1:43.

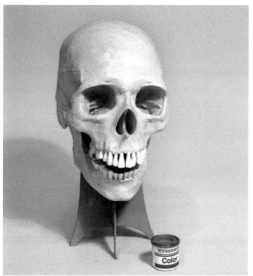

FAR LEFT A 1:1 scale example of a model kit, the human skull. Originally a Renwal kit, this was also issued by Revell.

LEFT Scales can be larger than life-size. This ant kit, from Heller, is in 6:1 scale, six times larger than a real ant.

BELOW 1:1 scale bird kits from Airfix on show at the IPMS UK Nationals.

Occasionally you may also see 1:1 scale, which would usually refer to the full-size object itself, for example, 'Here is a 1:25 scale model of car, placed on the hood of its 1:1 original'. But this could also refer to 1:1 scale replica, such as a fibreglass shell of a Spitfire used as a 'gate guard' outside an aviation museum. It may be full size, but it is still 'a model' in its truest sense. There are also some instances of 1:1 scale kits, but these are usually small animals and birds, although there have been instances of full-size replica guns being made in 1:1 scale. For various reasons, these tend not to be generally available these days.

Choice

The choice of scale has grown up with the industry and several acknowledged scales have become the norm for particular subjects. The most well-known has to be 1:72 scale, as is primarily used for model aircraft. This actually grew out of the scale used by aircraft recognition models, built so 'friend and foe' in the skies could be immediately distinguished, one from another. This, of course, meant they had to be in the same scale – the 'constant scale' – which had to include both fighters and bombers. For this reason 1:72 was chosen so the fighters would not be too small, nor the bombers too large.

These recognition models would have been made from wood, but it was almost certainly the reason why the very first 'plastic' scale model aircraft used 1:72 scale. These first appeared in the 1930s, and were the Frog Penguins; the name itself coming from the fact

CENTRE The default aircraft scale is 1:72, but this makes a large aircraft a large kit. This was unusually an airliner in 1:72, a Douglas DC-9, initially from Aurora and now being issued by Atlantis.

LEFT 1:48 scale is used a lot for small aircraft, both military and civilian.

LEFT Because modellers want to put the models side-by-side to compare, Monogram has made the most of the large American bombers in 1:72 scale – here the B-52. It is not the largest (that is the B-36) but it's still pretty large!

that the overall company name, Frog, itself made flying model aircraft, with the name Frog supposedly being an acronym for 'Flies Right Off the Ground', (though this is disputed by some!). Consequently, the static display model aircraft were called 'Penguins', being named after 'the bird that doesn't fly'.

Oddly, this good start with an adherence to 'constant scale' didn't last – especially when American model companies started to produce models, particularly of aircraft, in the very late 1940s and into the 1950s. The idea of 'constant scale' initially passed them by, and instead they built their models to fit certain sizes of existing boxes. They are invariably referred to as 'non-scale', though the term is inaccurate – they were all built to a scale, but most of the time their scale was arbitrary. They were not necessarily all to the same scale, and invariably their scale wasn't traditionally accepted. So these models are more correctly termed 'scaled to fit the box', or in shortened form, 'box scale', where the size of the kit box came first and the model was designed and tooled to fit it. Consequently, you did end up with odd scales – 1:69, 1:65, 1:75 – but these were all 'real' scales, they were just not 'conventionally accepted' scales or to 'constant scale'.

LEFT Some of the original Airfix 1:72 scale aircraft have been available in recent years – here the Comet Racer dates from the 1950s, though the decals are new this time around.

Imperial vs metric

One thing you may have noticed with most of the traditional scales already mentioned is that they are based on imperial measurements: 1:72, 1:48, 1:16. This is primarily as, firstly Britain led the Industrial Revolution, and secondly it created the British Empire. Therefore, when the technology of the former was exported around the world, due to the latter, the use of imperial sizes and measurements went along with it. This was also helped as the modern plastic kit industry really began, and was developed as an Anglo-American project, with both counties mainly using the imperial system at that time (and the US still does) .

Perhaps most intriguing these days is that the vast majority of the world, certainly the vast majority of the other model-producing countries, including Japan, China, South Korea, Russia, Ukraine, Italy, France and Germany, are completely metric. However, the vast majority of the model kit scales they use are still imperial based. Aircraft are still made in 1:72, 1:48 and 1:32 scale and vehicles in 1:32, 1:24 and 1:16.

The 'metric' world did, in fact, start the usage of 'metric-based' scales for models. One of the main players here was in the country that began the use of metric measurements, the major French model kit company, Heller. It initiated 1:50, 1:100 and 1:125 scale for aircraft. Slightly suspiciously, a lot of aircraft originally scaled by Heller at '1:50', have reappeared now listed as 1:48, but the difference is nominal unless you're a real purist, and it really depends if the scale was accurately calculated in the first place. Similarly, 1:100 scale craft have reappeared as 1:96. However, 1:125 seems to have stayed put, as it isn't really close to anything else. Slightly irritatingly, only Heller uses this scale, so when only Heller makes a particular subject in 1:125 that would be ideal to display alongside a similar subject, you cannot, as the scales differ too greatly. Some Japanese companies also started with metric scales. Some persist, but many have mainly moved to imperial again, with some older '1:50 scale' aircraft now reappearing as '1:48'.

Freewheelin'

The only country to still use imperial measurements is the USA, buoyed up to a certain extent by the country in which it all started, the UK. But this has led to an even greater oddity as in that last bastion of imperial, the USA (in which it is invariably termed 'English measurements'), the main model car scale is 1:25, which on the face of it is a bastardised metric scale. This actually originated as the early model car kit companies in the US: AMT, Jo-Han and Revell all worked alongside the

actual car companies: Ford, GM, Chrysler and – at that time – American Motors, to make 'promos' or promotional models; basically a toy version of the full-size (1:1 scale) cars the companies were selling. These would be given away to children of the potential buyers, 'promoting' the new cars they hoped dad would buy (and it would have been 'dad', not 'mom', at that time). But they were also scale models, and scaled down from the 1:10 clays used to design the full-size versions. Putting that aside, in an 'English measurement' country 1:10 is also a metric scale, but this led to a 2½ reduction. A x2 reduction, i.e. 1:20 scale may have been more logical, but would have resulted in a model car that was likely to be too large for little hands to hold.

1:20 was later introduced as a short-lived standard model car kit scale. Its introduction was mostly unsuccessful, but remnants of it still survive. Tamiya uses it for Formula 1 cars, copied by some other companies, though everything else it does is in 1:24. Lindberg and MPC also made a whole range of American machines in 1:20.

For a time in the late 1950s and into the 1960s, there was a slight variation in the way scales were noted, especially by the American company Monogram. Firstly, Monogram didn't have any connection with the full-size car industry and so did not make promos. Consequently, it also didn't use 1:25 scale, but it used 1:24 scale instead – a standard engineering scale. Monogram initially called it 'half inch scale' (there being 24 x ½ inches in 1 foot, hence the designation). This applied to aircraft and other subjects, where you would get the scale ruler printed in the plans, so you could measure the parts alongside it. This variation, however, did not last long and Monogram soon moved onto the more conventional way of describing scale: such as cars in 1:24 and aircraft in 1:48.

The first car kit scale was, however, smaller at 1:32, which came about from one of the very earliest kit companies, Gowland & Gowland. This really did typify the Anglo-American description as it was three Britons: Jack Gowland, his son Kelvin, and Derek Brand, working on the west coast in California soon after the Second World War.

The company initially designed and manufactured toys in 1:16 scale, a standard imperial scale (¾in scale) that included veteran cars. It then had the idea of producing model kits 'to put together yourself' and halved this size – hence introducing 1:32 (or ⅜in scale) to make some of the earliest model car kits. This idea was then 'borrowed' by Revell (which actually started life as Gowland & Gowland's sales team and called Precision Specialities) but also by other smaller US companies such as Hudson Miniatures. The scale was also copied in the UK by Airfix, when it started a similar line of veteran cars, and also Merit, which ran a kit division at the time and also made these veteran cars. (Some almost certainly copied from the others!)

Army manoeuvres

Scaling of other traditional model subjects has also had its ups and downs. One very popular subject worldwide is military army vehicles. If you go back to the start of the modern model kit industry, i.e. the 1950s, many came from Airfix in the UK and a variety of companies in the US. The Airfix kits were small and scaled at 1:72. They were able to be priced low, due to their size – most in Series 1 came in a polythene bag and were priced at 2/- (two shillings, or 10 pence). They obviously also matched the existing aircraft range, so you could use both subjects alongside each other. They were very close to the UK railway 00 scale of 1:76, so you also had a range of Airfix trackside buildings, rolling stock and sets of figures. The last used a catch-all scale of H0/00, so actually ranged from 1:87 - H0 to 1:76 - 00, which is, on the face of it, a vast range – 1:87 is roughly one-tenth smaller than 1:76. However, being figures as opposed to inanimate objects, they were far more adaptable and over the years no one has seemed to mind or query this difference.

Larger scales of army military and similar kits were initially left to the Americans. Here the main names in the beginnings of the model kit industry – Aurora, Adams, Hawk, Revell, Monogram and Renwal – all made kits of military subjects, tanks, self-propelled guns, soft-skinned vehicles and missiles. Of all these

names, only two – Adams and really Renwal – stayed true to constant scale, although these were different scales: Adams with 1:40 and Renwal with 1:32. In actuality, neither made all that many military kits (compared with the vast amount available these days), with less than a dozen each.

Revell also used 1:40, which matched Adams. In fact, at the time there was close cooperation between the two: Revell doing tooling and some design for the Adams kits, and in later years, much of Adams' catalogue moved to Revell. However, Revell also used different scales, many for its missiles, and some ended up in the unconventional 1:64 and 1:81 scales. Several larger originals dropped down to 1:110, so, for a time, this became a 'conventional scale' by default.

Monogram also made military in 1:32 scale, but suddenly in 1973 moved some to 1:35 (including some that were first listed as 1:32). At one point, in 1973, Monogram had both 1:32 and 1:35 military in the same catalogue. This could have been because Japanese model companies, particularly Tamiya, started producing military in 1:35.

The odd scale

Exactly why this happened, and why 1:35 became the de facto military scale is one of those modelling oddities, perhaps *the* modelling oddity of all time. It is not an imperial engineering scale, and although it could possibly be likened to model car companies using 1:25 (which also isn't an engineering scale but was based on the 1:10 scale clays), 1:35 hasn't really had any similar background. The reasoning behind virtually all other model scales can be rationalised, but not 1:35. One reason suggested it could be doubled (or halved – semantics here are not always clear) to 1:70, which originated in Japan and is linked to a person's height. But this theory has flaws: although some aircraft appeared as '1:70 scale', the main scale used in Japan for aircraft and smaller military subjects has been 1:72 (and 1:76 for some military), not 1:70. About the only company to ever use 1:70 was Tamiya for some aircraft, and for its only foray into the Apollo Program, where the company made its Apollo Lunar Module and Command-Service Module

BELOW 1:35 scale became the default scale for larger military AFVs, as seen in all these examples on view at the IPMS Nationals.

kits in 1:70 scale, not what would have been the conventional 1:72.

There is another suggestion as to its origins, which also involves Tamiya. Many early model kits from all Japanese kit companies were motorised – they had to have 'play value'. In fact, the motorisation aspect invariably came before any 'scale model' considerations. In the early 1970s, Tamiya started to make motorised military tanks, and, given that Tamiya was perhaps more devoted to 'scale' than some of the other early companies, it's likely that the model needed a be a size in which the batteries could be contained without compromising the scale aspects of the model. So as to contain the required batteries (B size is quoted, although this is not a conventional size of domestic battery), the tank scale ended up at 1:35. The reasoning still has flaws, primarily as to why the models weren't made to the existing 1:32 scale. After all, 1:32 was – and still is – an established model scale. Although, one could argue 1:32 is close enough to 1:35 for these two scales to be used side-by-side, especially in a diorama (and if any model subject is designed for dioramas, it is military setups) but that won't wash with scale purists. Consequently, it has led to a subdivision of aircraft models where some that are associated with army manoeuvres, such as helicopters, have been made in 1:35 not 1:32.

Once established, 1:35 was extremely difficult to shift, so all consequential manufacturers of military AFVs, from Japan, China, South Korea, Russia and Ukraine to the European countries, all use 1:35. But it still leaves that irritating question of why Tamiya (if it actually was Tamiya that instigated 1:35) couldn't have shifted its tooling up by around 8% to 1:32?

A life on the ocean wave

Ships (especially powered, as opposed to sail) were, with aircraft, among some of the first kits to be made. But here, because of the size of the originals, there was a slightly more rational reason to make them 'to fit the box'. This was especially so in the US, where naval and civilian vessels with engines ended up being made to 'box scales'. Airfix in the

UK were first to produce naval ship kits in injection styrene – as opposed to the Frog Penguins' examples in cellulose acetate – and they established constant scale for their naval ships using 1:600. This also applied to modern liners and some other smaller vessels. However, scaling was not constant for earlier sailing ships and galleons – in fact, this is the only overall subject matter in the whole Airfix catalogue over all the years of the company's existence that does not follow constant scale. One-time colleague, Heller, did try to retain more 'constant scale' with its galleons and sailing ships, variously using 1:100, 1:150 and 1:200.

Other 'conventional scales' have been introduced over the years. Although Airfix still uses 1:600 and halved this to 1:1200 for some models, other companies moved to 1:700 for naval vessels and doubled this to 1:350 for larger and more detailed models. Movement to traditional aircraft scales has also occurred, using 1:144, then up to 1:72 for smaller craft such as coastal patrol boats. Even the military scale of 1:35 got involved, with Italeri producing

ABOVE Ships can vary tremendously in scale, and the scales here are a mix of 'constant' and 'various'. From the bottom, Renwal used a constant 1:500 and Airfix 1:600, but the Lindberg is 1:888 and the Revell is 1:436.

a 1:35 scale Second World War German Schnellboot S-1000 that stretches to a fraction under 1 metre long – it is listed as '99.9cm' and (currently) holds the record for a static model of that type.

It figures

Model kits of figures have always sat slightly oddly against all other model subject types as they could be figures of any other subject, but generally they all get lumped together under this one heading.

Very generally they can be split into two factions. One is individual figures of a variety of subjects and made to a large scale. These individual figures can be positioned starting at 1:24 and moving up the scale, through 1:20, 1:16, and by the time you get to 1:13, every ordinal number up to 1:3. If you include pure parts of a figure, for example the head, you can add 1:2 and 1:1 to complete the set! The other main area is sets of figures, so you get more than one – usually a lot more, with sets of 20 or 30 or more individual figures available (some may be in duplicate poses, others in different poses). These are intended to be used in play sets, dioramas, railway settings and these days, wargaming. The vast majority of these

are scaled at 1:72 or 1:76, and being figures, the differences are slight. There are some sets available in 1:32 and others in 1:35, and again the scale differences can be mostly ignored.

There are kits containing individual figures that sit in-between 1:35 and 1:72, but these tend to be the very specialist 54mm or 120mm scales, corresponding more or less to 1:32 and 1:16. (There is more on this way of describing size and scale in millimetres, and how it is even less precise than most scales, explained opposite under the next sub-heading.)

Most companies made the larger figure kits to some degree, such as Pyro and Revell, but two tend to stand out. Airfix used the constant scale of 1:12, which again is one of the conventional imperial engineering scales – one inch to the foot. Subjects have mostly been historical, with Henry VIII, Anne Boleyn, Queen Elizabeth I and The Black Prince being favourites. These were British, though there was a nod to the neighbour over the Channel with Napoleon and Joan of Arc also being made. Perhaps the oddest, as it didn't quite sit 'historically', was the Boy Scout, available with traditional hat or the more modern beret. This has actually become one of the rarest to find.

Besides Airifx, and arguably even better known for its figure kits, is Aurora. It had a far wider subject range as it delved into the worlds of science fiction and fantasy as well as purely factual subjects. Aurora, however, didn't use 1:12; it used, almost universally, the scale of 1:8 for all its figures. But just to be awkward, of course there were variations. The forever unnamed 'Robot from *Lost in Space*' was made in the somewhat ungainly and certainly unconventional scale of 1:11. Consequently when, decades later, Polar Lights decided to fill in certain gaps of the Aurora catalogue with kits that had been planned but never produced, it made the 'missing' companion robot. This was Robby from the classic movie, *Forbidden Planet*, and Polar Lights also used 1:11. Consequently, although Robby and the *Lost in Space* Robot matched each other, they really don't match anything else!

Smaller sets of figures, as opposed to individual subjects, initially came from Airfix, though over the years have appeared from many other companies including Revell

Germany, Italeri, Hät, Hasegawa, Fujimi, Caesar, Imex, Dragon and Zvezda. Most are military in nature, intended for dioramas with other military subjects and also for wargaming. The vast majority fall under what has been variously described as 1:72/1:76/00/H0, but all end up roughly around 1in or 25mm tall. The only other scale really used for sets of figures is 1:35 to go alongside 1:35 AFVs. A few are listed at 1:32, although with figures it is far more difficult to be picky about size differences.

Using millimetres

Figures also bring in a slightly different way to describe their 'size'. Inanimate objects (vehicles, craft and buildings) are a set size, so calculating scales is purely down to measuring the object and 'doing the math'. But figures – initially assuming human figures, but also including animals and even aliens where appropriate – could vary in size quite considerably, especially between figures of children or adults. Consequently the 'scale' for some aspects of scale modelling is not quoted; instead, the height of a model figure is given in millimetres. This is mainly used for figures used in wargaming, where whole battalions are built up to wage wars in miniature, but it can also apply to larger individual figures.

This had to start somewhere, so it was decided that it would be based on a 'standard' 1:1 scale figure with a height of 6ft or 72in. And, just to complicate things, this uses imperial measurements while the 'scale' height is noted in metric!

So, using this as a convenient example to start, figures listed at '25mm' basically correspond to 1:72 scale. Consequently 1:72 scale figures can also be described as '25mm', as 25mm is almost 1in (25.4mm if you wish to be slightly more precise). This can be extrapolated up and down. 1:96 is also described as 20mm; 1:32 as 54mm; and 1:15 or 1:16 (note that variations are already creeping in) as 120mm. None are precise matches, but given the varying sizes of people, they are close enough 'for a figure in a particular scale'.

This hasn't been set in stone in the way, say, a conventional '1:72 scale Spitfire' has, that is 1:72 scale won't be described as '1:48'.

ABOVE Brother robots – the forever unnamed robot from *Lost in Space* (who variously acquired monikers such as 'B9' or 'YM-3') and Robby from *Forbidden Planet*. The *Lost in Space* robot is the original Aurora kit made to 1:11, so when Polar Lights made Robby, it used the same scale.

BELOW These various figures – from Revell, 1:87 (top left), Hät and Caesar, 1:72 (bottom) and Airfix, 00/H0 (top right) – could all be termed '25mm'.

However, 25mm has varied over the years with different manufacturers assigning different scales to their '25mm figures', which has affected scaling for other sizes. Consequently, you can find '25mm' quoted as being 1:60, even 1:48, while 1:72 scale has been listed as '20mm' although that is closer to H0 or 1:87. So in the case of 'figures' and 'scales in mm' it is really far more down to: 'does it look right?'

Off the rails

So far, all sizes of models (even with the slight sidetrack into millimetres) have been designated in 'scales'. This is true for all model subjects except one: railways or railroads. Here, the modeller not only has to contend with 'scales', as designated at the beginning, but also with rail 'gauges' (the width between the track rails) and the two are not necessarily the same. There is also the difference that most

subjects here are intended as static display models, while railroad modelling is invariably about a working layout with not only working locos and rolling stock running on tracks, but also putting them in a scene, in effect, a diorama.

The best example of scale vs gauge is to use the difference between 00 and H0 'scales'. 00 (or 'double 0') is the sole prerogative of the UK, and is only used in Britain. H0 ('half 0') is used everywhere else in the world, including the USA (although it invariably differs with every other country in many matters, here it is united.) The H0 scale is 1:87, along with the gauge. The 00 scale, however, is 1:76, but the gauge is the same as H0, so 00 rolling stock can run on an H0 track. This means that the bodywork of any 00 scale rolling stock is larger than any H0 equivalent. Consequently, it is in scale with other 00 scale objects, but not with the running gear, as the running gear is H0. And just to pile oddity upon oddity, H0 (half 0), used everywhere but Britain, is half the British 0 gauge (1:43.5), not the Continental 0 gauge (1:45) or the US 0 gauge (which is 1:48). (The last is the most convenient '0 gauge' as it is an established imperial engineering scale, also used for aircraft, military and civilian vehicles.)

This is just the beginning of railway scales and gauges. For the record, there are almost 100 'scales' used for model railways – many described with names or letters, such as 'G', not written in the usual scale ratio or fraction form. Many can duplicate one to another, depending on which country uses them, and many are only used by large scale 'ride on/ live steam' locos. All are 'scale' (to a greater or lesser degree) but in the context here, probably the most relevant are:

- Z – 1:220 scale
- N – 1:160
- TT – 1:120
- H0 – 1:87
- 00 – 1:76
- 0 – UK 1:43.5
- 0 – Continental Europe 1:45
- 0 – US 1:48
- G – 1:22.5

Even here, there are variations in scale, as demonstrated by 0, where all have been listed, while N, TT and G also being assigned to alternative sizes, and consequently scales, depending on the country.

One thing you may have noticed from the above rail scales is that, so far, scales have all been whole numbers and in the vast majority of cases, this still holds true. But in the list above there are two fractions of the denominator. One is the British 0 scale for railways – which is 1:43.5, a scale that is also deemed to be the traditional die-cast toy car scale, for Corgi and Dinky for example. Note that it is usually written thus and not 1:43½ (though it is pronounced 'one forty-third and a half'). Strictly and mathematically speaking, it should actually be written as 2:87 scale, but this variation never seems to occur. Also, in most cases the '.5' is omitted and you will just see '1:43' scale. (Just to repeat from above, as nothing is

ABOVE **Z-scale, or 1:220, is small enough to take with you in a suitcase.**

BELOW **The most widespread larger rail scale is 1:22.5, invented by LGB.**

straightforward with railway scales, '0' differs: the Continental European 0 scale is 1:45 and the North American 0 scale is 1:48!)

The other 'scale fraction oddity' with railway modelling is the Continental Europe G Scale (invented by German company, LGB, for garden railways), which is listed as 1:22.5 scale. Here 'G' actually stands for *Groß* meaning 'big' in German, but these days it's invariably interpreted as standing for 'garden.' These are the only two generally accepted scale fractions in modelling and the vast majority fortunately rely on whole cardinal numbers.

Space scales

For the last word on scale in this chapter, we move to the category usually lumped together as 'space, science fiction and fantasy'. This may be an odd collection, as spacecraft are 'real' while SF and fantasy are not (well they aren't as far as we're aware 'real' in the Known Universe…). But many spacecraft and rocket models were speculative, never built for real, so arguably fall between 'real' and 'SF'. In a chapter about 'scale', it also brings up subjects that have no scale, or more correctly have no assigned scale, or where scale is extremely difficult to calculate!

But as with all models, scales do come into it, and to start at the more straightforward end, factual spacecraft or rockets have indeed been assigned scales in the same way as aircraft, military or ships. Early missiles that fall between 'military' and 'space' have already been discussed with, say, Revell using a scale of 1:110 for many of its missiles. Later, space launchers as the two means of propulsion were basically the same, and many large ICBMs became space launchers. With the Apollo Project approaching in the 1960s, the famous Saturn V rocket was made in established scales – 1:144 for Airfix and Monogram, the former using the scale it had invented for airliner models, by halving 1:72 scale (now generally adopted as the standard 'traditional' scale, not only for airliners but for space launchers). Revell used 1:96 to make one of the largest model kits ever made (though not *the* largest…) while AMT broke away from its usual emphasis on car models, making all five American manned launchers in 1:200 scale (interestingly, a metric scale) later adopted as a smaller airliner scale by such as Hasegawa.

Other factual craft: Apollo, Gemini, Mercury and even the Soviet Vostok also used existing scales (1:24 or 1:48) while a few astronaut figures used existing 1:12 and 1:6 figure scales.

Out of this world

When it came to science fiction and fantasy, logic started to completely unravel. Here we were building models of what (if they existed, anyway) were models themselves, invariably built as filming miniatures for the latest blockbuster movie. So these were models of models, the originals of which were very unlikely to have been assigned a scale. They were built to do a job, and that job was purely to get an image on a screen. In more recent years it became even harder, as the originals were increasingly grown in a computer as part of a CGI program and weren't even built 'for real'. (Though in very recent years the situation is reverting back to 'traditional models' for movies – even if they are then scanned and then used as CGI – much to the relief of many professional model makers!)

If the SF design features recognisable 'human features' – doors and windows especially, scales can usually be calculated.

RIGHT The first *Star Trek* kit, made by AMT, but also issued by Aurora, initially had no assigned scale.

In fact, this precise approach was used when AMT made the very first kit of a *Star Trek* subject: the *USS Enterprise* NCC-1701. No scale was assigned by AMT, but Andy Yanchus, kit historian and past Project Manager at Aurora (that also issued the kit for the Canadian and European markets) took up the challenge. Using windows and other information, he came up with a scale of 1:635, which was later adopted as official, and has since led as a basis for the scaling of all other *Star Trek* craft, which now ranges across several other kit companies.

That was easy (or easier) as the primary *Star Trek* ships were Earth-based technology, so human attributes could be assigned. With alien craft it was far less straightforward, although some indicators were starting points. Arguably the whole of the 'Star Wars universe' is alien, but it appears to be conveniently populated by mainly human-size 'creatures' (even Jar Jar Binks), many of which are modelled piloting the various craft. So again, using the human form, scales can be allocated. Even craft that are far too large to have visible people – the Imperial Star Destroyers and, especially, the Death Star – had features, that coupled with published details (albeit fictional!) can be used to calculate probable scales. This has led to Revell Germany preassigning scales to many of its new *Star Wars* craft, though many do appear somewhat arbitrary. This actually comes down less to pleasing the model makers (although there may be some element of this) but more to tax implications. They are charged less on an education toy – a 'scale model kit', with the emphasis on 'scale' – than a pure toy, with no scale.

Sometimes, however, the model companies just have no choice but to compromise. When the official model kit of the *Liberator*, star of the BBC SF series *Blake's 7,* was made by specialist company Comet Miniatures in the UK, it was scaled at 1:5, *but* this was the scale of the kit, as compared to the main studio model – it was actually 1:5 scale to that. This was because no one had ever worked out the scale of the filming miniature (including this author, who worked on the series) and no one was even sure of where the flight deck was. So the Comet Miniatures kit is designated with a scale of '1:5 Millispacials' – the only ever example of this particular scale.

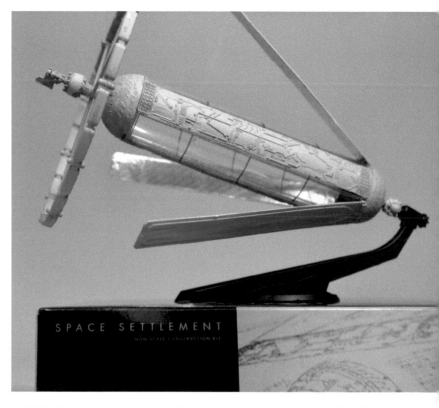

ABOVE The box says 'non-scale', but it does have a scale – even if it is likely the largest scale ever used in a spacecraft – or any kit. This Wave kit of a Space Colony is approximately 1:200,000,000.

BELOW Comet Miniatures' *Blake's 7 Liberator* was scaled from the large special effects miniature, so its listed scale is as compared to that.

Chapter Four

The range

If the question comes up, and it occasionally does, of 'How many model kits have been made?' you're on pretty safe ground that this is virtually impossible to answer.

The most comprehensive listings to date came from the late Rev John Burns of Edmond, Oklahoma, who produced several volumes of CVG – Collecting Value Guides, that dealt with 'collectable kits' (though John would have been the first to ask, 'How do we define "collectable"?'). John then also produced the books collectively titled *In Plastic*, which aimed to list all kits of any subject that had ever been produced (see also Chapter 11 – Collecting, pages 154–165).

For an example of the sort of numbers we are contemplating, the last ever issue of the CVG that John produced was in 1999. This ran to 456 pages of tightly typed text. His last *In Plastic* book on *Plastic Aircraft Kits of the 20th Century – and Beyond*, was published in 2003. This listed a total of 31,858 aircraft construction kits from 1,359 plastic kit companies, issued from 1936 to mid-2002. And that is 'just' aircraft. There have been no such books since, and John sadly died in 2015.

So that more or less puts into perspective the whole hobby. Can you get a model kit of a particular subject? The answer is 'quite probably', but of course you're going to have to search and there are always going to be omissions.

It is safe to say that the plastic construction kit was 'invented' as such by Frog in Britain in the 1930s, but lapsed after a few years due to the pressures of the Second World War. It resumed in its modern form after the war, starting around 1948, but in reality most of what could be termed the 'modern plastic construction model kit' occurred from the mid-1950s onwards. At that time, the number of scale model kits available was somewhat limited. But it very soon expanded with ranges of the most common model subjects, even introducing some very odd ones!

These days, the availability is even vaster, with virtually every subject matter that could be contemplated (and some that couldn't) being available in kit form. In its very widest sense, the subject matter for scale model kits can be contained under a few overall – and extremely general – headings: Aircraft, Ships, Automotive, Military (in modelling always used in the ground fighting sense, as obviously there are military ships and

ABOVE **John Burns'** *Plastic Aircraft Kits of the 20th Century.* **The amount of material in it can be judged from the thickness of the book.**

aircraft); Space and Science Fiction, Railways and Figures. However under those headings there are vast subdivisions and there are yet more subjects that don't fall conveniently into any of the above.

To move or not to move

There is also the situation that although most 'scale model construction kits' are static creations, they are not intended to move unless the kit does feature 'moveable features' such as a revolving propeller, moveable flaps or rotating wheels. However, there are sections of all model subjects where there are scale working models – railways being the prime example here. Although there are a few locos and rolling stock that are indeed intended as static display models, the vast majority of railroads are intended to work with animated rolling stock on tracks.

Then there are scale ships that sail on the water, scale submarines that glide under the water and scale aircraft and helicopters that fly in the air. Scale space rockets fly – well perhaps not directly into space, but certainly upwards – and many scale tanks are motorised and radio controlled. Radio control also applies to many scale cars and trucks, not forgetting those that run round slot car tracks. There are even scale drag racing tracks that race over a scale quarter mile.

OPPOSITE **One of Airfix's earliest aircraft kits, the Auster Antarctica (below right). Other issues can also be seen.**

51

THE RANGE

What you get within each particular range

Aircraft

Includes airliners – modern and classic; military planes: current, First World War, Second World War, all decades in-between and the more recent conflicts; helicopters of all types; gliders, hovercraft and all ACV (air cushion vehicles) and GEM (ground effect machines). Also, experimental planes such as the US X-Planes; dirigibles; balloons; very early historical aircraft such as the Wright Brothers Flyer; and some designs that never got built for real, including the notorious 'Luftwaffe 46', a category reserved for German war planes of the Second World War that were speculated, and occasionally even built as mock-ups, but in general could be said to have literally never got off the ground.

Ships

Includes modern warships, wartime vessels, ocean-going liners, cargo vessels, submarines, ferries, hydrofoils, research vessels, experimental vessels, old time galleons, sailing ships, yachts and even rowing boats! There have also been associated models of docks and lighthouses.

Automotive

Includes cars that are stock showroom condition; customs; racing, including everything from Formula 1, rally, dragsters, NASCAR; plus show cars and Hot Rods. Then there are trucks, with and without trailers; smaller vans; construction equipment: bulldozers, back-hoes and cement mixers; farm machinery with tractors, wagons and even ploughs. Also includes numerous accessory packs of custom, speed and garage equipment, plus figures that drive them, work on them and just stand around looking at them. There are even model kits of the engines that power them.

Military

Includes tanks, self-propelled guns, Jeeps, Land Rovers and other 'soft-skinned' vehicles. There are a host of figures and accessories in the common scales, and many standalone figures in larger scales. For dioramas there are even more accessories, buildings and general wartime equipment.

Space and science fiction

Maybe the widest possible choice from factual rockets and launch vehicles, satellites and space-probes, to space stations and 'factual futuristic' designs that could have been built

BELOW Airfix's first kit: the Ferguson Tractor.

for real. Then there is science fiction ranging from 'scientific' SF, such as *Star Trek*, through to 'science fantasy' such as *Doctor Who*, and onto the extreme realms of horror movies and Japanese anime. Here there is a multitude of craft and figures, many using limited-edition production methods.

Railways

These tend to be separated out, as they are primarily intended to be working scale models, as opposed to static display models, but again a very wide range of not only the rolling stock itself: locomotives, carriages and wagons, but buildings, natural structures, figures and vehicles.

Figures

The is the most difficult category to classify as it contains subject matter from all the previous categories. Figures can mostly be split between those that are of an individual, in sizes that are towards the larger end scales and sets of figures in multiples, usually a smaller scale, that are intended to be used together in military, and other, dioramas, rail layouts or wargaming.

Dolls' houses

To the above lists of categories one can also add dolls' houses, which, like railways, are a completely individual subject in their own right. Although the majority of ranges don't exactly fall under 'injection-moulded scale model kits', there are many crossovers. The main scales for, particularly, American dolls' houses, are 1:12 and 1:24 and these of course are two of the main model vehicle scales. Accessories for dolls houses have often been readapted for vehicles. Doll's house model companies also make such items as low-voltage lighting and electrics, which again can be adapted.

The Companies

The number of model companies that have existed over the years is also legion. There are the major brands that even non-modellers can likely name, to obscure, short-lived companies, some of which only ever issued one kit!

Very roughly, you can split the model companies into two types. There are what can conveniently be termed the 'mainstream companies', such as Airfix, Revell or Tamiya that have, more or less, become household names in their respective countries, and indeed, around the world. These companies employ a number of people, have commercial premises, and distribute to shops and stores in many countries. As with the overall number of kits ever produced, it is slightly easier to hazard a guess at the number of mainstream companies to ever have existed, though even here it has to be a 'rough educated guess', with numbers around 1,500.

At the opposite end of the spectrum are those that have been termed the 'garage, or cottage industries'. These are invariably one-man (apologies, but it usually is 'a man'!) presumably working out of a garage or a cottage, producing short-run kits or purely additions, modifications or accessories for mainstream kits. It is far less easy to count the individuals that have produced 'a kit' as many weren't full kits, many never really advertised their presence (which does makes one wonder how they sold their stock – it had to be only to friends or to their local model club) and others could be from countries that never really exported, so the products remained solely within that country's borders.

The garage companies started to appear in the earliest years of model kit production and it is many of these that remained obscure, even unknown. But one big – very big – change occurred in the 1990s, which was the opening up of the World Wide Web, thanks to the growth of the Internet.

The inter-web

Initially started as a somewhat esoteric academic method of communication, the Internet spawned the 'Web' primarily thanks to British engineer and computer scientist Sir Tim Berners-Lee. Although invariably quoted as 'Inventing the Internet', he did not – what he did was far more important. He made it function as the 'World Wide Web', as he devised the hyperlink. These days it is unthinkable to see a web page that says, 'Here is a list of model companies…', without the addition of, '…click link to take you to their individual sites'. It is the <http://> (hypertext transfer protocol – ironically, all but hidden these days in website URLs), that makes the Web work.

ABOVE Early transatlantic travel. Two Strombecker kits: the top example was made by Selcol in the UK, though the 'Strombecker' name was retained.

BELOW Early Frog aircraft kits – these are now moulded in polystyrene, not cellulose acetate.

This not only led to the large model companies having websites that could be published around the world, but any small company or individual could also take full advantage. Consequently, any model company – mainstream, garage or even that lone individual – can advertise their wares easily, publish online catalogues (so much so that many paper versions have disappeared) and announce new subjects immediately. None of these advantages were available when the kit industry first began.

Tooling swaps

Model companies, like everything else these days, have not been immune to change. Many companies that were thought to be 'here for life' found themselves being acquired by other model companies, or in many cases, holding companies, that bought up these older companies with the aim of turning them around and selling them on.

However, with the merger of various model companies with other companies, the tooling gets intermingled. A kit that began life with one manufacturer can crop up under a different kit logo, although it is the exact same kit. Alternatively, tooling was leased, usually from one country to another, so appeared under a different name, even if it was still available under the original name in its originating country. Some may think this is a recent phenomenon, but it actually goes back to the very earliest days. In the early 1950s, Airfix's first kit– the Ferguson Tractor – was reissued in the USA by the Thomas Toy Company of New York, presumably as the Ferguson was well known in the States. It had its own new box and packaging, although 'Airfix' is acknowledged in the small print.

In the opposite direction, the Strombecker series of futuristic spacecraft was reissued by Selcol for the British market. Selcol was not, strictly speaking, a model kit company. It was a general injection-moulding company, moulding anything in plastic from an injection tool. Here, the kit tooling purely replaced other moulds on the machine that could have been turning out anything mouldable – a comb, a bottle or a washing-up bowl. However, this was exactly the way other more-established model companies started, including Airfix, Glencoe and Jo-Han.

By the 1960s and 1970s there was a lot of two-way flow across the Atlantic, with Model Products Company (MPC) issuing Airfix kits for the American market and Airfix reissuing MPC kits. AMT and Frog had a similar arrangement between the UK and US.

Trade wasn't just Anglo-American – AMT also dealt with Hasegawa in Japan for US-Japanese kit-swap cooperation, as did Monogram with Bandai. In earlier years, Frog also had a two-way arrangement with Renwal in the US, and issued its kits for the UK market under the 'Frog De Luxe' name.

Revell even had divisions in other countries. First came Revell Canada, followed by Revell GB then Revell West Germany. It also had connections with companies in other countries: Lodela in Mexico; Kikoler in Brazil; Luis Congost in Spain; Lincoln Industries in New Zealand and Australia; and variously, Takara, Marusan and Gunze Sangyo in Japan. (Overall, this makes 'Revell' the best known and most travelled kit brand, likely with, at one time, the most tooling and the most widespread of all kit company names.)

Transatlantic moves

Up until the 1960s the vast majority of kit companies – although involving kit swapping with other names and a few original names disappearing – remained stable overall. But from the 1970s onwards, primarily due to the 1973 'oil crisis', everything began to turn around and major changes occurred. Now gone were the days when model companies owned themselves, such as Revell being owned by Revell Inc, Airfix by Airfix Ltd and AMT by The AMT Corporation.

Airfix found itself being taken over by the American General Mills conglomerate, which owned a wide range of products. Most were not model-related: General Mills's portfolio included food companies such as Betty Crocker and Cheerios (and a point of interest to anyone who has received a package – maybe with a model kit in it – through the post, General Mills invented the tear-open strip!) However, with all this emphasis on food, there was also another

ABOVE Cooperation between the UK and Japan, with the Hasegawa release of a Frog kit.

BELOW UK and US – Frog issued the Renwal Nike Ajax missile, using the 'De Luxe' name for these kits.

Revell interestingly moved the opposite way across the Atlantic, as it was taken over by French company, Jouef, in the 1980s. This saw the logo 'CEJI' appear alongside 'Revell' on kit boxes. The US side remained open as a business in Venice, California, but the French company had the option of putting the main European base either with Revell GB, which started way back in 1958, or Revell West Germany, which started a year later. Unfortunately for the British operation, it opted for Germany. This took over Revell GB, which became Revell Germany, UK Branch, while Revell US remained very much running itself.

Ironically, AMT also moved across the Big Pond, as Lesney, overall owner of Matchbox, took that over. Lesney started its own Matchbox kit division, so for some years the two lines became combined.

Later that decade, in 1986, Revell was sold again, this time to move back to the US and Odyssey Partners, a holding company in New York. This bought Revell's main rivals, Monogram, some months previously, and it moved Revell from Venice, California (basically a suburb of Los Angeles) to Monogram's headquarters in Morton Grove, Illinois (basically a suburb of Chicago). This somewhat belies the usual assumption that 'Revell took over Monogram', as it was Revell that moved to

ABOVE Revell and Monogram's names up on what was originally the Monogram factory in Morton Grove, near Chicago, Illinois.

RIGHT Lesney issue of AMT kits for the UK market (top) using both names; the US release just used the AMT name (bottom).

BELOW AMT kits in Europe in earlier years – Heller (left) issued them in France; Frog (right) in the UK.

BELOW An Airfix issue of an MPC kit, though both companies are credited.

Monogram's premises, so arguably it was the other way round and 'Monogram took over Revell...'. In reality, neither was the case. The two just became one company: Revell Monogram, or R-M (sometimes RMX). 'Revell' came first in the combined name, as although alphabetically it was the wrong way round, it was the larger and, worldwide, the better-known name.

Previously, Monogram had acquired most of the Aurora tooling when that company ceased in 1977, and Revell had acquired that of Renwal, which had ceased in 1979, putting four original major US model names under one roof.

LEFT An unusual Heller issue, the Breitling balloon.

BELOW Polar Lights first issue was a retooling of the Aurora *Addams Family* house.

More changes

Meanwhile, back in the UK Airfix was acquired by Humbrol (though itself owned by Borden in the US, that for a time also owned X-Acto tools). Humbrol had also acquired Heller in France, so uniting the two main Anglo-French rivals. In 1995, Borden sold its holdings to the Dublin-based holding company, Alan & McGuire and Partners, which reinstated Heller as a separate company, although it kept Airfix and Humbrol as one.

By the new millennium, however, things changed yet again. Airfix and Humbrol were up for sale and were eventually acquired by Hornby. Best known for its railway items, Hornby subsequently acquired Scalextric and Corgi, which gave it a very wide-based model remit – trains, kits, die-casts, slot cars -– and paint. Ironically, one thing it didn't get from Airfix was all its rail stock and trackside accessories. These had been sold off to the small UK company, Dapol, many years previously.

In the USA, there was an equal amount of trading. AMT was reacquired back to Stateside by The Ertl Corporation. They had previously bought MPC from General Mills, and had also acquired the Italian company, ESCI, along the way. The main US model paint company Testors had acquired Hawk, one of the original US companies, along with smaller US names such as IMC. Testors itself was owned by the larger RPM Company that also owned the CraftHouse Corporation. That acquired another original US name, Lindberg, which had started as O-Lin way back in the 1930s. Lindberg itself

had acquired other original US kit names such as Pyro and Life-Like.

Ertl was then itself taken over by Racing Champions, primarily dealing with die-casts, and later rebranded as RC. This was then revitalised as RC-2. Meanwhile, a new company was founded in 1994, initially as Playing Mantis, primarily making die-casts. A kit line was started in 1996 named Polar Lights, a play on the old Aurora name, with the original intention of reissuing retooled old Aurora kits (the first being the *Addams Family* house).

Playing Mantis was rebranded as the Round-2 Corporation in 2005. In 2008 it acquired AMT

ABOVE Glencoe Models started to reissue many old kits, but the Albatros is its only original.

and MPC from RC-2, and more recently in 2013, Lindberg and Hawk from the J Lloyd company, that had bought them from CraftHouse.

Over the years, some American-based companies first started to import and repackage overseas companies products. One was Entex, which reboxed a number of Bandai kits; another Paramount, which dealt with Japanese SF and fantasy subjects; a third was Minicraft, which is the only one to survive. It had a long association with Academy in South Korea, but with that link gone, now makes brand new kits of its own.

New beginnings

Four brand new names appeared in the US making injection-moulded kits up to and since the millennium. The earliest was Glencoe Models, which started in 1994 to reissue kits from old tooling – it has successfully achieved this over the intervening years. Atlantis Models, which started within Megahobby in Long Island, New York, was spun off as a separate company in 2009. Moebius Models was started in 2008 – one of those names to build on the old Aurora legacy, while Pegasus Hobbies started earlier in the mid-1990s. The most recent change has seen Pegasus take over Moebius, though the names trade independently from each other.

The biggest change – and the biggest surprise in recent years – was that Revell Monogram was taken over by giant US model

distributor Hobbico in 2007, which then acquired Revell Germany in 2012. But Hobbico itself went belly-up in early 2018. After some hiatus, a German holding company, Blitz, took over Revell Germany and also the assets of the American side, leaving the whole Revell name intact, though the US set-up was extremely reduced. Much of the American tooling not wanted by the new arrangement went to Atlantis Models.

Not all English speaking

Although the model kit market is invariably put down to an 'Anglo-American affair', and the majority of the early kits did indeed come from those countries, they didn't have it entirely to themselves. Germany's Faller started in 1946 and although these days could be assumed to have always dealt with Continental H0 gauge railways, in earlier times it did have a respectful model aircraft kit division.

France's main (arguably 'only') kit company, Heller, started in 1957. Heller has continued with slight 'ups and downs' to current times, with a range of similar kits to equal its original rival, then compatriot, then later returning to rival, Airfix.

Similarly Italy's Italeri still survives. Since its inception in the early 1960s, it has gone through two name changes: it was originally called Artiplast, but this was changed to Italereri. Later

LEFT Pegasus
Hobbies issued its
Luna (from *Destination
Moon*) in two scales.
These are moulded
in ABS, not standard
polystyrene.

FAR LEFT Moebius
Models issued its
own version of the
Frankenstein Monster.

LEFT Atlantis Models
has made a speciality
of flying saucers.

ABOVE Italeri is now the major Italian manufacturer, though the military Land Rover is an ESCI original (lower).

ABOVE RIGHT The best-known name of all Japanese kit companies, Tamiya.

still, this was shortened to become somewhat more pronounceable into its current, Italeri form. It continues to produce new kits, sometimes working in conjunction with Revell Germany. It also took over former Italian rivals ESCI (acquired from Ertl) and Protar along the way and works in conjunction with Testors in the US.

Not all American or European

Interestingly, over the whole of this time, while the US-European companies had gone through vast changes in size and ownership, the only other major country making kits in the earlier years, Japan, mostly stayed unaltered. This was primarily as the Japanese companies are – in the main – still family owned, and even though they had their own individual crises, they seemed to come out the other side more or less intact.

Many of the well-known Japanese model names began in remarkably similar ways, including Tamiya, Hasegawa and Fujimi. They all began in the 1940s, initially dealing with wood as the main model material. Tamiya actually started at a timber mill and lumber factory, created in 1946 by one Yoshio Tamiya and located in Shizuoka City, south of Tokyo and with views of Mount Fuji.

Tamiya's first kit was a wooden ship model, issued in 1948. These wooden ship kits were initially purely a sideline to the main business, but within five years had become the prime industry and the timber mill was closed. The plastic kit industry itself began in 1960. Intriguingly, Fujimi almost parallels Tamiya, also starting in 1948 by making wooden ship models and moving on to plastic in 1961.

Hasegawa started earlier, in 1941, with wooden education models, though it too started plastic kit production in the early 1960s. Its first models were gliders, reissued half a century later in its anniversary year. One of the perhaps lesser-known names, Aoshima (full name Aoshima Bunka Kyozai), started even earlier, as long ago as 1924, making model aircraft in wood but it too moved to plastic in the early

1:72　ロッキード P-3C アップデート II / III オライオン

UNASSEMBLED MODEL KIT
MAQUETTE PLASTIQUE A CONSTRUIRE

Hasegawa
Hobby kits

ABOVE More from Japan: Hasegawa.

RIGHT Another major Japanese manufacturer, Fujimi.

1960s. Its first kit, perhaps slightly oddly, was the British water speed record boat, Bluebird.

Perhaps the most intriguing feature of these four main Japanese kit manufacturers is that they are all based in Shizuoka City, making it a sort of 'Japanese model Detroit'.

Japanese kits were initially regarded – at best – as simplified 'toy-like' subjects, and indeed many were initially motorised, seemingly because it couldn't be imagined that any 'model' would not have some 'play value' in it. They were seen – at worst – as 'rip-offs' of what the western companies were making. But all that changed when it became apparent that

RIGHT One of the oldest model-making names anywhere in the world: Aoshima.

what the Japanese manufacturing industry in general was extremely good at was taking a product 'from the West', looking at it critically and then making it better! This has occurred across the range of manufactured products and one only has to look at the quality of a Tamiya kit, to see that they achieved it with the modelling industry as well.

Other Japanese manufacturers have covered a much wider range of 'toy products'; Bandai likely being the best known here, as over the years it has had lines of scale model kits of all subjects, along with other lines of standard toys. Recent years have also seen the appearance of other smaller, primarily model kit, Japanese companies such as Wave, Fine Molds, Zoukei Mura and Platz – all comparatively small in size, but producing high-quality models.

Although the Japanese kit industry paralleled what the West was doing with models of aircraft, ships and cars, because it was first and foremost Japanese it introduced to the West two specifically Japanese subjects. Firstly, kits of Japanese temples. These were significant and intriguing, as nothing like these existed in the West. But they were small in number, with a comparatively small number of models. Secondly, what rapidly overtook them and ended up far outnumbering them was the Japanese speciality, anime. This is purely a shortened form of the word 'animation',

LEFT Fine Molds makes an eclectic selection, including models of the machines that make the kits!

LEFT The Japan anime phenomenon has spawned thousands of kits. This is a tiny percentage.

so could refer to any country, but it has now become uniquely the prerogative of Japanese creations. This started with a penchant for 'monsters from the movies' specifically, of course, Japanese monsters, with *Godzilla* being the best known. But this then spread to the wider phenomenon of 'Japanese robots', of which the numbers are legion and likely beyond any meaningful calculation of the numbers of models that have been produced over the years. It does start to pale when you realise that very early on in the 1970s, sales of kits purely from one anime series, that of *Macross*, were well past the 200 mark and still rising.

We live in interesting times

In more recent years, there became a major – perhaps *the* major – change, with the rise of manufacturing from China. Although this applies across the board with any Chinese manufacturing, the model kit industry out of China began in Hong Kong. Still British-run in the 1950s and 1960s, when the Western plastic kit industry was starting, Hong Kong could be used to produce model kits more cheaply than

they could be produced at home. Lincoln was one 'British' model name, but the kits were 'Made in Hong Kong'.

China would have seen this, and its own fledgling model industry began under a variety of now virtually forgotten names, producing homegrown kits. Initially, the production mimicked early Japanese kits, in that they were not that well produced, very simplified,

BELOW One of the newer manufactures from China, Hobby Boss.

likely motorised and mainly of esoteric Chinese subjects. But China, as with Japan also learned, especially by the time it regained Hong Kong in 1997 – though in effect and for all practicalities, Hong Kong still runs as a 'separate country'. China approached the West, selling the ability to manufacture products – any products – far cheaper. The West (possibly unwisely!) took advantage of an offer which, at that point, they couldn't refuse. Much kit production was moved to China, including both tool manufacturing and actual production. All the Western companies then had to do was import the finished boxed kits and sell them.

China also learned from this and started making model kits that were to a much higher standard than originally, and of a range of subjects that could appeal to modellers across the globe. Many original names disappeared into the mists (does anyone remember Zhendefu?) but one name, that of Trumpeter, came to the forefront, though others such as Great Wall and Hobby Boss have come along in recent years. Products have been mainly military in nature, especially military AFVs, but also aircraft and warships. The range is worldwide, but does have a large percentage of Chinese craft, otherwise not obtainable from anywhere else. Occasionally, Trumpeter took some odd turns with its catalogue and branched out into making subjects that wouldn't be thought relevant to a Chinese company, particularly with some 1960s US sedans and convertibles and even an American fire engine! Other Chinese company names work primarily out of Hong Kong rather than mainland China, including Dragon, Meng and Bronco.

As with Japan and China, South Korea started by copying Western kits and issuing them 'as its own'. But – again similar to Japan and China – it soon branched out into producing its own subject matter at a very high quality. The earliest name associated with South Korea is Academy but now there are other companies, including Ace Corporation, working out of what is, after all, a relatively small country producing kits to very high standards.

Most recently, we have seen a growth in companies based in what were originally countries within the Soviet Union. Russia itself had kit companies such as Ogonjek and STC Start, but although these did have a certain charm of their own, they could hardly be said to have been of the highest Western or Japanese quality. But now there is Zvezda and Eastern Express in Russia and interestingly far more in the Ukraine, such as ICM, Condor, Master Box, Roden and Mini Art. Many of their kits are military in subject matter – aircraft, ships and ground vehicles – but ICM also makes early American Model T Fords and 1940s-/1950s-style cars from Germany, many released in both 1:35 and 1:24 scale. Master Box has also taken on a different approach to many companies, with figures and dioramas in not only 1:35 but also 1:24 scales.

Out of the garage

There has also been a blurring between what have been described as mainstream companies (the Revells, Airfixes and Tamiyas of the world) and the 'garage companies'. Many started in the Eastern European countries, especially Czechoslovakia (now the Czech

BELOW The Czech Republic's CMK, now Special Hobby.

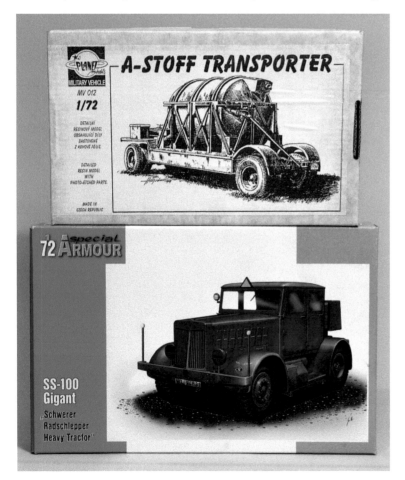

LEFT Major accessory manufacturer, now making full kits: Eduard.

Republic). Initially using low-production methods of manufacture (see more in Chapter 10, pages 140–153), many moved to styrene injection-moulding techniques, and kits in resin with white metal and photo-etched parts. One company stands out here: MPM (now known as Special Hobby), which has variously had divisions such as CMK, Special Armour, Cooperativa, Planet Models and Special Hobby itself.

Another major name is Eduard. Eduard started making accessories for kits but then started making its own complete injection-moulded kits, many in cooperation with other companies.

Mention needs to be made of Verlinden in Belgium, as for many years this company specialised in 1:35 military figures and accessories. It primarily used 1:35 scale, hence the military emphasis, and mainly in resin, though it occasionally branched out into other scales. Verlinden was one of the first companies to publish its own books on model making, and to include all manner of details on weathering. Created and run by Francois Verlinden, he closed the company in 2016.

Even countries not initially associated with model business now have appeared. In the past, Australia had small associations with model companies from other countries, but it now has homegrown Horizon Models, which manufactures US space launcher kits to 1:72 scale. Canada, although having had divisions from original companies such as Revell and Aurora, now has Hobbycraft as a homegrown company. This initially reissued other manufacturers' products, but over the last decades has started making its own.

So, to answer the question 'Is a model of this made?' the answer is 'probably', but you really will have to search!

LEFT Major accessory manufacturer, now making full kits: Eduard.

BELOW Entex reissued many Japanese kits for the US market. This was an Otaki original.

BOTTOM Minicraft has issued many 'different' kits of its own – including Noah's Ark.

Chapter Five

Tools, cement and a place to work

Unless your model kit is pre-coloured, snaps together and has stick-on decals, you are going to require some modelling tools, glues and paint to finish it. You are also going to need somewhere to work, and that will apply even if it is pre-coloured, snaps together and has stick-on decals. Where you actually build the kit is something that is purely personal, and obviously everyone's situation will be different and dependant on individual circumstances.

Where to work

Modellers have worked in places ranging from professionally equipped workshops in a specially dedicated area of the home, to working off a board placed on the kitchen table that has to be stored on top of a cupboard when dinner becomes the priority.

Purpose-built modelling areas could be built in a spare room, attic or basement, a spot in the garage, or even – as is common these days – an office-type structure in the garden (otherwise known as a shed…).

With working from home becoming more of a worldwide phenomenon, and consequently a home office space being common, perhaps adding a small extra area for a modelling bench may not be beyond the realms of feasibility. For the model maker a workbench next to the computer, scanner and printer could be very convenient, and for research, very useful.

It is beyond the scope of this book to actually detail the building of such an area, and a lot could also depend on the size of the model you are building. 1:72 scale aircraft modellers, figure builders and 1:25 scale car enthusiasts probably have it slightly easier than those going for 3ft-long galleons, 4ft-long aircraft carriers or 5ft-long submarines.

The main modelling area will probably need to cover no more than three feet/one metre wide by slightly less deep. If it is to be portable, it can built from any suitable wood: blockboard, plywood or MDF should all serve this purpose. You will probably need to seal both sides to prevent warping or even cover the work surface with a material such as Formica. Or, even easier, buy one of the finished wood surfaces from the usual DIY stores. A lip around the edge may be advisable to prevent small parts rolling off, especially if the work area is on the small side. If the board is to be moved a great deal, out of the way of the most inquisitive members of the family (small children and cats being the most inquisitive, especially with drying paint…), handles could be a useful addition and maybe even a cover.

The work surface

Assuming you have somewhere permanent, or even semi-permanent, to work, the first priority

ABOVE **A lamp with a magnifier, useful for detailed work.**

is the work surface. For the basic structure, purpose-built work tables can be bought, but it's just as convenient and certainly a lot cheaper to use an old table bought from a junk shop or garage sale. Direct working on such a wooden table or bench top is not ideal, especially when cutting, as scars are soon going to appear. It is better to use one of the many cutting mats available in a variety of sizes. These take general cutting blades in their stride, the surface being 'self-healing' to an extent. Alternatively, a sheet of mounting card could be used, available from art stores.

Lighting

One very important point is to have adequate lighting. If you are working from a temporary board, place it on a table near a window or a good light source. If you have a dedicated work area that has a window, position the main workbench under that. If there is no window, light sources will have to be fitted, and will likely be needed anyway if you intend to work when it's dark outside!

Fluorescent tubes

Precisely what you decide on as 'a good light source' is dependent upon your own needs. Workshops and the like tend to have fluorescent tubes fitted by default, and the tubes can be bought in various degrees of 'temperature', from mimicking indoors, which is

OPPOSITE **A workbench that started life as old desk many (many) years ago, placed by a window to give natural light. The window ledge is used for storage.**

towards the 'warmer' end of the spectrum (i.e. more red) to daylight, which goes the opposite way, towards the blue 'colder' end.

LED (Light Emitting Diode) bulbs

Much lighting these days is moving to LED and here the tube equivalents can often be found to be able to be 'set' to a certain temperatures, maybe via remote controls. Alternatively old style incandescent bulbs still have their uses – though remember these run 'hot' (some very hot), and invariably blow just at the most inconvenient moment. But again many are being replaced with LED equivalents that run colder, (though none run completely 'cold'). Although they are more expensive to buy in the first place, they use far less electricity and last far longer than what they replace.

Modelling lamps

There are also specialist 'modelling lamps' (though likely sold for anything that requires 'close work') usually on some sort of adjustable 'anglepoise-type' device. Many are based on a circular fluorescent tube, and there could also be a magnifier built in for really close up details. Others are now low voltage, perhaps using a quartz iodine bulb for brightness, though these run hot and are also being phased out. In fact, virtually all bulbs and fittings can be replaced with LED equivalents these days.

Cutting and trimming

Tools can range from the very basic to highly sophisticated (and invariably expensive) equipment that do very specific tasks. At the very least, for any standard (assuming such a word can be used) model kit, you will need the minimum of some method of cutting and trimming the parts from the runners and some way of cementing the parts together.

The cutting of the parts can be done in two ways. We ignore 'the third way' which is to twist the parts off, which will a) leave very ragged edges, b) likely break the parts or c) both! They can either be cut off using snips or sawn off.

To cut the parts there are specially manufactured 'modelling snips'. Frankly, an

BELOW Range of modelling tools, files, snips, razor saws and tweezers.

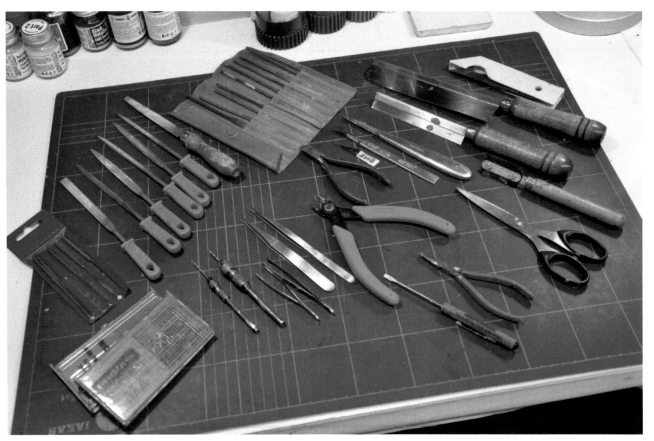

ABOVE **Using small side cutters to trim parts.**

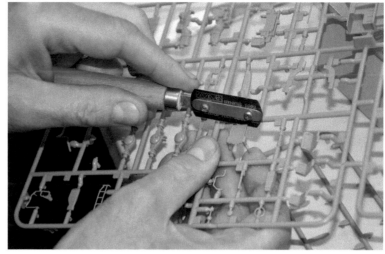

ABOVE **Using a razor saw to remove parts.**

LEFT **Using the small razor saw to do some modifications to the engine cowing of the Encore Pfalz biplane.**

old pair of nail cutters or electrical side cutters would also work – though the former may be too fiddly and the latter too large for small parts.

To saw parts, again there are specially manufactured tools, usually termed 'razor saws', which are specially made for delicate modelling tasks. These are more useful where the 'shock' of the snips 'snipping', can cause very small or thin parts to snap.

Whichever way the part is removed from the runner, it will invariably leave a slight edge at the gate, the connecting section from the runner to where the plastic was fed into the cavity. Here, a modelling knife or scalpel can be *carefully* used.

Knives and blades

Most model companies make their own-name model knives, though a wide variety of standard knives and scalpels are widely available from modelling suppliers. Many come in several sizes, with various blades for specific tasks. This particularly applies to scalpels, which are basically the same as those used for medical purposes, though they are listed as 'non-sterile'. Non-sterile they may be, but the blades are equally sharp – *very* sharp – consequently, it shouldn't be necessary to say 'be careful' and handle with respect (though this equally applies to any knife). When scalpel blades blunt or snap (they do regularly) carefully remove the blade from the handle. Specialist containers are available to safely store the blades so they can be disposed of correctly.

Larger knives can also be useful, such as what are referred to as box cutters, or by one of their major trade names: Stanley knives. It is preferable to use one with a retractable blade,

and they are useful for cutting larger runners, shaving parts and even just opening boxes.

Scissors will also be required when it comes to cutting up decal sheets. Get good-quality ones where the cutting blades are precisely aligned. You don't want precious one-off decals being damaged when all you are doing is cutting them apart!

Filing and sanding

Files

Small files are especially made for modelling and similar industries. These are made in various sizes and are available either individually or in sets. They come in various shapes – from the conventional flat to half-round, round, square and triangular. The smallest (the ones usually sold in sets) are usually referred to as needle files, and a set – even a couple of sets – will be the most useful for small model tasks.

Larger sizes will also find their use, and even some of the largest, conventional-sized, files could have uses for, say, removing bigger areas. They are particularly useful for dealing

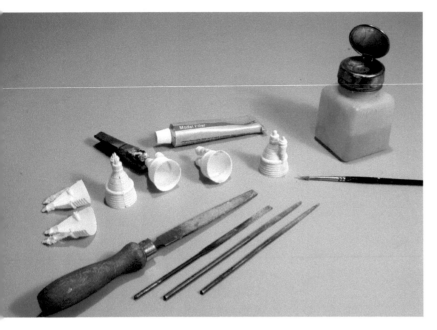

LEFT A build sequence of the F-1 engines from the Airfix Apollo Saturn V. Once the halves are glued together, the edges need filing (needle files are useful), filling with a good-quality modelling putty and sanding. Liquid cement helps blend in the filler.

with the gates of resin kits, which are far larger than the equivalent injection styrene kits, or for filing mating surfaces flat (pouring resin can sometimes leave a raised 'bump').

Sandpaper

Another very useful modelling tool is – using its most widely accepted term – 'sandpaper' (it hasn't used actual sand for decades, but the generic term remains). Many grades are

RIGHT Sanding set especially for model-making, using very fine grade sanding pads, polish and buffing cloth.

FAR RIGHT Grades of 'sandpaper'. The yellow and green sandpaper (left) is only suitable used dry; the emery papers (right) can be used wet and dry.

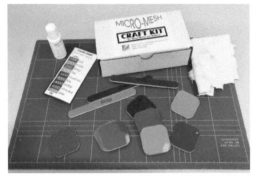

RIGHT For heavy-duty sanding, a mechanical version could be useful. For general sanding, glue a sheet onto a board (right).

available, and for your main supply there is no need to buy 'modelling sanding paper', just get the packs from the DIY store and cut them up into convenient sizes. A house builder will likely go through a pack a day, but for a modeller, one pack will probably last years!

Sanding papers can be basically split between that which is used dry and that used wet – though some of these can also be used dry and so are termed 'wet-and-dry'. Modellers will tend to find wet-and-dry the most useful, as sanding wet improves the cutting and cools the parts so the styrene doesn't tear. Most emery-type 'sandpapers' are fine for this task. These are waterproof and can easily be identified as they have a dark grey or black backing. Dry sandpapers (the type on a yellow or green backing) can also be used for some tasks – sanding the tyres on model cars is a favourite. These can't be used 'wet', as in water they will disintegrate into a soggy mess!

All sanding papers come in grades: the higher the number, the finer the grade. Course grades will be in the tens, medium grades in the hundreds and very fine grades in the thousands. There are also sets specifically made for modelling that concentrate on the finest grades, normally colour-coded for identification. These can be used with polishing powders or liquids for the very smoothest of surfaces.

Sanding devices can come in other forms. There are sanding sticks, some rounded for dealing with curved surfaces, and even the humble emery board (for fingernails) can be employed.

Clamping

Other types of tools that will come in useful are clamps for holding parts while cement dries, or for painting. There is a very wide range of small clamps available in metal or plastic and in various sizes from DIY stores, model stores and hobby shops.

Forceps and pegs
Medical forceps are extremely useful, not only for clamping but for holding small parts for painting. Because they have a slight amount of 'give' to them and are ratcheted,

they can accommodate a fairly wide range of thicknesses. Then there is that old mainstay – the humble clothes peg (clothes pin). Available cheaply in both plastic and wood, a box full should be a part of any modeller's tool kit. The wooden variety can even be easily cut down to points to hold very small very parts, again for drying or painting. For the plastic variety, many have holes in their handle section, useful as an aid to hanging up while drying.

ABOVE Clamps and other equipment.

BELOW Clamps – in the form of clothes pegs – are very useful, especially when you have to use a lot!

Vices

Small bench-mounted vices are also useful. Some of these have their own clamps or a vacuum suction base, so they can be temporally attached to the workspace, then removed.

Tape

Even humble sticky tape can be useful. Use a standard tape dispenser, so the tape can be pulled off with one hand – maybe even several dispensers with different types of tape in them. There could be white masking tape in one and regular standard 'sticky tape' in another.

Double-sided tape is also useful for holding small parts to a clothes peg for painting – these are available purely as standard thickness tapes that are sticky both sides. Even more useful is foam double-sided tape – a very thin layer of foam, also sticky both sides. The foam means the tape has a small amount of 'give' to it. It can be especially useful for attaching and holding parts that might have a slightly irregular surface. It is also great for adding to the edge of a wire holder to secure it inside, say, a model car body for spray painting.

Drills

Holes may have to be drilled, and here you have the option of hand-operated drills – usually called a pin-vice (or vise), or an electric drill. Both have their uses.

The pin-vice is invariably more precise, especially as it has very small drill bits for drilling tiny holes. However electric drill sets – besides being faster and time-saving when multiple holes have to be drilled – can also be fitted with other tools. These include sanding discs, cutting discs and polishers.

The electric variety can be mains or low voltage, and most will come with a speed control, as most of the time it will be vital to control the speed of the operation. Electric drill controllers often have companion tools that can plug in to the same transformer, such as a small jigsaw, which is invaluable for many other tasks.

Sticking together

Separating the parts from the runners and cleaning them up is the first task; the second is assembling them with the rest – and here's where gluing techniques come in.

BELOW Power tools can be bought individually, with their own low-voltage power supply (right) or as a set (left) – this one working off the mains.

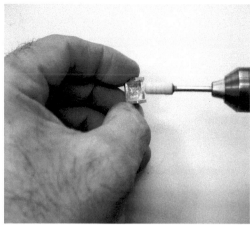

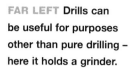

FAR LEFT Drills can be useful for purposes other than pure drilling – here it holds a grinder.

LEFT Using a small grinding wheel in an electric drill to smooth out the edges of the Airfix Saturn V LM Adaptor section. This has also been opened up using a razor saw so that the LM will be able to be seen inside.

FAR LEFT Using an electric drill to open up the windows in the building structure from the Pegasus 'Mercury 7' kit.

LEFT The miniature jigsaw can be useful for trimming large parts.

LEFT Glues: from liquid cement (upper left) to superglues (centre) and model filler (right).

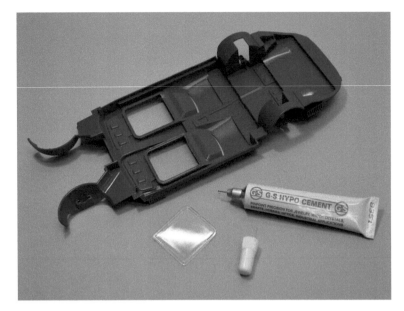

Assuming the kit is not 'snap together' (and, in any case, these can be glued as well), glue or cement is necessary.

Tubed cement

In early times there was just the one option – tubed cement. This was filler of styrene in a carrier solution (usually chlorobenzene or acetone), and you literally ran a bead of cement along one edge and held it against the other. It *mostly* worked (there was no other option anyway) but it had two disadvantages. Firstly, it could take ages to dry, depending on the thickness of the layer, and secondly, because it had 'bulk' you usually had some residue left over that squeezed out between the parts. Time was then required to allow it to dry thoroughly and you then had to remove the excess by trimming and sanding.

Liquid cement

Both these problems were solved with the introduction of liquid cement. This is (as can be surmised from the name!) purely a liquid that will dissolve the styrene and allow the surfaces in effect to 'weld' together. It is a much faster action than tubed cement and will not leave a residue of the filler as, well, there isn't any filler.

The liquids used can vary. Many chemical compounds will dissolve styrene, but most are based around an aromatic hydrocarbon solvent base. Most of these are unpleasant, if not actually poisonous, so although relatively small qualities are being used for model making, it is vital to ensure the work area is well ventilated. If you are particularly worried, wear a suitable mask with a filter. If you have a dedicated workshop area, you may even be able to fit an extractor fan, though ensure it is of an adequate size to shift a reasonable amount of air. (Fitting such fans – and where they vent into – may require special requirements depending on your locality. Check local by-laws if necessary. See also Chapter 6, on Paint, page 80.)

There are variations on liquid cements. Some still actually have a small amount of filler included, although these flow much more easily

ABOVE Applying liquid cement with the built-in brush.

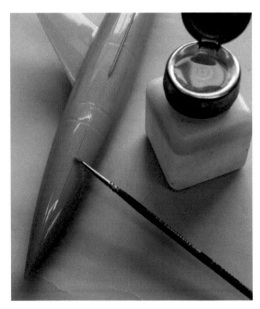

RIGHT Applying liquid cement with an old paintbrush.

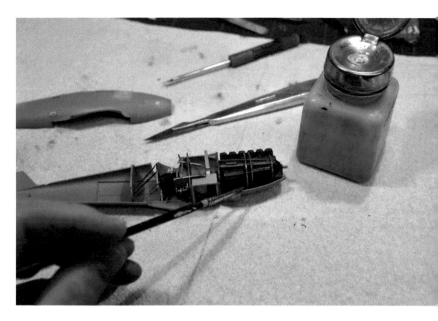

RIGHT Cementing the engine and cockpit of the Pfalz in place using liquid cement.

than the old fashioned type of tubed cement; others go to the opposite extreme and are sold as 'super thin'.

Application of liquid cement is slightly more involved than purely squeezing a tube. First, the container must be kept tightly sealed when not in use, as the liquid will evaporate very quickly. Dispenser pots are available with a lid and push-down spring to allow only a small amount of liquid to be free to the air, also minimising evaporation. Second, you need something to apply the cement with – an old paintbrush is ideal for this. Keep old ones when they are passed their paint-application days, so you double their useful life. Larger quantities, such as for cementing hulls of ships or aircraft fuselages, can be applied by using a pipette or syringe – though be careful it isn't made from materials that will dissolve in the liquid!

Superglue

Because many kits these days are 'multi-material', in that they come with additional parts not made from styrene such as resin, white metal, photo-etch or even flexible materials used as seat belts in aircraft and car kits, other gluing methods can be required. The main one here will be cyano-acrylate (CA), otherwise known as 'superglue'. For resin parts, this is really the only method, and it has largely replaced the older method of a two-part glue mix. This is somewhat akin to tubed polystyrene cement versus liquid cement. The older two-part adhesive has 'bulk', which will need to be removed when it squeezes out; the CA does not. However the older two-part glues still have their uses. Some resin kits are not as well cast as injection-moulded styrene, and here it can be occasionally useful to have some 'gap-filling' ability for holding the parts together.

RIGHT A sheet of plate glass is useful as a 'flat surface' when you're cementing parts together that have to be level. This is the base of the support for the large 1:20 scale Accurate Models' Saturn V F-1 engine.

ABOVE LEFT Curio from the past – Revell kits that had 'A', for acetate, on the box...

ABOVE RIGHT ...and then change to 'S' for styrene cement!

RIGHT Many injection
styrene kits now have
parts made from other
materials – usually
termed 'multi-material'
kits. Here the inner
screen for Moebius
Models' Robot from
Lost in Space are
photo-etched parts
that need to be slightly
curved before gluing
into place.

Superglue comes in various viscosities: thin, medium and thick, and a bottle of each will be handy – although if you only have space for one, go for the medium. Bottles are available in several sizes, but frankly, the amount a modeller will use is not that great so it's better to go for the smaller sizes. You'll almost certainly find, as superglue has a limited shelf life when opened, that most of the bottle has hardened over time with the larger quantities and only becomes fit for the waste bin. Keeping bottles in the fridge is suggested as a method of lengthening its usable life, but this may not be practical.

With superglue, 'little is more' is the adage. Use the smallest amount possible, as it will cure faster. Curing can be speeded up by the use of an accelerator, or 'kicker', usually available in a hand-pumped spray bottle. The chemical reaction gets hot – in some cases, very hot – so be careful to keep fingers away from the parts! Kicker also weakens the join, not that this is usually a prime consideration when building a model kit. Superglue is also excellent in gluing skin together (it is what it

was invented for in the first place), so a bottle of debonder should also be part of the tool kit – and kept to hand!

Superglue will also glue together photo-etched parts and other dissimilar materials. However, it is not suitable for gluing clear styrene, as used in cockpit canopies, car windscreens and headlamp lenses, for example. This is because it gives off fumes during curing that can affect and cloud the clear surface. It is better to use what is usually called 'watchmaker cement', a thin, clear adhesive in a tube that does not have the volatiles of liquid cement or superglue. Alternatively, for very small parts, small headlamps or lenses, a water-based adhesive such as PVA (wood glue) could be used, thinned down if necessary, or even clear varnish from a bottle or tin. These small parts don't require much tensile strength, so there is no strain on the 'glue' – all it is doing is preventing the part falling out!

For this type of glue application, there are superglue applicators that fit modelling tool handles and are designed to put a specific amount of glue in a particular spot. However, a cheaper alternative is to use the same 'second-hand' paintbrushes used for liquid cement application. This will invariably be the 'final use' of such a brush, as the superglue will cure on the bristles, rendering them useless. It is even cheaper to use cocktail sticks to apply drops of superglue. This, as with the paintbrushes, will cure on the end of the stick, but you can break off that section and continue to use the stick until it is, indeed, finally used up.

Cocktail sticks

Cocktail sticks are a useful – and cheap – tool in the modelling box as they can be used for a variety of tasks. They're handy for holding small parts for painting. If there is an existing location hole in the part, use that, or maybe drill one in an inconspicuous place. Their larger cousins, kebab sticks, are also very useful for holding larger parts.

Glue gun

There's one other gluing method that modellers can find invaluable, though this primarily comes into play if you are building dioramas. This is a glue gun. Using low-melting glue stick and powered from the mains, the gun part heats the

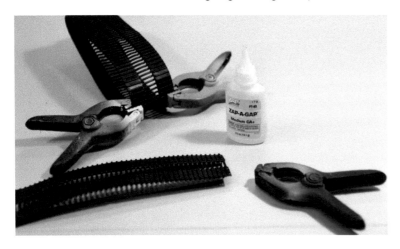

stick enough so that the glue will flow, directed out of the nozzle by applying pressure on the 'trigger' that pushes the stick forward. This method is obviously not suitable for gluing a kit together – it is far too thick and far too hot – but it is ideal for large-scale gluing of diorama parts. The guns are available in many sizes and some work at varying temperatures. There are even specifically 'low temperature' ones intended for children to use. The sticks are also different diameters, depending on the gun. Most types would be available at arts stores, DIY stores, maybe some model shops. There are even larger ones that are gas powered, though these are really only for professional commercial use. (Also see Chapter 9, Dioramas, pages 126–139.)

Cleaning up

With any modelling task, you will need to clean up, so a supply of paper towels is vital. The kitchen variety is the usual option, and if space allows, fit one of the holders so you just have to pull one sheet away at a time – just as they are used in the kitchen. Besides cleaning and drying paintbrushes, you will need to clean the parts before painting (using one of the proprietary cleaners or methylated spirits/ denatured alcohol) and there will be times when the brush cleaner container will get tipped over – yes, it will happen – and you'll need something immediately to hand to rapidly mop it up!

Fillers

The vast majority of model kits are extremely well engineered and the fit of the parts will be precise. However, there will be times when you require filler. Maybe it's an older kit, or the

tooling has worn, or the seams aren't quite as exact as you'd wish. With many resin kits, the fit isn't quite as precise as styrene, so again filler is necessary. Or perhaps you are doing some scratch-building and 'holes have to be filled'.

Most model companies that also make paint and accessories include fillers that are specially made for model kits. These are fine in texture, apply smoothly and dry reasonably quickly. Most are also 'one part', i.e. they do not have to be mixed to harden. Some fillers are two-part, such as two-part resin glues, so they have a filler and a hardener that have to be mixed together to cure. These are similar to the type of body filler you can get for full-sized car repairs – in fact, many of these car body fillers could be used instead. The advantages of two-part fillers are that they can be used to fill larger areas, as the curing does not rely on air drying. However, depending on how much hardener or catalyst is used, they do cure fast, so speed of assembly could be an important factor.

Model filler really began life as an addition to early American car kits. Here it was usually called 'body putty' and was intended to mould

ABOVE LEFT Model fillers are very useful for seams. Let them dry and then sand, preferably with wet'n'dry for a smooth finish.

ABOVE Model filler is used on figures, where you tend to find more gaps, due to irregularly shaped parts

BELOW Some older kits (and indeed many newer kits) may need a small amount of filler along the seams. This Airfix DH-88 Comet is from very old tooling – it dates from the 1950s – and benefits from filler around engine halves and wing roots.

custom parts into the main car body to create your own designs. However, the idea was soon adapted to many other model subjects, and standalone tubes of filler began to appear.

Both one-part and two-part fillers will require finishing in the form of sanding, and both types are ideal for wet-sanding to get the smoothest of finishes. Sometimes the use of both types is appropriate. For example, you can use the two-part car type to fill larger areas, but not right up to the surface, then apply the 'official' model putty to bring it up level with the kit surface, ready for sanding.

Storage

Where you store your tools and cement depends on your circumstances. If you're restricted to working from a temporary base that has to be cleared, you'll need a convenient box for tools, glues and paints. The type sold for fishing accessories or small tools, screws and nails that can be bought from DIY stores are the most straightforward options (these, of course, can also be used by those with more dedicated areas in order to keep their benches looking neat and tidy). If you're fortunate enough to have dedicated modelling area, tools, glues and paints should also be stored neatly and not casually scattered all over the place. It will be obvious when supplies are running low, will prevent damage to tools, and a neat work area almost certainly has a beneficial psychological effect!

Small plastic sets of drawers, again available at DIY or even office suppliers, can hold spare blades, drill bits and all the paraphernalia that every modeller will accumulate. Plastic trays, again either bought or recycled (such as Chinese takeaway food containers) can hold files and knives. Small glass jars, or even chipped drinking mugs, are useful for holding scissors, small rulers, pens and pencils – and again add to the whole recycling ethos.

With some tools it is especially vital that they are stored correctly. Paintbrushes in particular need to be stored either flat or upside down (i.e. bristles at the top!) in a jar or other container, so the bristles are not squashed. Storing them bristles down is the quickest way to wreck them. So more use for those recycled jars or chipped mugs!

If you use older paintbrushes for liquid cement application, it's best to colour-code them and store them separately. Colour-coding is extremely easy for any modeller with a supply of paints to hand. Just chose a colour that will immediately say, 'I'm for cement application, not paint'!

As your skills and expertise increase, you could find other more specialist tools and equipment are necessary. Many 'full-size' tools intended for woodworking, even metalworking, can be adapted for model making.

There is one other section that comes under 'storage' – and that's what to do with all the spare parts?

The bits and pieces box – or boxes

Many kits have optional parts that are going to be left over when the model is finished. Some may just throw these away, but most modellers

RIGHT Small sets of drawers useful for small parts – it helps if they are labelled.

BELOW Larger boxes for larger parts.

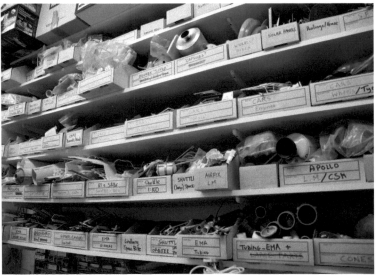

will want to hang onto them 'just in case'. If you only ever build one or two kits, the spares will be correspondingly small, but if not you'll be surprised how they can build up. They'll then need their own storage system.

The 'spares' will be of various sizes, so will need categorising and storing in a way that you can find the parts if you need them in the future. Logically, small parts are going to need small containers, and here again, small sets of drawers available from office suppliers are going to serve the purpose. For larger parts, well, any modeller is going to have a ready-made source – the box the kit came in. In the longer run, though, this solution may not be practical, mainly depending on how many kits you've actually built.

Again, recycling boxes such as takeaway containers or margarine tubs could be a source. There are also specific container manufacturers that make storage boxes in all sizes. These you'll have to buy, though, and if they are all the same size they could be easier to store – all one size on one size of shelf.

Whatever the storage solution, make sure they are adequately labelled. You don't want to spend precious time going though all boxes, only to the find the part you want is in the last box you check.

And while on 'spare parts', one question that does come up quite often is: 'Can I reuse the runners when all the parts are removed?' Here, unfortunately, the answer really is: 'Not really'. However, polystyrene is a perfectly recyclable plastic – the code of styrene is #6 (ABS, #9) – but that does not mean any local recycling centre will actually do this. Also the amount any hobbyist is going to generate is unlikely to make it worthwhile (see Chapter 1, page 17).

But there could be one use. Some modellers, those scratch-building spaceships, have used bits of the runners as parts. This is a very good source if you intend to build a Borg Cube from *Star Trek*. Yes, this has actually been done and yes, it uses up a lot of runners!

MODEL MAKING ON TOUR

There is a small sub-set of modellers who travel for work a lot and, to while away the evening hours, like to take a portable work area that can be set up in a hotel room. For many years, they could likely take any of the tools used at home on their travels. However, when travelling by air, recent legislations started making this impractical, if not completely impossible. Aerosol paints were definitely out in both hold and carry-on luggage. And if it was just carry-ons (and most business travel tends to be), blades and other sharp tools were also out and any liquids, such as paints and glues, were limited in volume and had to be in specified containers. The only possible option was to leave behind the tools, paints and glues and buy them from a local model store when you got there – though this, of course, assumed you could find one at your destination anyway. You would then have to discard them for the return flight, so it really became impractical to try and do any actual building! Perhaps instead use the time for research on the laptop?

ABOVE LEFT You may find installing an extractor fan useful.

ABOVE And yes, cats do get curious! Here Charlie is exploring; fortunately no wet paint was around!

Chapter Six

Paint

Virtually all models are going to need some paint applied at some point in their construction. To this end, a whole industry has grown up around supplying suitable paints and accessories. Best known worldwide are Testors in the USA, Humbrol in the UK and GSI Creos in Japan – the last using operating names: Gunze Sangyo or, more often these days, Mr Hobby.

Other model companies also have their name attached to paint products, such as Revell Germany, Heller, Italeri and, especially, Tamiya. Airfix long ago supplied paint in bottles, but it has been connected with Humbrol for many decades, so its paint supply is now down to the associated name.

Then there are the companies that make more specialised model paint. Hannants, the UK's main aircraft and military distributor makes its own Xtracolor, while Spain has Vallejo, AK Interactive and Mig-Ammo.

Paint basically falls under two headings as far as modellers are concerned, as most of the time it will either be brushed on or sprayed on. Brushing paint is consequently available in tinlets or bottles and spray paint is available in aerosol cans. Of course, there are variations on these. There has been an increasing use of what were originally termed a spray gun, now somewhat elevated to the more sophisticated airbrushes, developed from those used in the design and fine-art world. To this end, pre-thinned paints are increasingly available from specialist supplies that can be used directly in airbrushes, without having to do the mixing and thinning yourself. Then there are also an increasing range of posters paints that can be used for weathering, dealt with in more detail later.

The type of paints used, in both brush or airbrushing, also varies. The best known, and still used (started in the early days of modelling) is enamel, such as in the classic range of Humbrol tinlets. But you will also see acrylic, lacquer and maybe even cellulose. (The latter is primarily being used by flying aircraft models to 'dope' surfaces. However, it is rarely used by plastic modellers, as it affects the styrene surface.)

Brushing

Whether the paint is in tinlets or bottles, it is vital that it is mixed thoroughly. First shake well – and it shouldn't be necessary to say, but it is – ensuring the top is firmly on (yes, it has happened, shaking the bottle and the top comes off…). Then stir thoroughly using a cocktail or kebab stick. The non-brush end of the paintbrush is permissible if a stick isn't available. (Then, of course, ensure the end of the paintbrush handle is wiped clean!) Try not to use the working end of the brush – it won't help the bristles.

Any brush paint finish is only ever going to be as good as the brush that applies it. There are a multitude of brushes made for the model maker, and if you include those intended for fine-art painting, even more. The advice is always to go for the best quality you can afford. You don't want odd hairs dropping out and becoming part of that high-gloss finish you've just spent hours achieving. Designations vary depending on the brush manufacturer, but you will need a range, from the finest (invariably designated along the lines of 000) up to medium (3, 4, 5 and 6) and maybe larger. Then there's an extra-wide brush that is never used for paint, only dusting! Even the best brushes won't last forever, but dedicated care of them will certainly extend their life.

After use, brushes should be wiped clean of excess paint (this is where the paper kitchen towel holder is invaluable) and cleared of residue paint using a good-quality cleaner – white spirit or turps substitute. Keep this in a container with a lid, such as a cleaned-out pickle jar, so it won't evaporate and leave fumes in the air, and to help when it gets tipped over at some point (and, yes, it will…). With the lid in place, you at least have a better chance at not having to use the whole of the paper towel roll for the clean-up operation! The cleaner will eventually get too cloudy for further cleaning so either use it for more basic cleaning (such degreasing full-size engine parts) or dispose of it, with due respect to the environment.

OPPOSITE Storage of paint tinlets: colours are stored in individual trays, which are reused film transparency holder trays.

BELOW A range of tinlets and bottles from various manufacturers, plus the recycled pickle jar, now holding white spirit for cleaning. A selection of brushes and the vital roll of paper towel.

One thing not to do, of course, is to store the brushes in the cleaner, bristles down – unless you want shorten the life of the brush to zero as this will totally wreck the bristles! Ensure the brushes are dried and either store horizontally or vertically, bristle-side up, in a spare container. However carefully they are stored, all brushes have a limited life, but after their best painting days are over, they can be usefully employed to apply liquid cement.

Spraying

Aerosol or spray cans of paint for modellers became available in the US in the early 1960s. Initially, these were mostly intended for spraying model cars, and companies such as AMT and Pactra made a wide range in solid colours, plus metallics, metalflakes and candies or 'kandies' (transparent) shades. These were available as enamels but also as lacquers, which use a different base.

Worldwide legislation in recent years has meant an almost complete change of formulation in these cans, so although some still are enamel- or lacquer-based, the vast majority now contain acrylic-based paint.

Being water based (though formulas vary), acrylic was initially difficult to get to spray correctly, but refinement has meant that acrylic has now become the norm. It's easy to spray straight from the can (even for a novice), it's less toxic than enamel or lacquer-based paints (though adequate ventilation should still be used) and, in the main, it dries fast. It is also less reactive with other paints, so spraying one

type of paint on top of another is *usually* less prone to creating a reaction with the bubbling or lifting of the paint underneath, which could result from using enamel or lacquer paint. However, it's always advisable to test any paint on any surface before applying, especially if you haven't used that particular brand or type of paint before. Apply a little paint to an out-of-the-way part: the inside of a fuselage, hull or car body, or a spare part that's not going to be used.

Spray paint cans may have stood for ages, meaning the paint mix inside separates out and the heaver or denser elements settle in bottom of the can. Consequently, aerosol cans have a ball bearing inside. This helps with the mixing, and the rattling sound indicates the fact the paint is loosening. In fact, pick up a can that has been standing for some time, do an experimental 'rattle', and you won't hear a sound – the ball bearing will almost certainly be stuck in the congealed paint at the bottom of the can. (Some older cans of clear varnishes didn't have a ball bearing, but these were in the minority – modern cans all have 'a rattle'.)

Besides thoroughly shaking to mix the contents – and this needs to be done for longer than you think would be necessary – aerosol cans certainly benefit from being warmed. Stand the can in warm water for a few minutes, then do the shaking.

This 'shaking thoroughly' process also applies to prepacked bottles of airbrush-ready paint. As airbrush use has become more popular, there is an increasing range of these – again, it is vital to ensure that these are thoroughly mixed before any attempt at airbrushing. If you don't, the paint will almost certainly clog the airbrush nozzle, resulting in dismantling and cleaning!

Don't stop

Whatever the formula of the paint, and whether it's from an aerosol can or an airbrush, when actually spraying the golden rule is to *never* stop the spray on the model itself. Start the spray in front of the model, pass the aerosol mist over the model surface and only stop when you have passed the model. The exact speed at which you move the can or airbrush and the amount of paint you are spraying will have to come down to practise and experience. However, the basic rule is to apply a lot of mist coats to build up the layers rather than one 'heavy' coat. As always, there are exceptions. When spraying a high-gloss surface (model cars being the prime example) it is usual to apply initial layers as mist coats, but to apply the final layer as 'wet' as you can – without the paint running – to get the glossiest finish.

With any aerosol can, when you finish spraying, invert the can and spray for another few seconds to clear the nozzle. However, if the nozzle does block up – and they sometimes do – remove it and soak it in paint cleaner. In fact, it is useful to have a supply of spare nozzles, so recycle empty cans (many recycling centres will take aerosol cans) but salvage the nozzles. Keep these in an old lidded jar, filled with more brush cleaner, and occasionally shake the jar to persuade the cleaner to act on the paint in the nozzle. If you need a spare nozzle, remove one from the jar, wash it under water then fit it to the can. It's important to blast some paint through the can before you attempt to spray a model, firstly to check the nozzle is clear and secondly, you don't want any remaining paint cleaner sprayed onto the plastic!

ABOVE Salvaging aerosol nozzles for reuse. Keep in a jar filled with brush cleaner.

Airbrushing

Airbrushing is a complete subject in its own right and there are many books on the subject. Here, however, are the basic procedures.

Airbrushes are not specifically designed for painting models; they are generally used in the art and design industry and they all work on more or less the same principle of using a precise jet of air over the paint supply and propelling it out of a nozzle, usually variable as to the size and shape of the stream of paint onto the surface. They all consist of two main parts: the paint container and the body you hold, through which the paint flows via the trigger. The paint container can be variously positioned. It may be in a container or cup, above the handle, so the paint primarily uses gravity, some are below in a bottle and use the flow of the air to pick up the paint.

Airbrushes are also usually described as 'single or double action'. Single action uses a set paint flow – the trigger only controls the overall speed of delivery of the air. Double action varies the flow of both the air and the

BELOW A range of airbrushes, and – behind – compressors. Most of the latter will have regulators and air pressure gauges.

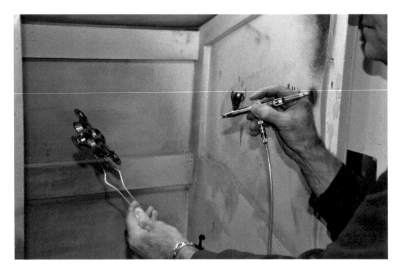

amount of paint, depending on the position of the trigger. With both methods, however, the airbrush has overall settings as to the amount of paint and air it will deliver in total.

Under pressure

The air itself needs a source. Most will use a small compressor, these days mains powered, with both a pump and a small air reservoir. They can be set to only send the sort of air pressure you would need. The pressure can vary according to personal preference, which is linked to experience – experimentation will show the sort of pressure you will need to spray the type of paint you are using. Some modellers will use pressures as low as 5psi, some as high as 40psi. Generally start with something between 20 and 30psi, and then vary depending on circumstances. Many pumps also have filters and water traps to remove water vapour from the air. You need the air

to be as dry as possible, as water vapour will affect the surface. If you only ever spray very small amounts, air canisters are available that will connect to an airbrush, though this is an expensive way to obtain an air supply.

Most airbrushes will take any paint, providing it is thinned correctly. Never try to airbrush with paint straight out of a standard bottle or tinlet of model paint – this will immediately clog up the airbrush. Always try and use the designated thinner for any manufacturer's paint – they all make the correct thinners for their own products. Modern acrylics can be slightly tricky as they have varying formulations depending on the manufacturer, so it's best to use that company's own product. However, if you're using enamel, it will thin with good-quality white spirit or turps.

Getting the consistency correct also can be tricky to begin with. If you're new to this skill, you're likely to make the paint still too dense for spraying correctly. The general advice when thinning paint is to make the consistency 'like milk', though exactly 'what type of milk' was never really specified – in reality, what you're looking for is the consistency of semi-skimmed or similar, not full-fat Jersey cream!

Next, practice on scrap plastic or a spare model to ensure you have the correct consistency, and also – if you're new to airbrushing – the correct speed at which you need to move the brush. Time to emphasise again that – as with an aerosol can – never start or stop the airbrush on the model; always start the spray before it starts to hit the model then pass along the length, keeping the movement as smooth as possible. Don't take your finger off the trigger until the spray is past the model, otherwise you'll almost certainly end up with runs on the surface. As with most things, the old maxim 'practice makes perfect' definitely applies to airbrushing.

Paint specific

Initially, airbrushes were expensive (and many still are) but overall prices have come down, and this has become an important tool in many modellers' armoury. To this end, several manufacturers started to make paint specifically for airbrushes, in that they would only work when applied by this method; they were far too thin to paint 'with a brush'.

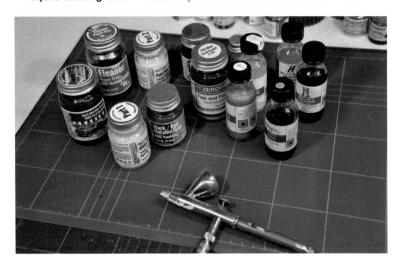

The first, and likely still the best known for this is the Anglo-American company, Alclad II, which only makes airbrushing paint, the majority of which are metallics and similar intended for aircraft. However, Alclad's catalogue also has a 'chrome', which is a finish virtually impossible to reproduce satisfactorily, other than by the vacuum-plating method used to make the 'chrome grilles and bumpers' for model cars. (The process actually uses aluminium powder, not chrome, but the finish is definitely 'shiny chrome' in its appearance.) The Alclad process, however, does an almost-perfect reproduction of chrome, providing it's sprayed over a gloss black base.

Other existing manufacturers have come on line with airbrush-only paints. Big names such as Testors and Humbrol make them, and smaller companies including MMP and Zero Paints make specific paints, the latter especially for race cars, where precise shades are invariably difficult to match in standard shades.

Spray booths

If you're contemplating doing a lot of spray painting, either using an aerosol or an airbrush, it's worth considering exactly how and where you're going to do this.

There are two basic elements to this: catching the overspray and disposing of the paint-laden air. The very simplest form could be a large cardboard box to take care of the first part, and spraying outside for the second. Putting to one side any environmental concerns for the latter, there is also weather to be taken into consideration. Avoid the obvious, such as if it's pouring with rain – paint doesn't like 'damp' air. It also doesn't like high humidity so it won't help either if it's too hot, even if it's dry, as spraying doesn't like extremes of temperatures. Too hot is just as bad as too cold, as the paint is likely to have dried long before it hits the surface of the model.

So we are back to where you do your modelling and the fact that any spraying may not be able to be located by the modelling bench. The ideal solution is a spray booth with filters to catch the paint, and ventilation to the outside to expel the air. Commercial modelling spray booths are available in a whole range of sizes and prices. If you're not intending to do

much spray painting, one at the lower end of the price spectrum will probably be adequate. If you intend to do a lot, it's worth investing in a more sophisticated device, or maybe even building your own.

It is beyond the scope of this book to go into precise details as to the building of such a structure, though bear in mind any extractor fan must be powerful enough to move a reasonable amount of air (which invariably rules out standard kitchen or bathroom fans – you really need something 'industrial'). It should also be certified that it will take the sort of paint aerosol mist that will be passing through it. It has been found that some cheaper spray booths aren't guaranteed to take such a spray, (though this then does beg the question, 'what are they intended for in the first place?'). It could also be worth checking if local legislation has something to say regarding the disposal of such aerosols into the air, even if adequately filtered.

ABOVE A small commercial paint spray booth. It has an extractor hose, which can be put out of a window.

BELOW Sorting out runners to minimise paint use.

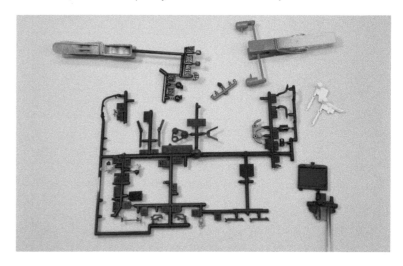

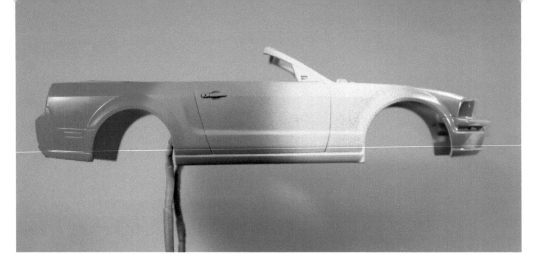

RIGHT The problem when painting over red (or yellow). From left to right, the kit is moulded in red, so first grey primer is used, then white primer and only then the final coat of light blue is applied.

Primers

A point about primers. Some may think them a waste of time (and money) but they do serve a very important purpose. Many models these days could be assembled from different materials, such as styrene, resin or photo-etch, and priming will 'pull' all these dissimilar materials together, making a coherent surface. Even if the model is all plastic, priming will still help the top coats of paint to adhere correctly. Dedicated primers slightly 'etch' themselves to the surface of the plastic – in fact many are termed 'self-etching primers' – basically helping them, and the subsequent layers, to stick to the plastic.

All the model paint companies make primers, usually in grey, white and black, though there are other colours that are listed 'as primers'. Choose the one that suits the top coat the best. Usually it is going to be the white or grey, but if the model is dark, or is going to be a metallic finish (usually a car, an experimental plane, or maybe a spaceship), these usually work best over a black base – it helps the 'sparkle'.

Although most kits these days are moulded in white or a neutral grey, some are still in pre-coloured styrene. This can lead to problems spraying over these colours, especially if the intended topcoat is diametrically opposite the starting colour. Most pre-coloured plastic kits these days are intended for the 'junior' end of the market, but there are many cases where these kits are vital to the more experienced modeller, as they could be the only examples of that particular subject.

However, what happens if the kit is moulded in red and you want it in white? Spray white over the red, even if you use a white primer, and you'll find that the red colour will invariably bleed through and you'll end up with a slightly surreal pink! The same can happen with yellow plastic. This is due to the colour dyes added to the styrene during the manufacturing process, and reds and yellows are particularly prone to 'bleed', even through primers. In some cases you have to go against natural instinct and for that white top coat, you have to paint the model with a grey, maybe even a black primer first, then matt white primer, and only then gloss white. This is usually the only way to stop the red or yellow dye bleeding through.

Cleaning

Whatever the painting method, though this especially applies to spray painting, it is vital to ensure the intended surface is not only dust free (which should go without saying) but – and this may be less obvious – is also clean of contaminants.

There is a lubricant that aids getting the parts out of the injection-moulding machine. This should not still be on the parts, but traces could remain. Resin parts, which usually come from garage manufacturers, tend to have more remaining containments on the surfaces – a combination of resin kit moulding using more lubricant and, being garage kits, there usually isn't any process to clean off the lubricant. Washing with warm soapy water is one option (allow to thoroughly dry, of course) or there is an increasing range of specially formulated cleaners for the purpose of cleaning plastic parts. Alternatively methylated spirits/denatured alcohol can be equally effective. Beware: these, and some cleaners, are highly inflammable, so never apply these near any naked flame. The washing, by whichever method, also helps to reduce the static on the plastic, which is the process that mainly attracts the dust.

To Hold

How you handle the parts while painting is also something to be considered. With the vast majority of kit parts being supplied still on their runners, this is the most convenient 'hand-hold' for painting. The usual process is to first assemble all the parts that will be the same colour (see Chapter 7, pages 96–100) then paint. Others will need individual application of paint. Most parts have more than one gate (where they attach to the runner), so remove all you can but ensure the part still remains held securely. Alternatively, the parts may have to be completely removed, in which case see if there is a locating hole where you can push a cocktail stick as a hand-hold. This may even involve drilling a specific hole for this task in some out-of-the-way place.

If there are many parts on one runner that will be the same colour, remove all the gate positions you can, then spray the whole runner, perhaps holding an edge of the runner with a large clothes peg.

Larger parts such as car bodies can be held by bending a suitable length of wire rod (a metal coat hanger is the usual source) so that it 'snaps' up inside the body. This can be held in position with doubled-sided sticky tape.

Besides providing a convenient hand-hold, it also supplies a useful method of hanging the part up to dry. This now brings in the question: 'Where do you put the parts to dry?' Drying paint is just as susceptible to dust as when it is

LEFT Using a wire coat hanger, bent so it can be used to hold such as car bodies for spraying. The liquids can be used to clean and degrease the plastics before spraying.

LEFT The coat hanger allows the painted body to be hung upside down to dry – this helps to prevent any dust settling, as the body is on the underside.

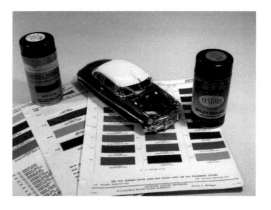

LEFT Original paint charts for the actual car can help when it comes to choosing the finished scheme – this for the Moebius Hudson Hornet.

RIGHT Use masking tape or an adhesive putty to mask parts while spraying.

BELOW Various methods of holding parts while spraying, including the bent wire coat hanger and clothes pegs.

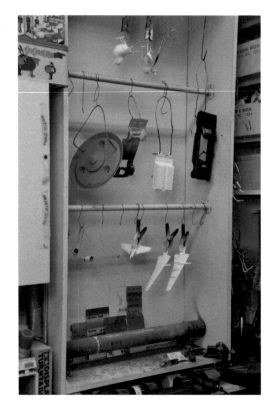

being painted – in fact more so, as drying takes a longer time.

As with spray-painting booths, the ideal solution for allowing paint to dry is a dedicated 'drying area', though this is also down to individual conditions. However, unlike spray-painting booths, dedicated drying equivalents aren't really available – so you'll need to devise a method of your own.

The home-made drying cabinet shown here has a simple box structure. It has rails to hold the paint hangers or clothes pegs, made out of small diameter rails, such as those intended for towels, from DIY stores. Then there is a tubular airing-cupboard heater fitted to the base, as warmth helps with drying paint. Warm air can then rise upwards by convection. Small parts can be laid on the base, receiving their warmth by radiation. This method also means that many drying parts, such as car bodies, will be upside down, so if there are any 'falling particles', they will end up on the 'inside' of the model.

If such a 'drying cupboard' device is not possible, ensure drying parts are out of the way of other work. Moving air is going to carry small particles you don't want on the painted surface while it's drying.

If the worst does happens and 'bits' do

fall on the surface, all is not lost. Small hairs and similar can be carefully removed with fine tweezers. If the paint is still 'very wet' it will likely flow back to fill any gaps, and it will obliterate the fact anything that wasn't supposed to be there was there in the first place! Other small particles may be able to be teased up and out of the drying paint using a small scalpel blade and tweezers. If this is impossible, the only option is to wait until it is completely dry then sand the affected area and repaint. Consequently, the best option is to avoid any of these particles falling onto the paint in the first place.

Masking

A model may be just one colour, but very many are two or more: two-tone cars, camouflaged aircraft and tanks, colourful civilian airliners…. This is where masking comes in.

Very basically, the process is as follows:

1) Apply one colour
2) Allow to thoroughly dry
3) Mask
4) Apply the second colour.
5) Remove masking.

Actually, and overall, that is it, but of course there are a few things to be aware of.

Masking in many ways is an art in itself. The tape has to be sticky enough to stick down so no paint creeps underneath, but conversely it can't be too sticky or when it is removed it is likely to bring the paint with it! To this end, most general 'masking tapes' designed for, say, interior decorating or even full-size cars, aren't suitable. Consequently, there are a number of specifically manufactured tapes made for modelling purposes that stick down well, so as to not allow the paint underneath, but can be removed without taking the paint with them.

They are manufactured in various widths, however they are not that cheap. So it can be better if masking a large area, to use the dedicated model tape for the actual edges to be masked, but if necessary, back this up with some of the cheaper tapes. Large areas can also be covered over with a polythene bag (more recycling, as runners in most modern kits are packed in polythene bags!), held in place with some of the cheaper tape. Check for holes in these bags (there to prevent anyone 'playing' with the bags!), and if necessary, apply tape over these holes.

If the masking line is curved, there are two ways around this: either lay the 'straight' masking tape and carefully cut through with a modelling scalpel to match the desired curve or buy the specially manufactured modelling masking tape available that can cover curves – this can take a bit of practice to get positioned correctly but it may be the only option.

Before starting any spraying, it is advisable to double-check ALL places where you've masked. Spray paint is extremely cunning and will get through the smallest opening, through those air holes or under badly positioned tape.

One the spraying has been done, the usual rule is to remove the masking as soon as is practical – in fact, while the top layers are still tacky. This will allow the top coat to 'flow' ever so slightly. It won't be enough to affect that carefully positioned line, but it will be enough to make the top surface 'become one' with the surface below, so you don't get a 'step'.

If, by chance, paint has crept under the masking, all is not lost. If the overspray is slight, it can be possible to 'tease' the line back to its correct position with a clean paintbrush, dampened slightly in whatever thinner/cleaner is appropriate – for example, if the spray is enamel-based, dip it in white spirit.

If the overspray is somewhat larger, using the same combination of brush and thinner, carefully wipe the excess away from the model surface. Continue this until it is gone, carefully wiping and cleaning the brush between every application. Cotton buds are also useful for this task. It may be possible to 'slice' the overflow paint using a small scalpel blade, though this will only usually work if the paint is dry. When the paint is thoroughly dry, model polish can also remove a thin layer of overspray. Polish is, after all, a very fine cutting agent.

Two-Tone

If you're dealing with multiple colours, it's always best to apply the lightest colour first. Say, for example, you are building a 'Luftwaffe '46 Haunebu flying saucer' (which almost certainly

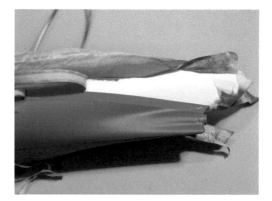

LEFT Two-tone masking here to get the lines on the hull of a ship. The white was sprayed, then masked and then the thin red was sprayed. That was then masked and the lower hull was sprayed.

LEFT Judicious use of masking tape on the AMT Northrop Flying Wing allows different shades of aluminium to be sprayed on, giving the look of slightly different finished panels.

LEFT A *lot* of masking was required on the fuselage of the Moebius Ranger from the movie *Interstellar*.

BELOW Masking for the Ranger starting to be removed.

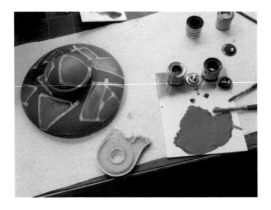

RIGHT Masking for the three-tone finish on the 'speculative' Haunebu German WWII Flying Saucer from Pegasus. The model was first sprayed green, lines masked and the purple hand painted.

RIGHT The finished Haunebu model with one further colour, black, also applied.

never existed in any form, but it's fun to speculate!). This is being finished in a classic Second World War German scheme of green, purple and black, with solid lines between the colours. First – having primed the surface, of course – apply the green. Then, when dry, apply masking tape and apply the purple. Finally – leaving the masking tape in position, as you don't want to repaint the green – mask the purple and paint the black.

There are two ways to approach this. If using bottle paints, the masking lines need only be applied to the actual masked edge – there's going to be no overspray, as the model is not being sprayed. The same applies when applying the third colour. However, if the model is being sprayed, the masking will have to cover the total area of the relevant colour.

Special masks

One area that is always tricky to mask and paint correctly is aircraft cockpit canopies. The scale is small and the lines are thin, so companies came up with the idea of supplying pre-cut marks that can be applied to the clear cockpit to allow for precise lines. This also applies to modern cars models where the window glass is glued in, usually leaving a black strip around the edge. Again, you can get masks to ease this painting task, and some manufacturers such as Tamiya even supply them in the kit.

It should go without saying that it's very important to line up these masks precisely, otherwise the paint pattern will be misaligned! Sometimes the styrene part is pre-etched with

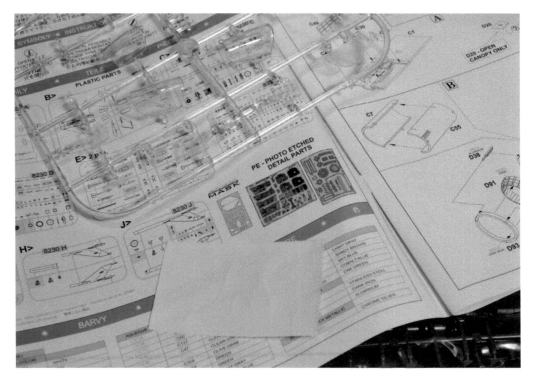

RIGHT Paint masks supplied with this kit, in yellow, are intended to mask the cockpit canopies (above) to allow the frame to be painted.

a faint line to indicate where the paint – and consequently the mask – goes. The masks usually come pre-cut on a backing sheet, so it's simply a matter of peeling them from the backing sheet, and applying. Small masks can be held with tweezers and you can line up one edge, juggling it slightly to ensure the other edges will follow. It's best to lay the mask down, gently enough for it to hold its position so you can check that it is indeed correctly lined up, but not securely enough that you can't lift it off and start again. Only when you are entirely sure it's aligned correctly, press down firmly to seal the edges.

If you do get it wrong, you can usually remove the mask a couple of times for realignment. Ease a scalpel blade under one edge to lift it, being careful not to damage the edge, otherwise it won't mask correctly. Don't try this too many times – after a few attempts, the mask will start to lose its stickiness, so won't form a good seal for the paint. Consequently, aim to get it correctly placed in the first place, before applying too much pressure.

Finishes

Intriguingly, paint finishes are 'scalable'. As an overall rule of thumb: the smaller the scale, the paler the 'look'. This applies especially to ships, which are some of the largest real objects that are modelled, so end up in the smallest of scales. It also depends on how close you are viewing them. The colours are going to be stronger and more vivid for a warship at anchor in dock, even if it is mostly 'battleship grey'! Take that ship out to sea, however, and the colours become far more muted. That dark grey becomes mid-grey, while the mid-grey becomes light grey. This is something to bear in mind when finishing – make sure the colour balance matches the size of the object.

All bright and shiny

Some models require the shiniest of finishes, so the top coat of paint could benefit from polishing. This tends to rule out military planes and ships, but could apply to airliners and, especially, cars. Polish is very slightly abrasive and here the intention is to literally take off the very topmost layer of paint, evening it all out, which adds 'the shine'.

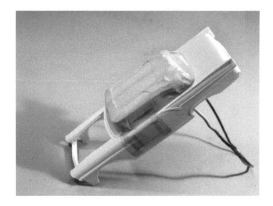

LEFT Masking doors and roof of a Revell 1957 Ford, which has been first sprayed gloss white, as the rest of the car will be black.

To this end, it's extremely important to check the paint is absolutely dry. Model paint formulation means the paint will dry quickly, usually faster than other paints, but even here it is advisable to leave at least a week – preferably longer – before any polishing is attempted.

There are liquid polishes specially made for modelling purposes. Alternatively, larger quantities are available for polishing full-size cars. Put a small amount of polish onto a lint-free cloth and apply in a gentle circular motion. You will immediately see the cloth turning the colour of the paint. This is what has been removed, so the advice is: don't rub too hard!

There are views as to how 'shiny' the shine needs to be! 'Shine' is also scalable, and there are arguments that if a model is too shiny, it can become unrealistic. Too high a shine on, especially, a model car can make it look more like a high-polished die-cast model than a representation of a full-size car.

When it all goes wrong

Even with the greatest care, paint finishes can go wrong. Runs appear, the surface wrinkles up, or you find loads of bits in the air have fallen on the wet surface. However,

ABOVE With the masking removed, the typical police 'black and white' can be completed.

ABOVE Paint removal using old brake fluid – and it works. Gloves, however, are advised!

ABOVE Paint removal using old brake fluid – and it works. Gloves, however, are advised!

RIGHT This is Model Strip, one of the alkali-based paint strippers – gloves are even more necessary in this case!

all is not necessarily lost – it can usually be recovered.

If the surface has just been painted and is still wet, or at least tacky, paint can be removed with the relevant thinner. If you have used enamel, use turps or white spirit; for acrylics possibly use water or methylated spirits (back to acrylics not all using the same base, see page 82). It's going to be a messy process, so do it over a sink or disposable surface and wear protective gloves.

If the parts are small or you have a lot of cleaner, tip some into a container and immerse the parts. Use an old brush (an old toothbrush is useful) to rub the paint off. If it's just been painted, you'll usually find the paint will dissolve away. Some corners may need extra scrubbing, but this usually brings the surface back to pristine condition. Then all you need to do is wash the cleaner away with soapy water, allow to thoroughly dry, and start all over again in the hope it all turns out better second time around!

If the paint has dried, a different technique will likely be needed. If the 'damage' is in one

small area, you could sand away the paint, leaving a smooth surface. Use various grades of emery paper, ending with the finest. Again, thoroughly clean and dry the model, and you should be able to repaint over the existing finish, masking areas that don't need repainting, if necessary. If the whole surface is wrecked, somewhat more drastic solutions are required.

Several varieties of paint remover are made, most based on an alkali, which is very good at paint removal. The surface under the paint is, of course, styrene and styrene is reasonably unaffected by solvents and the like – but not all of them. Some solvents that will strip paint will also affect the styrene surface.

The idea of paint removal on a model isn't new. It goes back to when model kits were new in the 1960s and methods for stripping paint were being contemplated. Most originated from building model cars, as they usually had this nice pristine showroom paint finish, but the technique could apply to any model where the paint finish had 'gone wrong'.

At that time, two methods came to the fore and both, in fact, are still usable. One was to use the glow fuel for model aircraft engines. This was an expensive method (glow fuel, even then, was not cheap) and involved a lot of oil. Glow fuel is a mix of fuel and oil, and the oil obviously left a very greasy surface, which really did have to be thoroughly degreased before any further painting was attempted. The fuel itself was also very volatile – it was a fuel after all! So, apart from the somewhat obvious advice of not to smoke in the vicinity (this was the 1960s!), it evaporated very quickly so you were forever topping up the container.

A cheaper method was to use vehicle brake fluid. There was no need to buy this new, though that would work just as well, but used brake fluid was equally effective. So if you'd just bled your full-size car brakes, keep the fluid in some suitable sealed container. Find a suitable container, pour in the fluid and immerse the parts, leaving for, well, a length of time that had to be ascertained by experience and by constantly checking! Then, *usually*, the paint would float off. All brake fluid cans warn you to avoid spillage on your car paintwork because of this very reason – it can take the paint off!

Brake fluid itself is fairly harsh, so there

was always the advice if you used it for paint removal to constantly keep checking as it had been known to, sometimes, start to dissolve the styrene as well. However, with care, it was a well-used method for many years, and in fact, still has its devotees.

Alternatives using an alkali-based paste came on the market in more recent years. Here, the paste was smeared all over the relevant part, which was then placed in a polythene bag, sealed and left overnight in a warm place (such as an airing cupboard). When the paste is washed away under running water, it should take the paint with it. The surface of the plastic, if it was originally white or a light colour, invariably was slightly tinted a light brown colour, but the model was going to be repainted anyway, so this was hardly a problem. The paste however is caustic, being an alkali, so warnings were always given about performing this task in a well-ventilated area, over a disposable surface, such as old newspapers, wearing latex gloves and maybe even a mask. There was also the related problem that, because it was an alkali, it could not be sent through many postal services, so obtaining it had to be direct, via a shop or model show.

Whether to weather

There is a strange situation with models and modellers, though one that it is safe to say is a reasonably recent phenomenon. This is whether you literally 'weather' the model? Also described as 'distressing' or 'dirtying down', it almost certainly had its origins in the movie and TV special effects industry where models – usually termed 'miniatures' in the SFX sense, as they really are smaller than the original would be – have been regularly 'dirtied down'. This is to make them look 'real', as nothing in this life is perfectly clean. Drive a brand new showroom-condition car out of the showroom, and immediately the tyres will start to wear and pick up road dirt. This will be transferred to the bodywork, and your showroom car starts to look not quite so pristine. Aircraft take on similar dirt from runways, then pick it up from the air they travel through. Similarly, locomotives and rolling stock pick up debris and dirt from the track, and if they were older

steam engines, from all the smut and smoke from the stack. Ships sailing in water are also going to accumulate weathering from flotsam and general sea conditions. And it is certainly the case with military – using the accepted modelling sense of ground-travelling military vehicles–- where 'dirt' comes into play naturally as tanks churn up fields and mud will get everywhere.

It is with this overall idea that everything in 'everyday use' will pick up a patina, that started the FX industry 'weathering' its miniatures. Here, although many of the model-building techniques would be the same, or at least similar to hobby model making, the final purpose was not to be pride of place on the mantelpiece, but to be integrated into an overall story arc, with the intention of becoming integrated seamlessly with the live action.

BELOW A selection of weathering materials – some specifically manufactured; others are artist's acrylic paint in tubes and tubs (back and right).

ABOVE An interesting use of weathering on train carriages: they are going through the washer, so the one on the right is clean! Model by Ian Peacock.

This dirtying down of filming miniatures started to occur from around the time of Gerry Anderson's productions in the early 1960s. Before that time, SF movies that featured miniatures – and here it was primarily down to spaceships that featured in many of the American 'B' Movies of the 1940s and 1950s – were bright and shiny with no sign of weathering.

With Anderson's various series, the miniatures were invariably well-weathered as although the characters were puppets, so

RIGHT Using mud and rust on a Galaxie 1948 Chevy – it's been round the racetrack!

RIGHT Very thin 'dirt' from Pro-Modeller was airbrushed onto this Tamiya Aston Martin DBS to match the scene in the Bond movie, *Quantum of Solace*.

were only realistic to a limited degree, the craft and vehicles matched 'real life' far more. Here places that could have leaked oil had oil leaks, tracks and tyres were scuffed, windscreens smattered with dirt and dust and engine exhausts had all the signs of being heated and worn by hot gases.

From the many model kits of the Anderson creations, where dirtying down became a prerequisite, this moved on to modelling of real aircraft, which started to be modelled as they would appear when sitting on the runway. Beside flaps drooping, as the hydraulic pressure was absent, various edges began to be finished with the sort of wear and tear even the most ground-crew pampered plane would take on. Leading edges would be dry brushed with aluminium paint, as would be created by travel at several hundred miles per hour through the air. Undercarriage doors, air brakes and air intakes received the same treatment, while fuel doors and engine inspection panels had dirt brushed into crevices.

Any model to be weathered starts with the model finished in its pristine state. There are a few odd exceptions to this, but it's safe to say the vast majority of models to be dirtied down will start clean. In the early days of modelling and weathering, any weathering products had to be taken from what existed in the paint cabinet. Although this would include 'black', it was really one of the least useful colours. Nothing is really 'black', especially dirt, so it would need to be mixed with other shades: browns, greens and, of course, greys, to get a more realistic look. Thinned down, it would

RIGHT Dry brushing aluminium paint onto the edges of the engine bell ribs, on the giant Saturn V F1 first stage engine bell. This is a 1:20 scale multi-material kit from Accurate Models.

be applied to a panel line, were it could run along due to capillary action as a start to the whole process.

Dry brushing

One very useful weathering technique, mentioned briefly before, is 'dry brushing'. This is almost precisely what you do. Take a brush and dip it into some paint. Let us use aluminium for the example, as it is a widely used shade for many areas. The first thing you do, having applied the paint, is to wipe most of it off so the brush is almost 'dry' (hence the terminology). Then gently wipe across, say, the leading edge of a wing. A small amount of the paint will transfer on to the model, but it is 'only a small amount'. This will then take on the look of wear on that edge. This can be extended to many other areas, and if you have a 'mechanical' structure, say the aircraft engine, it can be used over the surface, where there are dips and rises, or where pipes are travelling (and the vast majority of aircraft engines have a lot of pipe work surrounding the main engine). It doesn't all have to be aluminium, of course. Most paint suppliers do a wide range of metallic shades, so involve bronzes, steel, copper and similar for different effects.

More dirt and dust

Then there is the dirt and dust. Leaving large areas of dirt and dust to the diorama chapter (see pages 126–139), individual models can receive more than just dry brushing techniques.

Besides the established mainstream model paint suppliers, there have been many smaller companies that have lines of paints and materials purely dedicated to weathering. One major one is AK Interactive in Spain. This makes a vast range of washes and powders purely intended to weather model kits.

With some bottles, it doesn't quite look as if you are getting anything at all. The bottle will have a pale mix, with a label stating 'mud brown', and you may wonder how it is used?

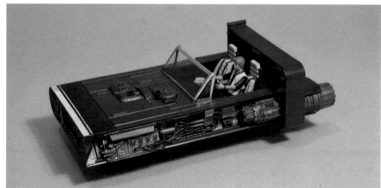

But it can be airbrushed to apply over 'dirt and dust', or brushed on in cracks and crevices in which the same dirt and dust will have accumulated for real. Most of these materials are also water based, so if you feel one area is a bit too weathered, it can be washed off and you can start again.

Incidentally, weathering has become such a part of amateur model making that there are many books, and even magazine series published by Mig-Ammo and AK Interactive, devoted to the whole subject.

ABOVE Dry brushing various shades on the 'mechanical' bits on the Revell kit of the Han Solo Land Speeder, from the movie *Solo*. This is actually intended as a beginner 'snap' kit, but the judicial use of paint and weathering can elevate it.

Chapter Seven

Basic building

It may seem a very obvious statement, but the first thing to do when starting the build of a model kit is to open the box and make sure it's all there! Older kits tended to be packed loose in the box, so the runners and any other parts, such as vinyl tyres or tracks, were mixed in. Movement could knock parts off the runners and if the kit was opened at any point (most kits were not shrink-wrapped at that time) parts could fall out. Their absence was then not noticed before the lid was put back on, and only discovered later when you tried to fit that part during assembly.

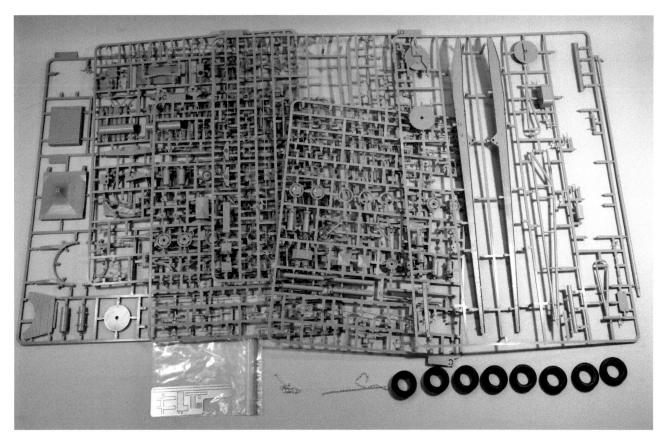

These days, quality control of modern kits is very good, particularly helped by the fact that most runners are packed in polythene bags and kit boxes now tend to be shrink-wrapped. However, this has to be balanced against the fact that many kits have far more parts than in earlier times, so actually checking 'if it is all there', may not be quite so straightforward. An obvious gap in a runner may signify the absence of a part, though many kits now have so many small – some very small – parts so this method may not be that reliable.

Also, you'll need to check that all the 'ancillary' parts are there. There is almost certainly a decal sheet, maybe a photo-etched sheet, with many modern aircraft or military kits, then small runners with clear or transparent coloured parts, metal axles, and possibly a pack of springs or retainers. The presence of all these need to be checked. Many plans now have a parts layout at the beginning, which should help. These layouts should also point out if some parts are not to be used for this particular version (many kits are now designed to be built in variations, available as separate kits). There is also the increasing use of multiple

runners, which seems to affect military AFVs more than anything. If, for example, three identical parts are required for the build and this occurs with a number of parts, these are all on one runner, and you get three identical runners in the kit.

The next stage is to read the instructions! Seasoned modellers invariably take a perverse pride in the fact they can build a kit without having to resort to actually reading the plans, but we have all come undone at some point where parts 1 and 2 really have to be dealt with before you try to attach parts 3 and 4.

First things first

It's worth thinking very early on about how the model is to be painted. In most cases there can be a lot of 'sub-assemblies' to do before paint is applied. Car, truck, tank or even some aircraft kits will have engines, which are likely at the very least to be split into two halves, and almost certainly a number of other parts in addition. These can usually be assembled first, then put aside for painting. The same could apply to fuselage halves, hull halves, car bodies

ABOVE Parts of a kit, not only the runners – quite a number – but vinyl tyres, photo-etch and real chain. This is the Meillerwagen that transported the V-2 missile, from Takom.

OPPOSITE Starting any build, get your tools ready.

RIGHT Possible fault with older tooling: flash. This is easily cured with a sharp knife.

BELOW Another fault that can occur where the moulding is fairly thick, as with figures: sink marks. Again, this is easily cured with a small amount of filler.

With the many reissues of old kits, some from tooling decades old, there are a few things to watch for.

Flash

First there could be the presence of flash. This comes about because injection moulds do wear over time. It occurs between the mating surfaces, which then shows up as a thin 'web' of styrene that spreads out from the runners and parts. Although somewhat irritating, it can be rectified easily with the usual range of modelling tools – scalpels and files. The overall problem can't really be cured: if the tooling is worn, the tooling is worn. If modellers want some kits, the original mould will have to be used, it will not be cost effective to make a new tool, and sometimes flash will occur and has to be dealt with.

Sink marks

Another fault sometimes apparent is sink marks. These tend to occur where the parts are thicker than others. One main example where it can happen is with figures, which, in smaller scale kits such as 1:35 and below, are going to be relatively small. Because of this they are usually moulded solid and the plastic therefore takes fractionally longer with these thicker parts to cool. This can sometimes result in a 'depression' at the thickest part, and with figures this is usually (though not always) on the backs. Again, although irritating, this is easily rectified with a small amount of filler.

Surface irregularities

Very, very occasionally there may be irregularities to the surface of some parts. This is likely because the tooling was not mothballed correctly. The steel tools can rust if a preservative has not been used, and these may be rust spots. Again, there is little that can be done with some of these old moulds. Sanding and filling is probably the only answer.

with bonnets or whole sections of figures.

You may very well find that many parts on one runner will all be the same colour, though will not necessarily end up being glued to one another. Here you can save time, effort and paint by keeping them on this one runner and spraying it as a whole. It is then neater if you can reduce the number of gates per particular piece down to as small as will support it, ideally down to one, as far less touching up will be

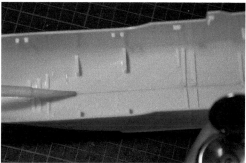

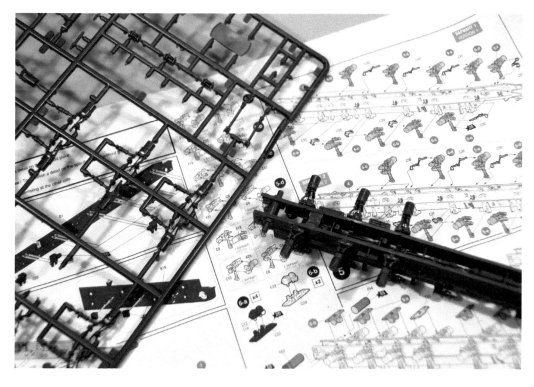

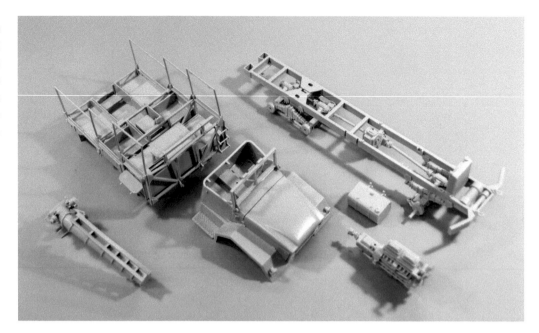

RIGHT With many kits – this is the Renwal LaCrosse missile – you can sub-assemble many of the parts to allow them to be painted 'as one'.

RIGHT With some very thin parts – this is the side trim from a Revell '58 Chevy Impala – it is best not to use snips, as the part is likely to snap. Use a razor saw instead.

BELOW This thin nose probe, for the Moebius *Jonny Quest* Dragonfly, is also best cut from the runner using a razor saw.

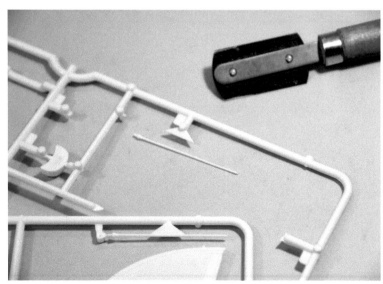

required. There may also be merit in combining runners that will be similar colours. Cut the runners from one section and glue them onto another. This will keep the painting area as small and compact as possible, and again will mean less wasted paint, especially if they are being sprayed.

If the primers and undercoat will all be the same shade, but the top colour different, you can still minimise paint loss with a bit of ingenuity. Combine runners and parts for stage one, and when the top coat is different, separate them out and deal with two or three separate runners for the individual finishes.

For the actual build, refer to the Tools section (see Chapter 5, page 69) and cut the relevant parts from the runner using snips or a razor saw. This will leave a slight amount of plastic at this gate position. To remove this, trim with a modelling knife or scalpel and finish with needle files and fine-grade sanding paper.

Glue the parts using your preferred method. Most these days use liquid cements, though some still prefer the older type of cement in a tube. Note where parts are painted. Glue won't stick to paint – it will instead turn it into a sticky goo. For some parts, this may be able to be hidden as it is inside or on the underside, but it's good practice to scrape or sand off the gluing areas before applying any cement. If the kit has chrome-plated parts, primarily vehicle kits, this is vital anyway as polystyrene

LEFT One of the largest aircraft kits produced: Revell's 1:48 scale B-1 Bomber, in its prototype colour scheme.

BELOW Camouflage pattern on this Dragon Horten Ho-229 Flying Wing in 1:48 scale.

BOTTOM Is it a plane, is it a boat? Well a bit of each; the uniquely Russian Ekranoplan from Revell.

cement of any type will not stick to the plating. Superglue will, however, and could be useful for tiny parts such as car wing mirrors or badges, which invariably find themselves on the chrome-plated runner and are sometimes difficult to cement using one of the actual styrene liquids.

The instructions show the best order of assembly. They will have been tested beforehand, so it really is best to follow these. Your own experience, however, may show that you can do this in a slightly different order, depending on your skills and way of working.

It is not the task of this book to take you through a complete build of any type of kit – that could be for later volumes. However, there are many general points that follow through over any particular subject.

Aircraft

Older aircraft models, especially military planes, had little in the way of interior detail – a pilot figure and seat, possibly a joystick and an instrument panel, if you were lucky. Modern kits, though, have a full wealth of detail here and most will have to be fitted inside the fuselage before the halves are brought together.

This can lead to alternatives of how to do the assembly to also allow for the most straightforward way to achieve the exterior finish. The interior details will obviously have to be finished before they are fitted in place, but this means a lot of masking will need to be involved with any exterior finish, particularly if it will be sprayed. Consequently, it could mean examining whether some parts could be fitted after painting. Perhaps the cockpit details could go in through the cocking opening, or engine position, or maybe the lower fuselage panels are separate and could be temporarily fitted without gluing, painted, then removed to fit the interior? This can only be general, as all kits are going to be individual and different construction methods will be needed.

Painting civil airline liveries can be one of the most complex, as the kits of airliners are almost universally split into left and right halves. You are then faced with the dilemma that the two halves need cementing together and possibly need slight filling and sanding before painting. But the passenger window glass has had to be installed before the two halves are fitted together, so they now all need to be individually masked before being painted!

Fortunately, many airline liveries have colour differences between the main fuselage and panels of a different colour where the windows are. It is this part of the overall scheme that is likely to be on the decal sheet. In this case, one would be able to finish the entire fuselage, including gluing, sanding and finishing of the join line, with the windows already in place. Then it is purely a matter of masking over these, keeping inside the decal line, painting the overall colour then removing the masking and applying the decals. Some kits have even got around this by supplying the window 'glass' as part of the decal, so there was no need for transparencies in the first place.

Dealing with windows

There is going to be slightly more of a problem if the overall fuselage colour is the same all over. Here you may find that the window transparencies can be slid in, perhaps through the cockpit area. But this is going to be tricky and will be stopped if there are any bulkheads in the way. If the model is of a small scale, such as 1:144 (the traditional airliner scale) or smaller, the holes for the windows are also correspondingly small. Here, one of the 'glass makers' such as Microscale 'Krystal Klear' could be used instead of the transparencies. Krystal Klear actually has the same base as PVA glue – it starts white, but put a drop into the window opening with a toothpick and it will spread out to fill the space and dry clear (well, more or less 'clear').

Larger window openings will be more of a

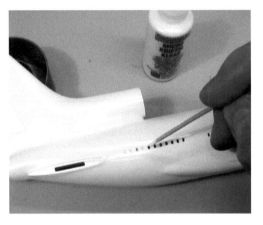

RIGHT One way to solve the problem of airline cabin windows: Microscale's Krystal Klear. This is an Airfix Lockheed Tristar.

BELOW Or ensure the plane has the windows on the decal sheet, as with this Minicraft Boeing 757 in NASA markings.

problem, such as in 1:72 and larger aircraft. Here, if the fuselage is one colour, it could mean individual masking, though latex-based liquids such as Maskol are available, which are brushed on, allowed to dry, the paint applied and then the masking layer peeled off. It is somewhat time-consuming, but this may be the only method. If the window area is one particular colour (and not on a decal sheet), first paint this, then add the window glass, assemble the fuselage, finish the joints, mask the coloured area around the windows and apply the main colour.

Military aircraft have varied considerably over the century or so since the first 'fighters' took to the air. Those from The Great War seemed to take pride in making them as bright and even garish as possible – take the Red Baron's bright red Fokker Triplane, or then many 'lozenge-type' designs. By the Second World War, camouflage became the main aim, so the classic green and brown evolved, though this was later adapted to other colour combinations. Two-tone greens, greys, sand for desert bases, even all-over black for night fighters. Modern combat planes seem to concentrate on greys, all over or patterns, some blended like their Second World War counterparts, others sharp-edged.

Military helicopters take on much the same patterns. Being a newer technology, some existed in the Second World War, but basically they are all post-war with grey or two-tone finishes. Civilian helicopters follow their airliner counterparts and kits will have a variety of decals with markings. All types of helicopter, however, are going to have one thing in common – and that is the rotor blades. These ideally need leaving off while the main fuselage is dealt with, painted and decaled, and only then fitted into place. Most also look more authentic if they droop. Most styrene blades are ironically too rigid, so some help may be required. You could soak them in hot water and then try to bend them – though styrene can be irritatingly stubborn when it comes to bending (polystyrene is an extremely stable plastic and is intended to resist bending!). Consequently, some perseverance could be necessary. Low heat could be applied – with the warning to be very careful, as once the blade is 'bent' too far, the shape will be difficult to recover.

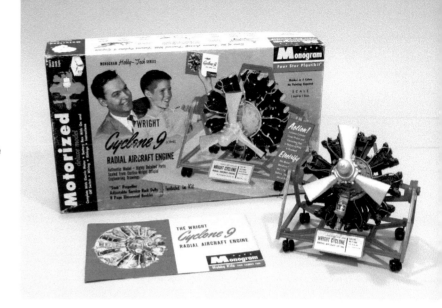

ABOVE One of those kits with a difference: Monogram's 1:12 scale Wright Cyclone 9 radial engine. This is the original kit that was motorised.

BELOW Colourful helicopters: the 1:32 Revell kit of the MBB BK-117 Spaceship. The scheme designed by Luigi Colani is fortunately all on the decal sheet.

BOTTOM The old ITC kit of the US Navy blimp, reissued by Glencoe. This comes complete with a small diorama base.

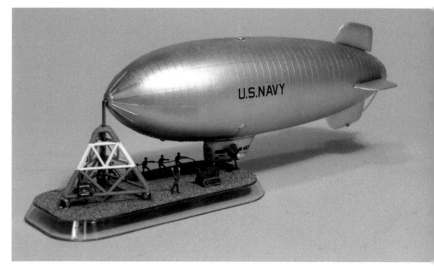

RIGHT Many military vehicles – AFVs and soft-skinned – can be assembled 'as one' then painted.

Military and AFVs

If building a military AFV, paint-wise you're almost certainly going to have a slightly easier job than with a civil airliner or helicopter, as the vast majority of these vehicles are painted with just one overall colour. This will mean a great deal of the kit can be assembled 'as one' before any painting is attempted.

Yes, there are tanks and the like that are camouflaged in two or more colours, so masking techniques may become relevant. With smaller scales such as 1:72 and 1:76, it is most likely any 'two-tone' will be hand painted, so masking may not be necessary. Try spraying one colour first (usually the lighter), then hand paint the second. The finished model can then be sprayed all over with a matt varnish to 'pull the finish' together.

Some details may be metallic or there could be idler wheels for a tracked vehicle and, if the model is of a soft-skinned vehicle, there could be seats, benches and tops in different shades.

Military vehicles are, of course, the main modelling subjects for dioramas. Consequently you may be building such a model in a 'weathered' state, and some parts may be omitted – been blown off in battle – while other areas could be damaged.

Vehicles

Building a showroom-condition car is diametrically the opposite of a military AFV. Here you are aiming for a glossy finished body, contrasting interior, seats and instrument panel, and in many cases a detailed engine and running gear.

Most car kits – and trucks for that matter – fall into three parts: the body, the interior and the chassis, engine and running gear. In most cases, they can be dealt with separately.

Engine blocks are usually assembled and painted 'as one'. There are stock colours that are used on particular manufacturers' engine blocks: the old BMC used black or dark green and in the US, Ford used a blue, Chevy an orangey-red and Chrysler a bright red, but this was not set in stone. Many modern, aluminium-based blocks are not painted at all but remain the silvery colour of the metal.

Chassis components are invariably black –

BELOW The Renwal model of one of the oddest AFVs ever, the Ontos. The three figures come with the kit; the base and accessories have been added.

and if the model is not destined to be turned over and examined closely, this may very well suffice. But many have separate details such as an older-style rear axle and differentials painted in a contrasting colour. Shock absorber/ dampers can be coloured blue or yellow, and drive shafts plain metallic. Exhaust systems mostly remain unpainted, due to the heat, and so vary throughout various metallic shades. Even if you're not going down a 'super-detailing' route, tyres look best if the tread is sanded slightly to give them that 'used look'. Gently sand each tyre on a piece of reasonably course sanding paper.

And this is purely stock showroom cars – if you're building a custom or Hot Rod, anything goes, and finishes such as metalflakes and candies (or 'Kandies') come into play.

Window surrounds can be finished in chrome, in which case Bare-Metal Foil (BMF) is the best option. Modern cars are almost universally black, so either use the black version of BMF or carefully paint by hand, masking if you wish.

Trucks can have an even more garish finish if they have owners' logos, or have been custom painted. Kits that feature such options will have these on the decal sheet. The same will apply to race and rally cars, with their own specific markings. Race cars especially have a wide range of aftermarket decal sheets.

Motorbikes tend to follow similar lines to

cars and trucks. Tyres can be sanded the same way, and usually motorbikes are made to larger scales so that extra details, piping, brake cables and the like can be included. The introduction of superglue has helped a great deal here, as trying to glue vinyl tubing to styrene parts was never easy.

One thing in common with all vehicle kits is the tyres. Primarily made in vinyl, sometimes they won't easily slip over the wheels. To fit them more easily, soak them in hot water for a minute or so to soften them.

ABOVE Ferrari, not this time in red, but a metallic grey. This is the Revell kit of the Ferrari 430 Spyder, the type used in the movie version of *Miami Vice*.

BELOW The classic 'split' of a model car kit – body, interior, and chassis and engine. This is the 1:24 Revell kit of the classic Monte Carlo Mini.

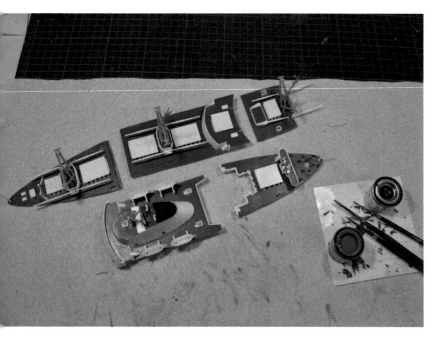

Ships

You can really draw a complete line down the middle of ship models: those that are powered and those that are not. The latter use sails for power, which brings in the whole subject of the sails themselves, how they are represented and how they are rigged. With the odd exception of aerials and the like, powered vessels are totally free of sails and rigging. There are a few examples of models of sailing ships that also have engines, but these really are few and far between.

One commonality of all these, however, is the hull. Whether you are dealing with a galleon from the 17th century or a modern aircraft carrier, the vast majority are in two halves and one of the first tasks in any build is to cement these halves together. Here liquid cement, applied with a pipette, comes into its own, as trying to do this with a brush will leave some areas at the start of the task dried before you've got to the other end. Remember some galleon models – and aircraft carriers for that matter – can be 3 feet/1 metre long!

Then there is the matter of fitting all the other parts according to the instructions. Decks – again galleon or warship – may have to go in at this stage, or can be finished separately and only fitted at the final assembly stage. Modern warships are going to have a wealth of details with superstructures and gun turrets, aircraft and missiles. With galleons it could be cannons, deck fittings and the giant ship's wheel. Both types are also the subject of any aftermarket parts, even crews can be available in some of the smallest scales, made from photo-etch parts.

Modern civilian vessels have always been dwarfed in number compared to naval, but there have been a reasonable number. Airfix's first ship kit was the *Southern Cross*, after all. These can be treated somewhat as with the distinction between military and civilian aircraft. Here the civilian vessels are going to be far

more colourful, and many will have the specific markings for the owners on the decal sheet.

Sails for galleons are either supplied as vac form parts – about the only time you will get such parts in mainstream kits, or furled as injection styrene parts. The former look more realistic, the latter are far easier to deal with. Then there is the rigging, but that really is a completely separate subject.

Spacecraft

Much of the building of spaceships – factual ones, at least – follow similar lines to aircraft. For example, the Space Shuttle was a large glider and although it featured an exterior of tiles, it had wings, a tail and relatively conventional landing gear. Construction of the many kits of the Shuttle in many scales could follow much the same lines as an aircraft kit. Larger-scale kits have cockpit details, and here it could be fitted in through the cargo bay doors – this being one exception to a 'standard' aircraft kit.

Rocketry tends to be directly split down the middle of the rocket stages. Care needs to be taken that these halves are precisely lined up before cementing. Many are helped by pins or tags to aid the location, but it can still be advisable to check that they remain 'lined up' as you go along with the cement, otherwise you'll get a step one edge to the next. This can be filled or sanded, but getting it exactly lined up in the first place will save time and effort. This is admittedly no different to lining up any other 'halves' in kits, such as aircraft fuselage halves and hull halves, however rocket body halves tend to be longer and straighter and will more obviously show up if not done correctly.

Until recently, there were not many models of unmanned spacecraft, satellites and probes. In fact, until at least the 1990s these could be counted on the fingers of one hand, as there were precisely three model kits. These days there are a number from Japanese companies featuring, mainly, Japanese craft, although Hasegawa surprised everyone with a kit of the Voyager probes. Many of these models tend to be 'bitty' in their approach, with lots of sensors and instruments that, being free of an atmosphere, don't have to follow the

LEFT The Airfix 1:144 scale Saturn V rocket. This can be built similarly to a ship in many ways, in that the rocket structures come in halves that need cementing together.

BELOW An interesting addition to the space modellers' collections in recent years is a growing range of unmanned satellites from Aoshima in Japan. This is Selene, a Lunar probe, in 1:72 with two small sub-satellites seen in the foreground.

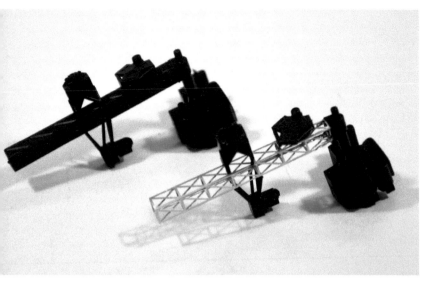

ABOVE Replacing injected styrene parts with a photo-etched equivalent. In this case, the scan platform boom of the Hasegawa Voyager planetary probe, using the LVM-Studios PE set.

BELOW From Polar Lights, build the 'real' Batmobile (left) with the actual V8 engine, or the 'reel' Batmobile (right) with the fictional jet engine.

streamlined shapes of aircraft, but this is precisely as their 1:1 scale originals. These are also craft that can benefit from thermal covering – invariably the classic gold foil – to cover many of the surfaces.

Science fiction and fantasy

This tends to run across the board of subject matter, as it can include both craft and figures, and this is one area that is a favourite with the Garage Companies. Most tend to be spacecraft, but there are vast swathes of Japanese robots that fall between 'figure' and 'craft'. There are SF submarines – Seaview, Nautilus, Proteus and Stingray, and even almost conventional vehicles.

After all, is the Batmobile a 'real car' or

'science fiction'? Arguably it is both – the vehicles in the TV and movies all existed 'for real' and were all driveable (to a certain extent), but they were powered by a convention internal combustion V8, not a jet engine. So the car is 'real' in the sense of being a 'real driveable vehicle', but can also be described as 'reel' (a play on the dual pronunciation, and the fact you got – and still do – 'reels of film'). So much so that the Polar Lights kit of the original Barris TV Batmobile could be built with its 'real' V8 or its 'reel' jet engine. But overall, and as modelling is concerned, it is a model of a car so can be built as a model of a car.

Many of the SF craft – the spaceships – are at the other end of the scale. Though scales have a slight problem coming into this, as they were never really established for the SFX miniatures, scaling that to the scales of the model kits mostly had to be invented (see Chapter 3, pages 48–49).

In many ways, the nearest SF spaceships they can be likened to are not aircraft, but Earthy seagoing ships, especially when size and whatever scales have been allocated are taken into consideration. Consequently, many of the building techniques are based on how models of ships are built. Hulls have to be glued together and painting small details comes into the same league as painting fixtures and fittings on aircraft carriers.

For spaceships of even larger dimensions – the Star Destroyer and Death Star from *Star Wars* are the ones that usually spring to mind – it can be even more difficult to retain a sense of scale. Ironically, these kits tend to be simpler in construction (the original AMT kit of the Death Star is, after all, only eight parts) so far more work has to come into the finishing. However, we are struck by the oddity that the hobby model is a model of a special effects model, not a real object. What is more, that SFX miniature will likely have been built in many different scales, each made to perform a particular filming task. These varying sizes, and consequently details, will almost certainly vastly differ. For example, the *Star Wars* Millennium Falcon was built in many sizes: the smallest the size of a dime (10 cent coin), the largest was full-size, with many more sizes in-between.

Rail

Most rail modelling is going to be working layouts where, perhaps ironically, the rolling stock is likely to be bought already assembled and the modelling effort is going to the ancillary equipment, buildings, scenery and the like. But static kits of rolling stock are not unknown, with examples from Monogram, and most famous in the UK, Kitmaster. These were acquired later by Airfix, then later still by Dapol, and many are still around. There are even odd examples such as MPC's The General 'Wild West' wood-burning locomotive that was made in 1:25 scale, as MPC primarily makes car kits in 1:25.

Here the choice is to build the model completely clean, or to weather at least the 'rolling' part of the structure, which is never going to remain in pristine condition on the track. For many years, both Humbrol and Testors made separate 'railway colours' and although Humbrol combined its ranges, Testors still makes a specific railroad range of paints: both brush and spray.

But most of the whole idea of railways is the layouts, so all the other modelling subjects come into play. Buildings abound from many companies. If you are a 1:87 Continental railway builder, Faller makes a very wide range. Many are pre-coloured, saving painting, and many are even pre-built. The US companies (the largest is Walthers) also make a wide range and most, being buildings, are made up from flat structures.

Assembly follows very similar lines for most, if not all, buildings; the only differences being the number of floors for the building

and whether it is a private house, commercial premise, industrial building or maybe even a hospital – these will especially vary in their number of windows and doors. The latter will mostly be separately moulded, making assembly easier, and they can be painted separately and then fitted into place. Most buildings are also – unlike, say, cars or airliners – not pristine in condition, so weathering comes into play with most permanent railroad layouts (possibly less so for those that are only assembled temporarily). The permanent layout can also involve landscape and scenery, though for more on this see Chapter 9, Dioramas (pages 126–139).

ABOVE Trackside accessories with a slight difference from the original Airfix range: the three-wheeled Scammell Scarab lorry in British Railways markings (right) and Watneys (left).

BELOW Not an American 'trackside accessory' per se, but Moebius Models' Mel's Diner (from *American Graffiti*) is the same H0/1:87 scale – here with the main roof removed to show the interior.

Figures

'Figures' are the models that go across the board of subject matter. Whatever the subject, most can be treated in the same way when it comes to the build. Unlike the majority of previous subjects where the general rule is to paint separate parts or sub-assemblies before final assembly, with figures it tends to be the other way round: assemble everything first, then paint. This is obviously a very rough generalisation, as there are many examples where you do indeed keep some elements of figures separate until final assembly – maybe they are holding something or even sitting down on a seat. In a very general way it makes sense, as figures are usually hand painted and areas that are different colours then have to be blended in, one with the other.

This tends to hold true for individual figures, but the whole subject also includes the sets of figures that are either used for military dioramas or for wargaming. Few need 'assembly' in the general sense – there may be separate weapons or small vehicles, possibly horse-drawn, which need some assembly.

One problem with these sets (in particular, the original Airfix sets) is that they were not moulded in styrene. The figures were one piece and had to come out cleanly from one mould. Undercuts, which could be common with figures, would prevent ease of ejection from a standard steel tool. Consequently, many

of these sets were moulded from vinyl plastic, so they would be flexible enough (to a certain extent) to pull straight out of the mould. There is also the reason that some of the sections would be very thin and fragile, and rigid styrene would easily break. However, vinyl and similar can't be glued with standard polystyrene glue and standard enamel paint wouldn't adhere to the surface.

Later, when superglue and acrylic paint came into fashion, these problems could be solved. Some figure sets started to be moulded in polyurethane, which is less flexible than vinyl, but as rigid as styrene, and would take enamel paint. Many these days are moulded directly in styrene so, although superglue and acrylics are generally available to solve the original problems, these original problems have mostly been got around.

Many fantasy figures are from 'garage companies' and are cast in resin. This will tend to make them solid in nature, so mating surfaces will likely be the areas where the resin was poured, which will invariably be slightly proud of the surface, where resin has been poured in. This will mean sanding them down flat so they can be joined.

Examine the whole of the outside of any resin cast for air bubbles. If present, they will be at the uppermost surface where the resin was poured, which will likely be the base or joining surface, so any bubbles won't be noticeable. However, it's not unknown for the odd bubble

BELOW Not all kits are of powered vehicles. Adams made a series of 1:48 scale wagons from the 'Wild West', here in a desert setting. The kit has been reissued by Glencoe models.

RIGHT Following the idea of 'famous figures' originated by Aurora, Polar Lights continue the tradition with The Three Stooges, in a scene from the short movie, *We Want Our Mummy*.

RIGHT Following the idea of 'famous figures' originated by Aurora, Polar Lights continue the tradition with The Three Stooges, in a scene from the short movie, *We Want Our Mummy*.

to appear anywhere on the surface of resin castings. These are mostly small and can be filled with the usual model filler. Plus, given that the resin is immune to liquid cement, you can use a brush dipped in liquid cement to smooth the top surface of filler, with no danger of it affecting the resin. When dry, it will only need fine sanding to achieve a surface smooth. Some joins of resin figures, such as attaching arms or legs, are perhaps not as precise as injection styrene, so again model filler is useful for filling any gaps.

Animals

It hasn't always been the human animal for model figures. Other animals have also been a firm favourite with model companies, and one of the most popular has been prehistoric creatures. Several companies really specialised in these, primarily Airfix; Pyro, later Life-Like, then Lindberg; Aurora, later Monogram and Revell; and Tamiya. Construction follows the lines of any other 'figure', with the definite advantage that all can be assembled 'as one', and only then painted.

LEFT Animal figures: a recreation of the Aurora American Bison from Atlantis. Note the two prairie dogs.

With the possible exception of mammoths (which are not really 'prehistoric, but generally get lumped into this category) and those for which preserved specimens have been found frozen in ice so we know what they really looked like, there are no 'complete' dinosaurs. We only have skeletons to go by, so the exact colouration of the skin has always been a mystery. They generally got painted 'lizard-type' colours. But various theories now suggest they could have been far more brightly adorned, which makes paint schemes far more interesting. So you could end up with a bright red Tyrannosaurus Rex – and who's to say you are wrong?

RIGHT What colour do you want your T-Rex? Here is the Revell kit based on *Jurassic Park*, in the usual scheme – but could they have been brighter?

Chapter Eight

Decals

Virtually all model kits will contain a sheet of water-slide decals. These will provide national markings, panel lines, access hatch markings, licence plates, instrument panels, pin-striping, airline logos, badges and even areas of solid colour, depending on the kit.

LEFT A set of decals with an aircraft kit. This is an old reissued Revell Vought Cutlass, with new decals including extra markings.

They are produced by a very thin layer of the decal itself, held onto a backing sheet with an equally thin layer of glue. The decal has been printed, usually by silk-screen methods, onto this layer, which is transparent. Then it is simply a matter of cutting out the decals in a rough shape from the backing paper, soaking them in warm water for 10–15 seconds to loosen the glue and then sliding them onto the model surface.

Decals have been around since there were model kits. In the early days they tended to be called 'transfers' in British English, in that they were 'transferred' from one place to another. But the American model industry tended to use the older English term 'decal', which gradually took over worldwide and seems to have literally stuck!

Decals themselves are by no means unique to model kits. The idea is generally accepted to have been invented by a French engraver, Simon Ravenet in the 19th century, who produced the very earliest 'decals', coining the word 'décalquer' (which means 'to copy by tracing') to describe the process. He had

OPPOSITE Revell supplies both water-slide (left) and peel-off/ stick-on decals (right) for some of its kits.

LEFT The garish lozenge markings that cover many First World War aircraft. Here they are for a 1:32 scale Pfaltz, so are large one-piece printings that will require careful handling.

ABOVE **One solution to storage of decals: an office-type paper filing set of drawers.**

BELOW **Requirements for decal application: water container, sheet of polystyrene, wetting agents and brushes.**

moved from France to England and the word was Anglicised to 'decalcomania', from which we get the shortened form, 'decal'.

Initially, they were associated with a wide variety of methods of applying labels to, well, anything. They could be used as warning labels on machinery, 'push' or 'pull' signs on doors, personalised flowers, 'Ban the Bomb' logos for school books (this tends to indicate the era of the sixties…) or bumper stickers for cars. Many of these would be peel-off vinyl 'stickers', but the process to produce them is much the same. Model kits mostly use the water-slide variety, although there are variations.

Application

For most decal application, you will need:

- A small container for the water
- A clean flat surface; a piece of sheet polystyrene is ideal
- Small scissors to cut out the decals
- Small tweezers for handling
- A small paintbrush to aid manoeuvring
- A lint-free cloth or sheets of kitchen towel for blotting excess water.

The process is fairly self-explanatory. Most decals are printed onto a shape that mimics the shape of the decal itself, albeit slightly larger (this is to allow for slight misalignment during printing.) Usually, it's simply a case of cutting the decals out from the paper backing. Occasionally, and most usually with aftermarket decal sheets, the markings are printed onto a continuous sheet. This is primarily done as the modeller would likely be more experienced with building models and applying decals, and more used to cutting as close to the decal marking's edge as possible, thus alleviating any 'decal line'.

Next, working one decal at a time – or certainly no more than a few, if they're all going to be positioned in a similar area – wet the cut decal in warm water. Don't leave them in there! Instead place them on the plastic sheet to allow the glue to soften. This is usually only a few seconds – not minutes! – but there can be exceptions. Older decals may need longer to soak, but this is really a matter of experimentation: there are no hard-and-fast rules.

With the decal loose on its backing paper, either carefully slide it onto the model with a finger, or carefully lift it with the tweezers, place it in position over the model and slide, maybe with a brush dipped in the water, into position. When it's correctly positioned, blot away the excess water with a paper towel or lint-free cloth. Ensure there are no air bubbles trapped: these might need 'sliding out' to an edge using the brush. Finally, pat down and then leave to dry.

Misbehaviour

Occasionally, the decal misbehaves and tends to curl up when being applied. The main reaction here is: Don't Panic! Try and slide the

decal off the model and back into the water. Here it will *usually* uncurl by itself. Then place the original backing paper underneath and slide the decal back on. (This might take some perseverance, as surface tension tends to come into play and the decal perversely floats away from the paper, so you need to be firm!) Reapply the decal back on the model, ensuring, maybe with tweezers, that it doesn't curl up this time. If this persists, you may have to tease the part of the decal that is curled underneath back to the correct orientation with small tweezers or a brush.

Additional techniques

Preparing your painted surface

The decals will, almost 100% of the time, be applied to a painted surface. Firstly, you need to ensure that the paint surface is thoroughly dry. Secondly, check that it's free of any contaminants – remember fingerprints tend to be greasy and the work surface may have been contaminated by some other source of oil or grease. If so, carefully wash the surface with water, maybe even with a drop of washing-up liquid.

Decals work best when applied to a gloss paint surface. This is fine for your high-gloss custom car, but may not be so applicable for a camouflaged warplane. For the latter you

UNHELPFUL ENGRAVING

Many early aircraft kits from American model companies engraved the position of the decals and even the pattern of the artwork into the plastic. This was to help modellers to position the decals correctly, but of course left a somewhat odd 'pattern' under them. This process lasted a good few years but, of course, is now not the style with any manufacturer. Old kits with this feature do get reissued from time to time, so the usual advice is to sand them off first!

ABOVE The stars and bars on the decal sheet compared to the equivalent pattern engraved on the wing of the Revell Convair Tradewind seaplane. The kit itself dates from the 1950s.

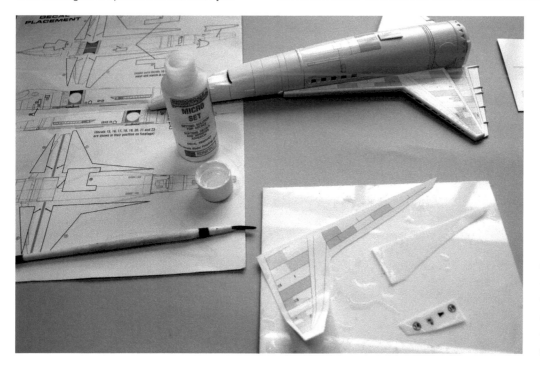

LEFT Decals are best applied over a glossy surface, otherwise you could get silvering, especially in this case of the Moebius 2001 Orion, where the markings cover most of the wings and fuselage.

can overspray with a gloss varnish, allow it to thoroughly dry and then apply the decals. Again, allow to thoroughly dry (you don't want water trapped underneath), then finally overspray with matt or satin varnish, depending on the required final finish.

Silvering – and how to avoid it

When decals are applied directly to a matt surface it can produce an odd effect called 'silvering', where indeed there is a 'silver' appearance to the decals. This is caused by minute amounts of air being trapped in the rougher surface of the matt paint and causing the light to refract – hence the advice to apply decals over a glossy surface, which is far smoother!

There are ways around this. There are what

are generally referred to as 'wetting agents': liquids that are primarily designed to break the surface tension of the water under the decals (which trap the air), allowing the decals to sit closer to the surface, thus avoiding silvering. Most model accessory companies make wetting agents – perhaps the most famous being Micro Sol, which makes the wetting agent 'Micro Set' (in the blue bottle).

Layering decals

In older kits, you will likely find only a few decals, for aircraft showing the very basic layouts of national markings, registration numbers, maybe the odd 'warning triangle' and similar. These days you will find that the overall number on the sheet will have risen, some by quite an amount,

maybe even ten-fold. This may also mean that decals might be applied over other decals. The 'lowest' layer is applied first and only, when that layer is dry, the top layer should be applied. This might even be repeated a few times. There are some cars kits, representing racing versions, that have four layers of decals!

Using decal softener

Many decals these days produce highly complex markings, some of which are intended to be applied to surfaces that are not completely flat or curve only in one direction – these are irregular compound-curved surfaces. Here, a decal will not sit 'flat', it has to be 'stretched' – and this is where liquids that will actually partially dissolve the decal are a necessity. Micro Sol (in the red bottle) is a useful decal softener.

This is a simple procedure, but one that to the uninitiated is somewhat alarming. First apply the decals as above, using the wetting agents to seat it in place. Ensure the decal *is* in the correct position (once the next stage is in process, there's little you can do and there's no going back!). Apply a drop of the decal solvent and *leave it* (what invariably happens – somewhat alarmingly if you're unfamiliar with the process – is that the decal will start to wrinkle up. The immediate response is to try and 'correct' it, but do not – you will likely wreck the decal. Instead wait and it'll eventually sort itself out. It will stretch to take on the irregular curves and, if necessary, shrink to fill recesses (or both) and dry in the correct place. The only permissible action if the decal appears to be settling in the wrong place is to very gently tease the decal with a fine brush, using plenty of water – that's about all you can do.

There are some manufacturers that make various strengths of decal softener. If the surface is particularly irregular or the decal appears to have been printed on thick paper, it could be useful to have a bottle of this on standby. Try the regular solvent first, and if that does not appear to be working, add a drop of the 'heavy duty'. But these stronger solvents are just that – use with care.

Recovery

Decal wetting agents such as Micro Set (*not* solvents such as Micro Sol) also have an

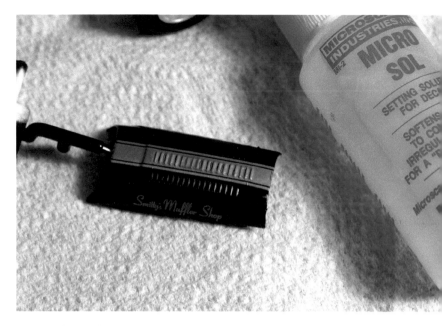

additional use. If you've applied the decal and it has dried, but you realise it's in the wrong place, you can use Micro Set to soak the decal and it will *usually* loosen the glue enough to allow it to be peeled off (maybe with the help of the tip of a scalpel blade under one edge) and either moved to the correct place or temporally transferred back to soaked decal backing paper while corrections to the model are done. BUT this is only a temporary measure and almost certainly won't work if a solvent has been used, as the decal is no longer flat.

Don't leave decals in Micro Set, or similar, for any period of time, as they will almost certainly start to dissolve. If you need to be a longer delay before reapplication, soak the decals in plain water, place back on the backing paper and they will probably work a second time – though this is not guaranteed!

Some manufacturers did start to add a disclaimer in the instructions that their decals are 'not decal solvent compatible'. This was really to protect themselves in case someone does make a mistake using such solvents and blamed the kit company. Usually all decals work perfectly fine with commercial decal solvents, though as per usual the advice is: 'If in doubt, test first'. There is usually a spare decal on the sheet that could be used, maybe even the name of the kit, which is usually done as a decal instead of being purely printed on the backing sheet.

Old decals

There's an increasing discovery of old kits, from swap-meets, sold-off collections, closed-down model shops and online auction sites, or just kits from your own collection that have never been built. If you put aside the notion of whether you can afford to build this old model anyway as it could have increased in value (see Chapter 11, pages 154–165, for more on this), and decide you are building it, there won't be any problem with the plastic parts themselves. Styrene is an extremely stable plastic and, providing the parts haven't been subjected to extreme heat (i.e. they've melted), there isn't a lot that can affect them. Even being soaked in water (the oft-quoted 'flooded

basement' scenario) will invariably trash the box, plans and decals, but the plastic will be left unscathed! There are some oil-based solvents that can dissolve the styrene, but this wouldn't be a usual scenario.

Yellowing

With old kits, the instruction sheets (even in the water-soaking scenario) can probably be recovered, or if not these are easy to replace – many companies have started putting a pdf of the plans online. What are far trickier to recover are the decals. Putting the water-soaking scenario to one side, as that almost certainly will have completely wrecked them, there are two other factors affecting older decals. First they could have 'yellowed', which is particularly noticeable, perhaps not unsurprisingly, with the whites. There is a way around this – use sunlight! It is an old trick but it actually works. Tape the decal sheet to a window facing the sun and leave it. Check it regularly, as the sunlight bleaches the colours, so you have to basically balance the removal of the 'yellow' only, without allowing the other colours to also fade too much.

Cracking

The second problem, which may not be so immediately visible, is that the top layer of the decal can crack with age. This will become immediately apparent when you try to soak the decals in water and they literally fall apart. This obviously has to be corrected before soaking – afterwards is far too late!

First, examine the decal surface, maybe in oblique lighting, to see if there are any visible cracks. If so, make sure the decal surface is clean of dust and overspray the decal sheet with a varnish, maybe twice or more. Microscale even makes a special product for this task. Whichever method you choose, it's certainly a good move even if no cracks are obviously visible, as some cracks and defects could be microscopic.

When the overcoat of varnish is dry, cut the decals apart – this will have to be done individually, as any initial separation will have been lost with the covering of clear varnish. They should then work 'as intended'. This cannot be guaranteed to work every time, but it does have a good track record.

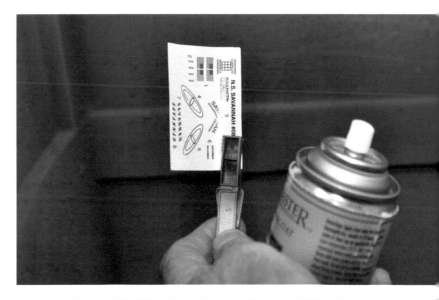

RIGHT Spray decals with clear varnish if you are unsure if they are cracked or not.

If the decal sheet is unsalvageable by the above methods, all may still not be lost. Don't, however, expect the original model company to be able to supply a new sheet. For a start, if the kit is that old the company may very well not still be in business. Even if it is, its decal collection – assuming it still has any – could very well be in the same condition as yours. However, online auction sites often advertise old decal sheets as well as complete kits, so you never know, you may be lucky and find a sheet.

Remaking

There is also a technique you can use to remake the decals. This requires some computer knowledge, the right computer programs, and a suitable scanner and printer.

First scan the decal sheet. Use a high resolution, certainly at least 300 dpi – you may have to experiment with settings such as whether descreening is on or off. Scanning can be either as a pdf or a jpeg (or other image file) – again, some experimentation might have to be done for the best result.

With the decal now as a digital file, any corrections or touching up can be done. Enlarge the image to make small corrections easier. Even removing yellowing can be done with an image manipulation program and the 'replace colour' command. If you make any changes it's advisable to save them under a different file name so you can go back to the original if necessary.

With the decal sheet as you would now like it, it can be printed back into usable form onto suitable decal paper. With the advent of modern computer systems, manufacturers started to produce decal-making papers that could be

CENTRE Making decals, in this case using a photocopier.

RIGHT Using a more modern colour laser printer, here with some experimentation of typefaces on the sheet, before the final version was applied to the AMT Dodge Deora (right).

printed out using home equipment. Before that, it could only be done using expensive commercial printers.

Decal paper is primarily available in two 'colours': white and clear. The white is denser and the colours will print better on it, but of course the backing is white, so unless the model itself has a white finish, or the decal has straight edges so that it can be cut out right up to the line, this isn't going to be usable for many models. The transparent decal paper is obviously the one to go for here, but this can sometimes show up light colours as being too 'thin' against a dark background.

The vast majority of home printers are either inkjet or laser, and decal-making paper is made specifically for either type. The main difference is that laser printing is 'dry'; the toner itself is dry, it transfers using an electrostatic charge and it is fused to the paper by heat. With inkjet printing, the ink starts wet, so the paper has to be slightly more porous for this to work. (However, experience has shown that most decal papers will print satisfactorily on the other type of printer.) Regarding which one to use, inkjets will usually give more vivid colours (being inkjets), but lasers usually give perfectly acceptable results. Laser printers – although more expensive to buy in the first place – are far cheaper to run and don't block with the monotonous regularity that occurs with many inkjets. This process will also work using older-style laser photocopiers, though

these were really limited to black printing on white or clear paper, and have largely been replaced with printers.

It is then advisable with either type, to overspray the paper with a varnish. Many companies make their own, though frankly any modelling varnish will usually work. Again the old adage: allow to dry thoroughly, then cut up and use as commercially produced decal sheets.

Other types

Dry-type rub-down decals

Although model decals started as the water-slide type, for a time in the 1970s some companies experimented with dry-type rub-down decals, as demonstrated with Letraset. Before computer word-processing became widespread, the only way to get 'professional'-type lettering was by this method, and the process was widely used in earlier years. Here the letters, numbers and symbols were on the back of the sheet, and applied by placing the sheet over where it was required and rubbing the top surface, ideally with the correct 'rub-down pen' (though most used a ball-point pen). This transferred the letter to the surface. The system generally worked very well – the transferred 'letter' was even thinner than a decal and it would generally adapt to irregular surfaces. But the application process was extremely time-consuming and the decal had to be exactly positioned the first time – there was no 'going back' with this method! If the decal wasn't in the right place first time, it would have to be laboriously cleaned off (a pencil eraser would usually work) and the whole process started again.

Some model companies, such as Matchbox at the time when it owned AMT, used rub-down decals for a few years. They were soon abandoned because of this required accuracy. Applying rub-down decals to a flat, even if rough, surface was one thing; trying to apply it to curved and irregular surfaces was something else. And, as pointed out, these decals were a one-time use. With water-slide decals, you can make adjustments before blotting down. With dry-type, you couldn't – it had to be right the first time.

ROUND THE BEND

The only potential problem that could occur while printing, is where printers (or photocopiers) have to take the paper around bends during the printing process. Most inkjet printers will take the paper in a direct straight line through the printing process. However, some older laser printers or photocopiers could take the paper on some tortuous route involving 180-degree turns, which could sometimes smudge the not-yet-fixed image. So check the route the paper will have to take!

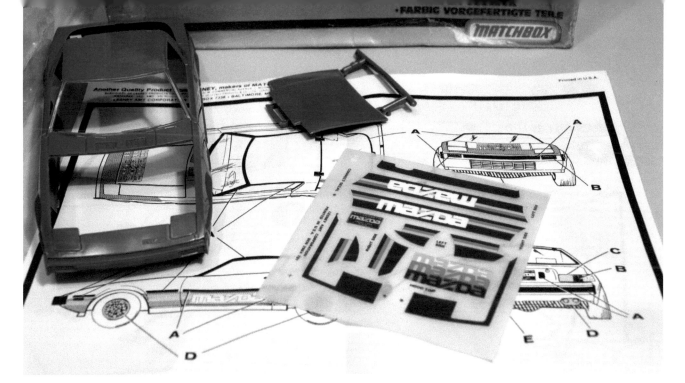

Peel-off/stick-on decals

Some kits will also have peel-off/stick-on decals. These are usually at the simpler or beginner's end of the market, coupled with snap – not glue – kits, where kids (of any age) didn't want the bother of having to cut out, soak and apply water-slide decals – they wanted to peel 'em off and stick 'em on as quickly as possible! There has also been the reasoning that in the US, where mom (and it would invariably have been 'mom' most of the time buying model kits for their kids) didn't relish the idea of glue being spread around the dining room table (hence the 'snap kits') but also didn't want the bother of water, which would almost certainly get tipped over – snap-together kits with peel-off decals got around both these potential problems.

There has been an intriguing development in very recent years where some manufacturers – Revell Germany being one – began to introduce kits that, although were snap together (Revell terms it the 'easy-click system') were also, for all intents and purposes, fully detailed glue-together kits. As these could be of interest to both ends of the market, satisfying both the beginner and the more experienced builder, two decal sheets were included with the kit. They both basically had the same details and markings, but one was peel-off while the other was traditional water-slide. So, depending on your skills, you could use whichever you wanted!

Another approach is that car, and other vehicle, models usually supply licence or number plates for vehicles on the decal sheet. These can be cut, soaked and applied as standard decals, but more often as not in recent years, the advice has been to simply cut them out and glue them directly onto the model using a white glue or similar, with the backing sheet still in place.

For the shine

There is one more type of 'decal sheet' that can be found in some kits (also primarily for cars, trucks and motorbikes) and these are what are generally called 'metallised decals'. This was originally developed for car badges that needed to be 'chrome' in appearance and rear-view

ABOVE **When Lesney (Matchbox) owned AMT, it experimented with rub-down-type decals for a time, but this never really caught on.**

BELOW Peel-off metallised decals, supplied for some versions of the AMT *Star Trek* USS Enterprise.

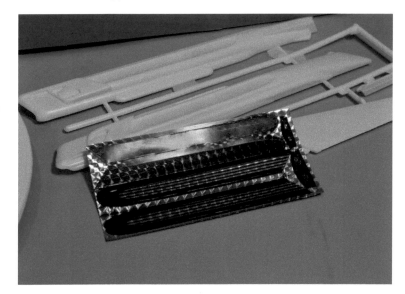

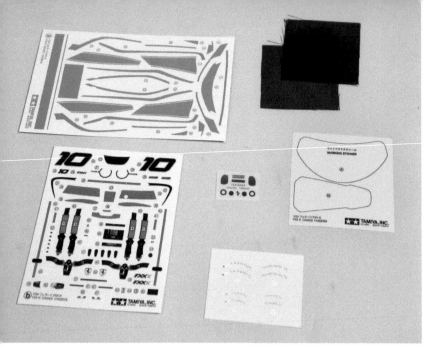

ALPS printers

In a chapter on decals, mention should also be made of ALPS printers, produced by the ALPS Corporation of Japan. This was more correctly called the 'Micro Dry Process', but tends to be universally known by the company name, hence 'ALPS'.

The system involved special printers that used a wax-resin transfer system and individual colour cartridges. These consisted of the standard individual printing colours – cyan, magenta yellow and black (CMYK) – but most importantly also made cartridges that would print not only white but metallic colours, such as silver and gold. None of these, at the time, could be printed satisfactorily (or at all) with inkjet or laser printers.

There was also a major difference in the operation of ALPS printers, compared to laser or inkjet, in that each colour was printed separately. The colour cartridges were stored on a rack. The printer would pick up each cartridge, print that colour, return it to the rack and pick up the next. Besides the decal paper having to be precisely located so the printing was accurate, it consequently involved a much increased time required to print all the

ABOVE Some modern car kits give a host of different ways to produce decals and lettering. In this Tamiya Ferrari kit you have two sets of decals (left), mesh for grilles (top right), paint masks for the windows (right), special tyre marking decals (lower right) and 'metallised' decals for wing mirror glass and instrument bezels (centre).

mirror 'glass' that needed to be shiny. These were an extension of the 'peel-off' decals approach, in that they were not soaked in water, instead the badges etc. were pre-cut with a sticky backing and held onto a backing sheet. Carefully removed with fine-tipped tweezers, they can be transferred to the model and buffed down with a soft cloth, giving a far more realistic appearance than standard decals. Car name plates and emblems bring another method of 'labelling': that of photo-etched parts – more in Chapter 10, Advanced Methods (see pages 140–153).

RIGHT Some kits also supply printed paper markings. This Ebbro Citroen 'Kitchen' has both water-slide decals for such as the cans on the inside shelves, and paper cutouts for the magazines on the counter.

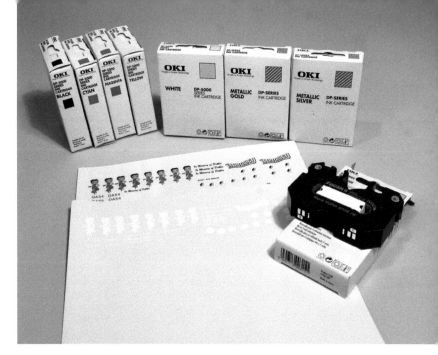

RIGHT The ALPS process. Here besides the four standard printer colours – cyan, magenta, yellow and black (back) – there are also white, silver and gold. The decal sheets show the way the layers are built up; the bottom one only has the white printed, while all colours are printed on the one above.

required colours when compared to a laser or inkjet printer, which would print all colours simultaneously. Although inevitably producing superior results, this increase in time spent printing meant that it never became popular with commercial printing companies. It did, however, especially find favour with decal sheets for model makers (and to a certain extent, those that printed logos onto T-shirts), as it could print white and metallics. But this was not enough to keep ALPS in the printer business (the company itself still exists as it is far larger and far more diverse than just producing printers) and although elements of the printers still exist in Japan, worldwide those that use them invariably have to rely on second-hand machines and dwindling stocks. The technology was licensed to other manufacturers such as Oki, Citizen and Kodak, but with the withdrawal of ALPS as the principal manufacturer, these companies too had to stop their participation in the system. If, however, you come across an aftermarket decal sheet with metallic in the printing, it almost certainly will have been done on an ALPS printer.

There have been developments in recent years of laser printers that can print white, termed CMYW printers: cyan, magenta, yellow and white. These have started to be used by some decal sheet companies, but as the printers are far more expensive than standard CMYK printers, their overall input into the market is currently still very small, though this will likely increase in the future.

Aftermarket

As soon as the first model kits began production, ideas for additional markings soon became apparent. Initially, this was primarily aircraft – these were the majority of the first kits and aircraft are a worldwide interest.

LEFT What can be done with ALPS. Here, a standard decal sheet (left) can be compared to the 'shine' you get with the ALPS printed sheet (right).

BELOW A very small selection of aftermarket decal sheets.

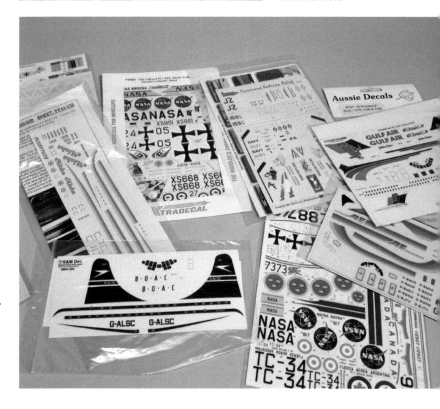

RIGHT Examples of the 'plain' kits from AMT and Revell of race cars, intended purely for aftermarket decal sheets.

ABOVE One specific set for the NASA Chase Car, with the Lindberg Police Dodge Charger as a donor. Note the print-outs of the actual car found on the 'net' and downloaded.

An aircraft produced with the national markings for one country was likely flown by other countries, so the appropriate markings would be required. Airliners were also a particular favourite here as they are a worldwide product flown by numerous airlines, each displaying their individual colours and logos.

Companies then began to be set up that concentrated purely on this aftermarket situation. Initially they won out as – invariably run by enthusiasts – they could concentrate on every single mark found on a particular plane, even down to markings a millimetre or so across on an individual notice found stencilled on a hatch. However, even mainstream companies have begun to issue decal sheets with literally all possible markings on them, some sheets running to hundreds of individual decals.

Aftermarket decals have been made for most modelling subjects; for the aforementioned aircraft, military and civilian, as well as another big customer – model cars. Race cars are the favourite, and this went so far that both AMT and Revell issued racing car kits without their own decals – they were solely intended to be finished with aftermarket decals.

Science fiction has also benefited from the aftermarket approach. The USS Enterprise from *Star Trek* began with an original basic kit (from AMT) with no external decals, apart from the 'USS Enterprise' name and a couple of red stripes. The filming miniatures, however,

RIGHT The completed kit with the aftermarket decals in place.

started to get more and more complex and decal sheets began to be available that would reproduce all these vessels. The same applied to the 'alien' craft from the Klingon and Romulan Empires. These ended up with what was termed 'Aztec Pattern', as it reproduced patterns that resemble the designs devised by the Central American civilisation. Creating Aztek patterns 'from scratch' wasn't the most straightforward of tasks, but the 'Aztec' decals made it considerably easier.

Make your own

The technique of replacing old, damaged decals using modern computers and printers can also be extended to making your own. So if you can't locate the decals you want, you can always make them yourself. This is an extension of scanning and reproducing existing old decal sheets, explained above, but this time you are starting with literally a blank sheet of – decal – paper. If it can be generated as a computer file, it can be printed onto decal stock.

You can make a decal of anything that is an image: lettering, diagrams, colour panels, drawings or even a photograph. Of course, the image has to be generated first. In earlier years, you didn't have much of an option if you wanted different lettering on a model. It was down to either attempting to make up the lettering you wanted from existing decals – alphanumeric sheets of letters and numbers were one of the earliest aftermarket decal sheets available – or maybe using one of the dry lettering systems (such as Letraset). These days, it is an entirely different story. Lettering and text can be generated using a word-processing program. With the vast range of fonts and typefaces available, it would be extremely surprising if you can't locate something to your satisfaction. These can be generated in any size and, of course, colour. And if you just can't find an existing style that suits, there's even more on the Web.

For more than just letters, if you are adept at drawing, you can make you own design. This can either be done in the old fashion way of literally drawing on a piece of paper and scanning it, or by drawing within a computer program.

Images can come from something you have photographed yourself, an image you have taken yourself or downloaded from the web, or a combination of both. Photo-manipulating programs such as Photoshop (though there are others) can change shapes, change perspective, stretch and squeeze the image and even flop it left-right or up-down – useful if you want an identical image but reversed for either side of a plane or car.

Sponsor logos likely abound on the web and although it can usually be taken that these are 'free to use', it's advisable to check that copyright is assigned and they are indeed free to use. Although it could usually be taken that individual use for your own personal model would probably not attract litigation, this is not a blanket free-for-all if you were starting a production line for decal sheets. If in doubt about any project, check first!

BE CAREFUL OF COPYRIGHT

A word should be said about copyright, and how it can affect modellers. Just because an image, photo or plan is on the Internet, does not automatically mean it is free to use. Some may be indeed 'in the public domain', meaning they are indeed free to use, but most are not – the copyright is held by someone, somewhere. Because the World Wide Web is precisely that – 'worldwide' – that copyright holder could be in a different country, and copyright laws are not necessarily the same country to country.

Very generally – although no legal interpretation should be made from this – if you download an image or plan and print out purely for your own use, for reference, painting schemes and similar, that is generally accepted as being 'fair usage'. Plus, in the very practical sense, how can anyone stop you? But if, say, you were planning on producing sets of decals that used that image, this is on far less safe grounds and the advice would have to be: get legal advice.

Chapter Nine

Displays and dioramas

Building models is one thing, but what do you do with them afterwards? Of course, individual models of an object could take pride of place on the mantelpiece or bookshelf, but there can be more to it than that.

Recreating an Apollo Moon mission, using the 1:32 Vista Replicas Lunar Module and the EVA Lunar Rover. The Moon dust is made from ceiling plaster.

ABOVE Some kits come with card dioramas. AMT's 'Man in Space' kit that featured all five – at that time – manned spacecraft, also included an impressive card base representing Kennedy Space Center.

Some models, and in fact some from very early years, came with certain diorama accessories. Both Revell and Monogram, long before they became the same company, did this. A favourite of both was an airliner, with access stairs, crew and maybe a baggage handler or two. There was no base as such, but it was a simple matter to find a square of wood, paint it grey to match tarmac and place the pieces in position. Monogram even made 'the first aeroplane' (with the priviso of 'heavier than air, powered and piloted') of the Wright Brothers 'Flyer', with all the equipment that can be seen in the classic photograph. Then there was a version of the Ford Trimotor with Antarctic equipment of figures, dogs and sleds, and these were both kits from the late 1950s.

Most figure kits come with some semblance of a base, even if it is to purely ensure the figure doesn't fall over! Airfix 1:12 scale figures all have bases, some more simple than others, while Aurora's 'horror monsters' figures all had bases that emphasised the subjects' usually macabre background. So there is Dracula with bats, The Wolfman with rats and a skull, and The Mummy with a serpent and broken Egyptian columns.

ABOVE Monogram's Wright Flyer. All the equipment in the famous photograph of the event was reproduced in the kit. Here, only the circular base has been added.

LEFT Mimicking what Aurora started, when Moebius created its own line of 'classic monsters from the movies' it used some diorama elements for the Frankenstein Monster.

LEFT Monarch Models produced very few kits, but it made one Aurora never did – that of the 'earlier' Dracula, Nosferatu – but in a very similar way, with a suitably decorated base.

RIGHT The Pegasus *War of the Worlds* comes with its own diorama base.

BELOW Creating water effects, here representing an Apollo recovery.

BELOW A simple base cut from MDF to make a support for Pegasus' *My Favorite Martian*. Modelling grass was sprinkled on top of wet paint.

Aurora even made 'Monster Customising sets', with additional creatures and details that you could add to your own bases.

Some models will obviously be more appropriate diorama in the amount of details in place. Military modelling is probably the most famous for this, with tanks, other AVFs and figures all fighting their way across a mud-splattered landscape. Add in bomb craters, barbed wire and trenches, and you have piece of history, forever giving up minute details not previously spotted.

But a diorama need not be that complex. A simple wood base with a top of scored plasticard sheet to represent paving slabs or concrete, could be an ideal base for a car or a taxiing aircraft.

Ships spend most of their life in water, so many kits are made as 'waterline' models. Here the lower hull – the part underwater – either isn't there in the first place or can be scored from inside the hull on pre-scored lines, and the lower sections removed. Bases can either be simply made from plaster on a wood base, painted a 'water shade' (which invariable is not 'blue'!) or using more sophisticated methods such as clear 'model water'.

Railway modelling is the other 'big' in dioramas, for by their very nature, railways/railroads tend to be working scale models, built on a base incorporating scenery. Consequently, they have many dedicated items at their disposal. These can range from an English country branch line from the 1930s, to the desert landscapes of the Wild West with wood-burning steam locos opening up the frontiers, to modern cityscapes with up-to-the-minute modern trains running on overhead gantries. Buildings, structures, landscape materials, trees, scrubs and bushes are all obtainable either ready-built or easily made.

All the above scenarios can then be expanded to science fiction and fantasy, where frankly, anything goes.

Simple dioramas

The simplest diorama is a flat base on which to stand your finished model. Bases can be bought pre-cut and pre-finished, especially intended for models, but in many cases it's just as simple and cheaper to go to your local DIY store and buy a piece of wood!

MDF

Actually, the most versatile material is not really 'wood', it is MDF (medium density fibreboard). This consists of wood fibres that are combined with resin and compressed into sheets of various thicknesses. It's not as strong as 'real' wood, and is mainly intended for panels in furniture, where it will be attached to a real wood frame. However, model bases do not exactly require much strength, and MDF's one main advantage is that it has a smooth finish on both sides with no grain. It ideally requires priming on both sides, so it takes any further painting better and to ensure it doesn't warp.

Many timber or DIY stores sell offcuts of MDF or will cut sheets to size. Otherwise it cuts easily and cleanly with a home-type bench circular saw. Sand the edges to remove any rough spots, and maybe put a chamfer on the edges. MDF does 'chip' quite easily, so rounded corners might be a benefit. The base can either be used 'as is', with purely paint and maybe some texture, or it can be covered with plastic sheet, spray glued into place. To save the edges, these too can be covered over with plastic sheet, using a file to chamfer the edges.

Foam board

Another very useful material is foam board. Available from art stores and similar, it is two sheets of card with expanded foam in-between. It's available in a variety of thicknesses and its advantage is that it is very light. It will cut cleanly with a sharp knife and will glue face-to-face with contact adhesive. It will also easily glue with a hot-glue gun – useful if you are gluing the board on its ends. It's useful for flat bases, or stand on end and create walls and whole buildings. These can then be covered with textured plastic card, plaster or similar.

Roughing it

Expanded polystyrene

MDF and foam board dioramas are fine for flat structures, but if you want a base with a rough irregular surface, the easiest and cheapest material to use is expanded polystyrene. This has the same chemical composition as the styrene found in model kits, but it has been aerated to make it much lighter.

ABOVE The old Aurora *The Invaders* UFO settles in a somewhat sparse forest. The base is purely a piece of wood; the trees are from one of the specialist suppliers.

BELOW Simple drag strip set-up using the IMC/Lindberg racing Dodge pickup, with an early-type TV camera from AMT's Drag Strip Accessories pack and a white metal figure.

BELOW Using foam board to build Gotham City, with kit bashed parts, and the Polar Lights' TV Batmobile.

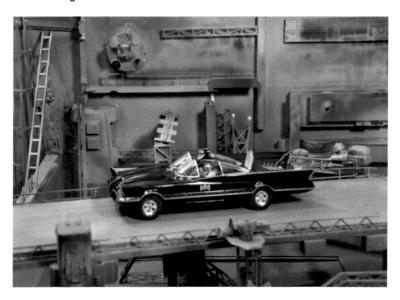

ABOVE **The Italeri F-117A flies over a section of the Nevada desert, here made from painted expanded polystyrene.**

of white expanded polystyrene. Alternatively, buy some insulation and you will have enough material for many bases. This can either be used by itself, or glued to one of the wood bases for additional strength.

Cutting

Expanded polystyrene can be easily cut with a sharp knife or thin saw. Be aware, though, that this will generate a lot of granules of polystyrene. These are not poisonous as such but can be an irritant, so if you feel it necessary, wear eye protection and a mask. The granules are also very prone to static electricity, so will stick to virtually anything, making cleaning up a chore. If you try sweeping they will just 'stick' to the bristles of the broom – a vacuum cleaner is easier.

Often known generically by its trade name, Styrofoam, initially its main use was as ceiling tiles and insulation, but now the tiles have gone out of fashion and the insulation is only made in large sheets. Now an easy – and free – source is found in a multitude of packing materials. Buy a new refrigerator or washing machine and it will certainly be packed around with sheets

Sanding

Shaping of expanded polystyrene can be done with course files or course sanding paper, moving to fine grades if you want smoother surfaces. This, of course, will generate even more 'dust', so is best not done in the family sitting room! A garage, shed or even outdoors will be better (with adequate attention paid to not getting too much into the atmosphere). If possible, lay the nozzle of a vacuum cleaner near to where you are sanding, which will probably get rid of about 75% of the dust.

MODEL MATERIAL

Sheets of white expanded polystyrene also have another modelling use – in fact, a general photographic use. They are often used in professional photography and filming to bounce light, fill in shadows and the like. In a model photo studio (see Chapter 12, pages 171–174) they can also have a similar use.

BELOW **The Renwal LaCrosse missile on a simple expanded polystyrene base, with some 'stones' and 'gravel' over a grass base.**

Melting

Expended polystyrene can be melted by heat, which can make interesting shapes. This comes with the very important proviso that heated polystyrene will certainly give off unpleasant fumes, and could catch fire – and burning polystyrene is extremely unpleasant to get near. If you need to resort to this method, do so in a safe environment, wear protective gear with a suitable face mask and have a fire extinguisher handy!

Cementing

Expanded polystyrene is still styrene, but it will not cement using standard styrene glue – this will purely melt the surface. Instead, one of the non-methyl-based glues is required. These are PVA (white glue) or latex based, and will not melt the surface. Instead coat both surfaces, allow to part dry and press and hold together.

Sealing

Unless you are building a snow scene – in which case, the bright white of the expanded polystyrene is a good starting point – the sanded surface will not really be adequate 'as is' for the base or diorama. It is prone to damage, and you need to seal it to prevent further granules sloughing off.

Consequently, it needs sealing. One option is a coat of plaster. Plaster of Paris or dental plaster could be used, but it usually dries far too quickly and you end up with a very hard surface that can easily crack. Instead, use what are usually termed 'ceiling plasters' (trade names such as Artex). These are still water-based mixes, which dry much slower and are softer – you can drill into the surface without it cracking, and they take paint very well. In fact, pour some paint into the mix, so the basic colour is already there.

Painting

If you are painting a large area, household paints will work out far cheaper than model paints. Alternatively, buy large tubes or tubs of artist acrylic paints. The artist-type acrylics are the type used for fine artwork, and are available from art or craft stores in various sizes. They are available in a wide range of colours; many suitable 'diorama colours' such as greens, browns and greys. They are far more expensive than household paints but will go a long way and, volume for volume, are still cheaper than using the specific small bottles of modelling paint.

If you want to add 'bulk' to this ground surface mix, simply add some sawdust. Bags can be bought at pet stores (used as bedding for guinea pigs and hamsters, for example). This is an expensive way of buying it; it's cheaper to get a bag from a woodyard or – even cheaper still – if you have a bench circular saw at home, tip it up and there will almost certainly be an adequate supply underneath!

ABOVE **Here, dry ceiling plaster was sprinkled over the base and car – an Italeri VW Beetle – representing a scene from** *Gremlins.*

Building up the detail

With the base covered with its ceiling plaster, you can set about building up your desired details. There are many manufacturers of 'scenic materials' to aid this, one of the largest being Woodland Scenics. This company supplies bags of virtually any type of surface you could want: brown earth, sand, green grass and all shades in-between. Some have coloured bits mixed in – representing small flowers in the grass – or you can add your own.

BELOW **Sets of greenery from the UK company, Treemendus.**

> ### CEILING PLASTER PLUS
>
> An additional advantage of using one of the ceiling plasters: because they dry far slower than traditional plasters, it becomes easy to embed anything – figures, vehicles, etc. – into the surface. Wait until it is generally dry, but still has some 'give', and simply push the object into the plaster. Either leave the model in place and paint around it, or remove it and the indentation will stay to allow the item to be placed in later.

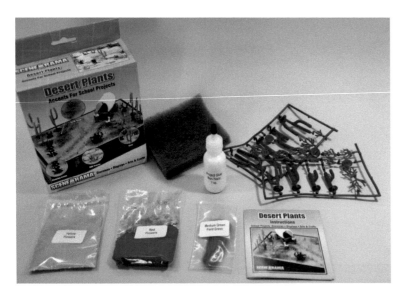

ABOVE Start your desert scenes with items from Scene-A-Rama.

Rocks and gravel are available in many sizes, so you can use a mix of several sizes in one diorama, or adapt to different scales.

There also nothing stopping you using 'full-size' sand and gravel, perhaps the small

amount left in the bottom of the bag after that garden makeover. Ideally wash and dry it before applying it to a model base. You can purely paint the surface and sprinkle on the sand. Much, however, won't stick, so will need tipping off once the base is dry. Alternatively, mix some sand with white PVA glue and 'paint' it on – the glue will dry transparent. Or you could even mix the sand in with the paint that will form the base colour and apply that. Other details can then be added on top.

Greenery

Many dioramas benefit from greenery – grass, bushes, hedges, trees – and these are also things many of these aftermarket companies supply, either ready-made or as kits. These are invariably expensive, though if time is of the essence, they're likely the easiest option. However, there's nothing stopping you making your own.

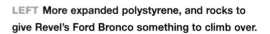
LEFT More expanded polystyrene, and rocks to give Revel's Ford Bronco something to climb over.

BELOW LEFT The English countryside in the form of Bridge Farm in Ambridge, home of BBC Radio's long-running series *The Archers*. Here Tony Archer shows off his Ferguson tractor, courtesy of the Heller kit. Animals come from the Tamiya sets (that is 1:35, but with animals it matters less when used in 1:24). Other parts from various sets and the trees and hedges produced by the methods given in the text.

BELOW Small bushes can become larger shrubs in real porcelain pots. The surface is real slate; the car is Revell's '83 Hurst Oldsmobile.

It is very easy – and very cheap – to find some real wood twigs, spray the top part with spray glue and dip into the 'grass' mix to make ready-made trees in leaf! Bore a hole in the polystyrene base – again, another side to the flexibility of using a ceiling plaster and polystyrene base – and push the miniature tree in place. Real twigs can also make bushes or can be cut down for hedges. Polyurethane foam (the type used in furniture) also works for hedges – even wire wool will work! Again, spray both with spray glue and dip in a 'greenery' mix.

Nothing in building dioramas is set in stone. Use whatever material comes to hand – it may even be 'stone'! Packs of 'stones' are available from the aftermarket companies, but – as with the sand – small pebbles and the like are available from gardening centres, which are a far cheaper source.

Flowers and plants can come from a variety of sources. There are many ready-made, which are not exactly cheap but can allow you time to be spent on other matters. Most have allocated scales, but plants, even more than humans or animals, are extremely varied in size, so 'scale' as such doesn't really come into it. Something listed as 1:48 will probably still work 'larger' for 1:72 scale and 'smaller' for 1:24. For extremely detailed plants and leaves, many are also made as photo-etched parts. These are more difficult and time-consuming to work with, but the detail is exquisite.

Desert scenes

One general species of plant often found in modelling is the cactus, as desert scenes often seem to find themselves modelled, from wartime scenarios to settings for suitably themed custom cars.

For the 'desert' itself, real fine sand can be used – the type used in aquariums is the finest, though a mix of grades of sand will be more authentic. Mix in some 'rocks and gravel' for even more realism, and hold the lot in place with a PVA glue. This can either be painted onto the base – maybe mix some colour into it, paint and sprinkle the mix. Not all will immediately stick, so you could shake it off when the PVA is dry and reuse, then spray over with a clear varnish (even clear hairspray will work). Alternatively, mix the sand, rock and gravel in

ABOVE Real sand to create the desert for Monogram's Rommel's Rod. Palm trees are from the old Britains sets.

BELOW Monogram's Boot Hill Express also in the desert. Here cacti and plants come from the Scene-A-Rama and Pegasus sets.

BOTTOM The famous scene from *Back to the Future Part III*, with a converted MPC The General wood-burning loco pushing the Aoshima DeLorean up to 88 mph. The ground is carved expanded polystyrene with real twigs as 'trees'. The track is modified LGB.

with the PVA glue, possibly watered down, and paint that on. PVA dries clear, so the 'white' colour will vanish when dry.

Water features

'Water' in the form of the oceans, rivers and ponds is a subject that also comes up frequently, with several solutions for modelling. Large areas of water, such as ships 'sailing on the ocean blue', can usually be done with a solid surface, using paint to represent the water. But here water is rarely 'blue', usually more a murky brown-green, and although the usual adage of 'the further away the object, the lighter it will appear' can follow through to water, it will still need to be fairly dark – after all, light doesn't percolate though the sea for more than about 12 feet.

Water also has no 'scale' as such, hence it being virtually impossible to 'miniaturise' it in special effects miniature sequences. (This has led to the usual reasoning of: 'If in doubt, avoid water completely in model filming!') For a model diorama base with a model battleship, aircraft carrier or liner, the water scale will be extremely small. However, some scale can be added with the white 'tips of the waves' – the mares' tails. Apply a base coat for the main water base using the ceiling plaster, or if the sea is reasonably calm, perhaps just some filler in the base paint. If some waves (and be aware of scale) are required, very carefully 'flick' the coating onto the base, so as to form the waves. Then allow to thoroughly dry. Once the base coat is dry, carefully add white paint on a fairly loaded brush to the edges of the waves. With larger scale ships the surface can be rougher, and the painting of the mares' tails slightly easier.

For larger dioramas, a pond (or small lake or section of a river) can be made by literally digging out the pond itself from the base, finishing it with suitable mud, plants and anything else – maybe the odd shopping cart! – then fixing a sheet of clear acrylic (Perspex or Plexiglas) as the water's surface. The edges can be filled in with a small amount of the base mix, painted to suit, add plants, gravel and maybe the odd water lily – the sort of thing available as photo-etch – on the surface of the water.

Finally, there are special acrylic mixes available from a number of aftermarket weathering paint companies. Here you literally pour the mix in thin layers onto the surface, and it dries hard and – more or less – clear. This is really only suitable for small areas, or in fountains, troughs or buckets, as it is an expensive method.

Mountain views

Scenery is rarely flat, so if you require a diorama involving hills, cliffs or mountains, you will need to build up the base. Using expanded polystyrene could be the best bet for this. If you have a large block, carve to shape using the previous methods (see page 130). Lacking a large block of styrene, alternatively build up the shape using thinner layers – use PVA glue to hold it together, or place the layers in position using thin sticks such as kebab sticks to hold them together and use ceiling plaster over the whole lot.

The older model railway technique for scenery was to build up a shape with chicken wire and cover it with plaster bandage. Any plaster bandage would do, though there was a modelling version called ModRoc (however, for all practical purposes this was identical).

Buildings

So far these have all been 'natural' scenes, but many will also involve buildings – either still standing, or in most military applications, almost certainly not. Here the modeller has a vast choice, though arguably in limited scales. Unlike ground and natural vegetation, buildings do not scale so easily and the vast majority are tied to just two modelling subjects: railroads and military in 1:87, with a slight nod to 00 gauge in 1:76, and military in 1:35.

Railway vistas

Specific railway buildings in H0 scale are available from many companies, for example from Faller and Heljan in Continental Europe or Walthers in America. All are intended to be used in conjunction with railway layouts, are generally fairly simple in construction in that they – being buildings – are flat sided, usually with separate windows, doors, roofs and the like, and moulded in colour. (And they all tend

to be very expensive!) Most are designed to sit on a flat surface, so don't need to be moulded into any diorama base. Then there are other kits, to the same scale, that are more 'engineering' in their subject matter so could be adapted to other scenarios. Girders intended for building, say, a crane, could be used as a load for a truck or alternatively piled up in a scrap-yard.

Completed buildings can, of course, be adapted to a wartime scenario and demolished to a certain extent. The two main scales that military AFVs are available in – 1:35 and 1:72/6 – are almost certain to be the sort of sizes in which most dioramas will be built. Buildings are less slightly specific than aircraft or cars as far as scales are concerned and given that most buildings generally available will be rail accessories in 1:87/H0 scale, they could likely be adapted to the 00/1:76/1:72 sizes without too much of a problem.

For the main military scale of 1:35, railroad buildings are not generally available, so can't be adapted. However, there are many aftermarket buildings made, primarily in resin, and many are pre-wrecked to varying degrees. Some even come from mainstream companies such as both Airfix and Italeri, which make pre-damaged resin buildings alongside their injection styrene models.

Many accessories, such as telegraph poles, fences, walls, barrels and road signs, are also made. Some of these could even be adapted to other scales, most noticeably for 1:32 scale aircraft or car dioramas. For buildings and

accessories, the difference between 1:32 and 1:35 is hardly going to matter, even to the dedicated scale guru. Given that scaling of these types of objects is reasonably flexible, they could possibly be scaled up to 1:24/5 for larger car scales. A large fence in 1:35 can become a small fence in 1:24/5.

Building conversions

Most of these kits are just that: kits. By definition, they are in several parts, so the parts themselves can be cut and adapted to other structures, or cut apart and reformed. Rubble can be added in the same way as general earth and ground – mix bits with PVA glue, add some colour and paint or stipple in place. The AFVs can be pushed into the surface while it dries, and then

ABOVE A New England township, with railroad, buildings and vehicles. This is 1:87 scale and part of Gulliver's Gate in New York City.

BELOW Recreating a clandestine landing in occupied France during the Second World War. The 1:72 scale Airfix Lysander, with one of the same company's wrecked buildings and cows.

ABOVE Rat Rods demand an equally chaotic setting. Here the Lindberg kit uses leftover parts of the actual kit, such as the fenders, as part of the setting. Rust out of a bottle.

a cutting board as the knife needs to cut through the foam board cleanly.

Foam board can be glued, if face-to-face, with standard contact adhesive, but if you are standing parts on end, a glue gun is the best option. Be aware that the heat from the gun (even the 'low temperature' ones) could start to melt the foam, but a bit of juggling with gun and board usually means there's enough glue on the card edges to hold everything firmly in place.

With a basic structure in foam board or balsa wood (or both), details can be added. Windows and doors can be built from balas or plastic. There are packs of plastic shapes available from companies such as Evergreen and Plastruct that could be used to build frames. Embossed plastic sheet is made in many brick and stone patterns for walls. You can even get embossed sheet for roof tiles, from the more conventional flat slate to pantiles so often seen on Mediterranean style buildings. Other embossed sheets could provide wooden doors, or simply scribe a pattern yourself into a plain sheet.

Clear acetate sheet can form window glass, and you could even add curtains or drapes where appropriate from cast-off material in the sewing box, or alternatively and more to scale, from dolls house accessories. Here dolls houses and their catalogues can come in very useful. Admittedly there's a lot of dolls house equipment that is somewhat oversimplified and probably doesn't work in a 'realistic' setting such as military – or other – dioramas, but

add weathering techniques to the vehicle, if not already applied. Figures can also be added at this time, just push them into the drying 'mud'.

Although many buildings, of any type, are available as kits, others can be built from scratch. The main materials here are going to be foam board and wood – balsa wood is a favourite as it is extremely easy to work with. Foam board, as mentioned before, can be bought from art stores, as it is used a lot for mounting photographs and paintings. It is, however, an extremely useful resource for building dioramas. It's basically a sandwich: two layers of card, with a layer of foam in-between. The thickness of the foam varies, and sizes can be bought from a few millimetres up to ½in or 1cm thick. It cuts very easily with a standard modelling knife, best over

RIGHT If anything is intended for dioramas it is military AFVs. Here, an example from the New City Scale Model Club.

search around as some items can be very useful. Many companies make real pottery flower pots and tubs, which are adaptable to many scales as flower pots come in all sizes. The pottery ones could even be broken up if they are meant to be damaged.

Building buildings

There are commercial model companies that make architectural items for those that still build 'proper' architectural models. Some design companies still like to see 'real models' of their latest designs in reception.

EMA/Plastruct make a wide range of architectural model-making items and the Irish-based ArcKit make 'do it yourself' architectural kits of parts for budding architects (or even professional ones) to play about with building designs. These parts are intended to be used then broken down and reused for new designs, but there's no reason why their parts can't be adapted into dioramas.

Aircraft dioramas tend to find themselves displayed in a far tidier situation – the plane emerging from a hanger or sitting being readied for flight on the runway. Here, the base is almost always going to be mainly flat, as bumpy runways – even for military aircraft – are hardly the norm. Sheets of plain polystyrene are available from many manufacturers; Slaters and Evergreen being the most well-known. These sheets tend to be universally around 12 x 8in. However, commercial suppliers of plastic usually stock larger sizes, which although trickier to handle can be cut down and will be more economic.

Whatever the source, the polystyrene sheet can be stuck down to a wood base, with spray

TOP Using specially formulated 'acrylic water', this from **AZ Interactive**, to produce the stream into which, in typical fashion, Lieutenant Horatio Caine of *CSI: Miami*, is gazing.

CENTRE Creating a display base for the Dragon 1:48 Bachem Natter, here Tamiya acrylic paints are used on a slightly raised base.

RIGHT Both the prototype and what could have been a production version of the Natter. Vehicles from Tamiya.

ABOVE **Combining kits: the 1:32 scale Revell Bell X-1 with a Gowland & Gowland , later Revell, MG-TC.**

glue, available in aerosol cans. (Spray with the awareness that it tends to get everywhere....) Once firmly stuck, lines for slab bases and the like can be scribed into the surface. There are special modelling tools that will do this, and special blades are made for Stanley knives, for example. Finally paint – start with a coat of grey primer, then brush on details such as dirt in cracks and maybe the odd piece of vegetation if it's a somewhat under-used runway. Figures and accessories can then be added, and there are a vast amount produced in all traditional

aircraft scales from both the mainstream and aftermarket companies.

Don't forget that modelling subjects can be mixed. If the aircraft scale is one of the larger ones, such as 1:24, there's similarly a vast amount of cars and trucks that could be positioned alongside it. For an Airfix 1:24-scale Spitfire, the Monogram 1:24 MG-TC could be used as the pilot's personal transport. There are many 1:32-scale vehicles for aircraft in that scale, and even quite few in 1:48. 1:48 scale aircraft can also be displayed with the growing range of 1:48 scale military. And down to 1:72 and 1:76, there is a vast range of aircraft, buildings, and even some vehicles that can be mixed.

Science fiction and fantasy

Everything to date has been based on reality – here, everything goes out of the window and you can let your imagination run riot! You have, of course, the multitude of existing commercial kits of SF and fantasy craft and 'beings', and this is the one area where scratch-building really comes into its own.

For diorama settings you have everything that has gone before in this chapter – plus inventing anything else you like. Building techniques for bases is much the same – expanded polystyrene, plaster bandage, plasters and paint can all be adapted, though the colour of the grass may be blue not green!

It's also an ideal time to explore materials and objects that would possibly not be used in more terrestrial-based scenes. If you want an odd-looking building shape for some far off planet, you could look at the many vac-formed shapes used for packing. Usually discarded, these shapes could take on a new life. Most will be clear to begin with, so you already have windows of sorts. Mask and paint frames, or add some wooden and plastic shapes. Odd pieces of existing kits can be adapted – in the special effects world, this is called 'kit bashing', where you take one part from a kit and use it on your scratch-built creation as something completely different. This is done all the time in building special effects miniatures, and even with the growth of CGI for many effects, effects miniatures are still being made, so scratch-building and kit bashing still comes in to play.

Another thing about creating special effect miniature sets is they are usually built 'soft', in

COMPETITIONS

Exactly what comprises just a 'display base' and when it becomes a 'diorama' has taxed many competition devisers, leading to confusion as to which class to place a model. Some rules and regulations have stipulated that a model aircraft entered just as an 'aircraft' can only have a maximum of two figures, though it can be on a plain base, 'for handling'. But what if you add an entry ladder or a single toolbox – does that now make it 'a diorama'? The question is rhetorical, as obviously it's down to any competition – and how liberally the rules are interpreted! It can be a minefield of uncertainly, but overall it only really matters if you intend to enter a model in a particular competition. If in doubt, ask! (See also Chapter 12, page 170.)

MOON DUST

Interestingly, Artex and other ceiling plasters match Moon dust pretty well, so if you're recreating the Moon landing, Artex could be a good lunar surface – the landing legs of the Lunar Module can be indented into the surface of the dry powder, just like the real Apollo missions. You can even create authentic-looking craters by dropping a small ball into the dust and carefully removing it. This also works in wet Artex, if you're building a more permanent base. Or you can do this in the dry powder and spray water from a handheld spray to wet the surface, leaving it to dry thoroughly, when the pattern will be retained.

that they're not built as a permanent display – this is one main difference between what the professional and amateur model maker generally will be doing. Most of the latter will be built 'fixed'. However, there may be a situation in which you want to take a series of dioramas for photography – or even make your own SF movie on your iPhone (it has been done), so the miniature sets would not be permanent and would need constant alteration. The same materials can come into play – expanded polystyrene, sawdust and plaster.

Futuristic cityscapes, à la *Blade Runner*, can be created by more kit bashing or existing structures, mixed in with broken girders, pipes and walls, to get that derelict look. If you want a more *Blade Runner* look (where it was constantly raining) use some of the 'clear water' (see page 134) for puddles, gutters and the like.

Chapter 10

Alternative and advanced techniques and the future

Given that making injection-moulded construction kits requires a lot of engineering effort, from making the tooling to running it on an injection machine, other methods of producing kits have been explored using all techniques – except injection moulding.

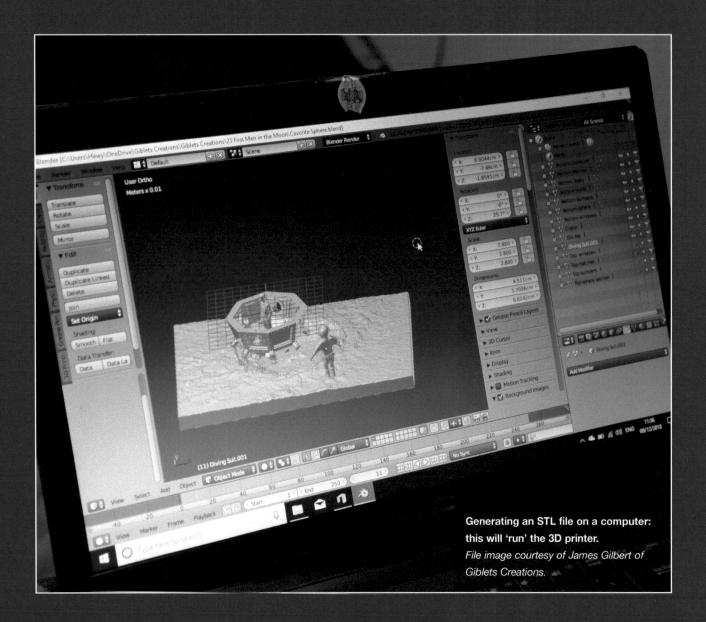

Generating an STL file on a computer: this will 'run' the 3D printer.
File image courtesy of James Gilbert of Giblets Creations.

Other techniques

Many kits have now been issued from specialist model companies that involve a wealth of alternative materials, so much so that they are usually referred to as 'multi-material kits'. But it all started in a slightly simpler way.

It wasn't long after the first model kits came onto the market that enthusiasts started to adapt them. It began purely with conversions by individuals, but then perhaps someone decided a few modelling friends would like similar items, so a small production line was formed. This was firstly how the cottage or garage industries started and secondly was the first usage of techniques not used by the kit manufacturers themselves.

These very first ideas were not exactly 'high-tech' – in fact this very first method was especially lo-tech. But it was the first alternative to injection-moulded polystyrene; it used the same basic material and could be used to make parts and, in many cases, whole kits. This was vacuum forming.

Vacuum forming

Vacuuming forming (otherwise known as vac forming) uses the simple notion of taking a sheet of polystyrene, heating it enough so that it is flexible, and quickly pulling it down over a shape or former to take the form of that shape. To aid this, draw the air out from under the sheet with a vacuum, so the sheet is pulled down directly over original shape – the 'former'. And that is it; with the vac-formed shape generally being referred to as the 'pull'.

There is, perhaps, slightly more to be added. The resulting sheet has to be removed from the former, so undercuts have to be avoided (otherwise the pull will get stuck over the former!). The excess styrene around the shape then has to be cut away using scissors or scored with a knife and snapped away. But it is styrene, so it will glue with the same cement and will take paint and decals in the same manner as conventional kits.

You have be dedicated to deal with vac form kits, as they are not the most straightforward. Besides the cutting out of the parts, they don't have locating lugs, so joining fuselage halves together – and the vast majority of early vac form

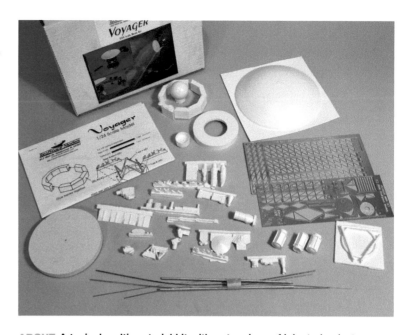

ABOVE A typical multi-material kit with not a piece of injected polystyrene in sight – the nearest is vac-formed styrene (top right). The rest are resin and photo-etched parts, with some metal wire and tubing (bottom). The kit is the RealSpace Models' **Voyager** space probe.

kits were aircraft – involves extra work fitting lugs out of scrap plastic then lining up the thin edges.

It didn't help that most were made in the way described above. The former was male, meaning that the final object that was pulled over it was female. Any details on the outside of the former would now be on the inside of the pull, so would only show through the thickness of the styrene sheet. There was a way around this, though it doubled the effort. After the original – male – former was made, a female

BELOW Building a vac-form kit: this is a Welsh Models' E7-A. Parts have to be carefully scored and snapped away from the backing sheet.

RIGHT Vac-formed parts do crop up in commercial kits – the circular grey base at the top of this image is a vac-formed part. This is the MPC kit for the *Space 1999* Nuclear Waste Disposal Area.

BELOW Vac forming is still used to produce more authentic-looking billowing sails for galleons.

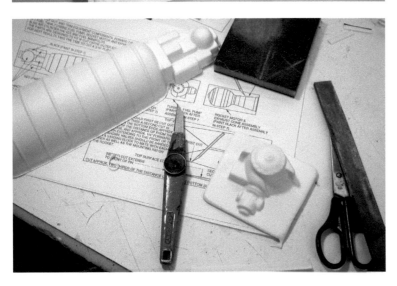

mould had to be made from this and the vac forming was then pulled into this female mould. Only then would the detail be on the outside of the final part. Even then, the detail wasn't going to be that great, and certainly not the sort of quality that you'd get with an injection kit.

You also had to decide on the thickness of the styrene sheet used. Too thin – and yes it would 'pull' into all the nooks and crannies of the former and was better at picking up the details – but it was far more likely to tear along the way. Then the final piece, assuming it did vac form correctly, would not be that strong. Conversely, a thicker sheet was far more hard-wearing and strong but had to be heated more thoroughly, with the danger of melting before it got anywhere near the vac form machine. Even then, it might not pull into all the nooks and crannies.

Because of a lot of these problems, vac forming has really fallen out of favour with modellers in recent years, although there are the odd exceptions. There are still some dedicated companies using the method, and some aftermarket cockpit canopies are made by this method, which results in a part that is

LEFT Trimming the vac-formed parts on the Apex 1:16 scale kit of the V2 missile. The edges here needed quite a lot of cleaning up.

far thinner and closer to scale than its injection styrene equivalent.

Vac forming has found its way into some of the diorama features supplied with mainstream kits. MPC has used it a lot with its dioramas for *Star Wars*, *Raiders of the Lost Ark* and most recently with its new *Space 1999* moon base scene. Vac forming is also used to create the billowing sails in kits of galleons.

Home vac forming

Vac forming is also something that can be done at home. Some basic vac forming machines are made, though they mostly just supply the working block, and you have to supply your own heat and vacuum sources. The former can actually be made in a kitchen oven – needless to say, set on *low* – or with a heat gun or even a reasonably powerful hair drier. Meanwhile, the vacuum source can come from a domestic vacuum cleaner.

You will need some former to mould over. For example, if you wanted a thin dish as an antenna for a spacecraft, this could purely be moulded over a bowl or dish. Place the former on the moulding bed and attach the vacuum cleaner nozzle. Heat the plastic sheet – the machine manufacturer usually supplies a frame to hold it. Then, in a coordinated movement, pull the now flexible sheet over the former. Switch on the vacuum to remove the air from under the sheet. Much will depend on the power of the cleaner and the sealing of the pipe work and it can help to seal it with gaffer or duct tape. You have limited scope with such a device, but this method can be used very successfully to make relatively simple shapes.

Home vac forming was – and still is – very much a process of trial and error. The main trick is to get the sheet heated to the correct degree

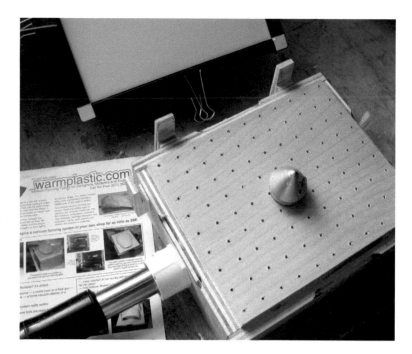

TOP Using a small commercially made home vac former from warmplastic.com to make a part for the Apollo Saturn V. The former is in place and the vacuum cleaner hose (left) is attached.

CENTRE Heating the plastic sheet using a hot-air gun.

RIGHT Pulling the heated sheet over the former.

WOOD CARVING

Parts for other shapes that can't be sourced can be made, for example, by carving wood. Balsa wood is probably the best known wood for model making, being light and easy to carve, and is consequently used a lot in flying model aircraft. But it has grain, which can show up in a vac form, so this will need sealing and then sanding to get a smooth surface. Another wood often used for modelling is jelutong. This is somewhat harder so is less easy to carve, but as it has very little grain it likely won't need as much sanding before use.

of flexibility. It needs to be flexible enough to draw down over the former, but not so hot that it will tear, or worse, catch fire! Consequently, be sure to have lots of styrene sheet cut and ready to go, as you'll almost certainly get through a good percentage of them!

Using resin

The next 'aftermarket technique' to appear for model makers after vac forming would have been resin. Given that this is a book on 'plastics', resin is not far removed. Styrene is a polymer, and so is resin, albeit one that cures and can't be melted down for reuse.

Initially individual parts were made: a new nose for an aircraft or a different body for a car. Unlike an original former for vac forming, there

needs to be slightly more to making the original former to then make the resin castings. Most had to be made exactly as an injection styrene part would be made, and precisely the same size. This then needed to have a mould made from it.

Moulds were usually made from a hard rubber, though the life expectancy of these was short. If a longer run was planned for the parts, a fibreglass mould would be more robust. Either way, the original would be pressed into clay, up to approximately halfway. Locating lugs could then be pressed into the clay, so when the upper half was poured they would help locate the two halves together. Pouring channels would also need to be built in, the equivalents of the runners in a steel tool, so the resin could be poured to make the eventual casts.

The mould material was then poured around this top half and allowed to cure. The whole lot was then inverted and the clay removed. A mould release agent or 'separator' layer then needed to be painted onto the mould surface so the other half of the mould didn't stick to the first. The other half of the mould rubber would then be poured in and finally, the two halves were separated and the original removed – you now had the mould.

The resin for the actual kit part could then be poured in and ideally the mould was 'jiggled' slightly to remove any air bubbles. These bubbles are the worst enemy for resin kits, as the mixing process for the resin – unless done extremely carefully – will trap air. Resin is fairly viscous, so air bubbles can get 'stuck', but they can rise to the surface while the resin is curing in the mould, resulting in an air bubble. There are methods and practices to minimise this: one is 'degassing', where the mix is done in a low pressure tank that draws out the trapped air. Another method, often used where there are many similar parts (such as small figures), is where the mould is rotated slowly, thus moving the air out by centrifugal force to the other edges, which are – if planned correctly! – the base of the figures, so any air bubbles will be on the underside and out of sight. Minimising the overall intake of air, and consequently bubbles, is ultimately down to careful mixing and pouring.

If the mould for the resin is rubber (as opposed to fibreglass), it does have one

BELOW Many accessory parts have been made over the years. These are from Belcher Bits.

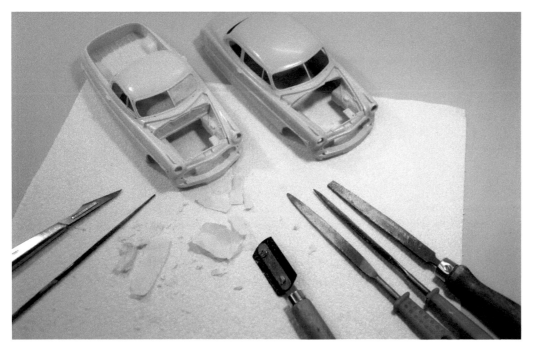

advantage to a steel injection styrene tool in that it is flexible to a certain extent. Consequently, small undercuts that had to be avoided with conventional steel tools (or else involved complex 'sliding' parts within the tooling), are far less of a problem. The mould can be simply peeled off the parts. Resin moulding is an extremely slow process, depending totally on human action as it can't exactly be automated. Therefore it can only really be used for small runs of kits, resulting in proportionally far higher costs than their injection styrene counterparts.

In the main, a resin kit can be dealt with very much like a styrene injection kit. The same methods can be used for cutting parts from resin runners, filing edges and sanding smooth. But, of course, it won't glue with a standard polystyrene cement.

Gluing resin

Initially, the only way to glue resin would be using two-part resin glues. The early versions of this took hours to cure, although modern versions will cure in minutes, if not seconds. These all still have 'bulk', so the excess would need trimming away, sometimes involving a lot of trimming. The introduction of superglue, which cures in seconds and has, in effect, no bulk, can make resin kits more appealing to the general modeller.

Resin types

The resins used to make the parts can vary. Early resin kits used polyester resins: usually dark orange in colour, where small parts especially could easily snap. In more recent years, resins have moved to polyurethanes, which are lighter in colour – sometimes even pure white – and far more resilient to breaking. In fact, some polyurethane kits can be made to look almost indistinguishable from styrene, so much so that if you're not sure of its origin, to tell them apart you have to carefully apply some liquid cement on an unseen surface of a part and see if it has been affected. If it has, it's styrene; if it hasn't, it's resin!

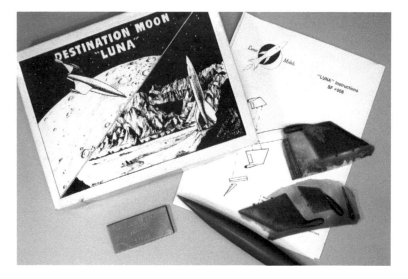

Most modern resin kits are made in a similar manner to conventional injection styrene equivalents. The bodywork, hull or fuselage is hollow so these parts are moulded in two halves, with separate small parts moulded on the resin equivalent of injection runners, attached via gates. These are usually somewhat larger than injection kits and pressures involved are far lower than with injection styrene, so the resin has to have a large enough gate area to flow. This then means more excess to saw and file off then sand smooth.

If there is a large area is where the resin was poured – usually the underside of a base or stand – you may find the resin bulges outwards where the resin was in effect 'over-poured' to ensure there was enough to fill the mould. This tends to require considerably more sanding to remove the excess: use coarse sanding paper, a woodworking file or even a motorised sanding disc (see page 70). Be warned: a lot of dust will be generated. This is generally inert as such, but could certainly be an irritant, so perform such a task with adequate ventilation and, if necessary, wear a protective mask.

Slush moulding

Some resin kits are moulded solid, usually referred to as 'slush moulding'. Frankly, this is the easiest option for turning the parts out in the first place – just pour the resin in the mould. This works for some craft, such as aircraft that don't need a visible interior, and especially figures. However, some cars kits have also been slush moulded, which you can only build without a visible interior. Consequently, go for a finish with heavily tinted windows!

White metal

Around the same time resin was introduced,

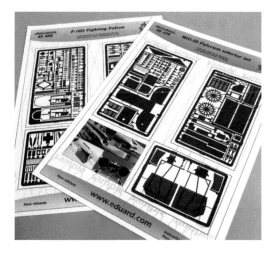

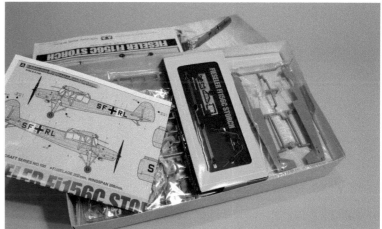

another material started to become reasonably widely used in model kits, and that was white metal. It was used to make the toy soldiers of the time, which were called 'lead soldiers' as they were originally made out of that metal. Conveniently, as lead melts at a (comparatively) low temperature, it can be poured into the same sort of hard rubber moulds used for resin.

After the toxic effects of lead were acknowledged, other materials had to be found. This new compound ended up being made from a mix of primarily tin with other elements mixed in such as antimony, copper and cadmium. (Various compositions are also used to make pewter.)

Besides its use in such as wargaming figures, it was realised that it could be used to reproduce the one main weak point of all model aircraft: the undercarriage. If anything was going to give way on a static model aircraft, it was the landing gear. The comparative strength of plastic wheels and legs, especially holding up a top-heavy body, being far less than a metal equivalent. Aftermarket companies began making such undercarriage kits from white metal, and this even started to extend to the commercial kit companies themselves, who started to add white metal castings of these parts into their own kits.

There are also many companies that use white metal to produce complete kits, though, because of the cost compared to injection styrene (or even resin), they tend to be at the smaller-scale end of the market. For example, there are many white metal car kits, but with very few exceptions, they are all 1:43 scale, not the more conventional 1:32 or 1:24/5 scale. There are also some far larger, far more

expensive (and far heavier) model kits made entirely in white metal, but these are beyond the scope of this book, as we are primarily dealing with 'plastic'. Consequently, white metal is a very useful factor in the plastic kit industry, but only for small accessory parts.

Limited run

There is actually a way of injecting styrene into rubber moulds. This results in a similar kit to

BELOW **Photo-etch used to produce the antennae on the nose of this Dragon Horten Ho-229 Flying Wing. These would be very difficult to make in injection styrene, as they would be far too fragile.**

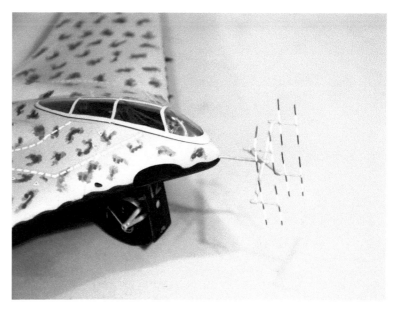

extremely fine details, although they are basically two-dimensional, so they're ideal, for example, for instrument panels in aircraft, where the details on individual dials can be picked out, and on disc brakes and badges for cars and trucks, or railings for ships. They are also used to make larger scale architectural parts, such as fencing and railings, clock faces, weather vanes and – for the more natural world – extremely detailed leaves and flowers. However, photo etching can also be folded to make three-dimensional parts.

Most modellers will buy their PE parts ready-made. Photo etching can be done at home, though it's beyond the scope of this book to go into details on the procedure. For details on this, check out the various videos available on YouTube. However, very briefly, photo etching is achieved by first generating the artwork. This is then attached to the metal sheet and sealed down then the metal is placed in a bath of chemicals. These remove the areas not protected by the artwork, and the metal surround that is not required is 'etched' away. Once clean of chemical residue, the parts can immediately be used.

The metal used can vary. Most modelling parts are produced either from brass sheet or stainless steel, easily told apart by its colour and flexibility. Brass is, well, brass in colour and bends easily, while steel is shiny silver, is far more resilient to bending and is consequently stronger. Brass is far easier to work with: it cuts with scissors or a strong knife blade and can be soldered easily, besides being attached with superglue. Steel, being far stronger, can be more difficult to work with and to bend, unless etched 'bends' are built in or a special 'bending tool' is used. Both types will be found either in kits or as aftermarket accessories.

Both brass sheet and stainless steel need to be handled with care. Working with brass PE is somewhat easier as it will cut with scissors, and if a slight bend is required this can be done by hand, but watch out for sharp edges where it is trimmed from the surrounding. Steel PE parts need more careful handling, as sharper edges can be left where it is cut. Both types need these areas carefully filed and sanded away. To achieve any required bends in steel PE parts, you'll need to firmly hold the parts in pliers.

If you intend to do a lot of work with PE parts, especially if a lot of bends will be

ABOVE The tiny badge for the Fujimi *Blade Runner* Spinner (held in the tweezers), which can be glued in place using superglue or contact adhesive.

BELOW A special photo-etch bender, vital for bending PE parts, especially long lengths, as otherwise it is very difficult to get a 'clean' bend.

the standard steel tool injection methods, but with thicker parts, larger gates and invariably less detail. The tools do not last that long either, so kits made by this process are in limited numbers and are usually termed 'short run'.

Photo-etch
Another non-plastic material that found its way into model kits is photo-etched parts. Again, this primarily started with aircraft, though these days you can find photo-etched (PE) parts in kit subjects across the board. Injection-moulded polystyrene can be extremely detailed, but small parts can be difficult to work with and can never quite reproduce the very fine details that are demanded. PE parts can reproduce these

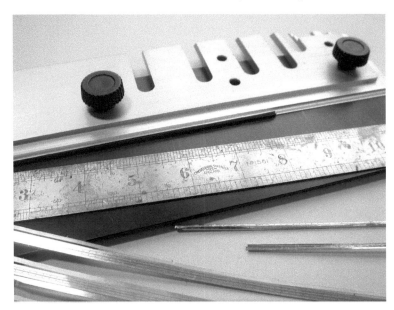

involved, one of the dedicated 'PE benders' could be a good investment. These are not exactly cheap but are invaluable when it comes to bending lengthy sections. They clamp the PE part firmly down, and using such as a steel rule, the exposed edge can be neatly bent, keeping the bend even along its length.

There is also a growing trend in kits that are entirely made from photo-etched sheets, such as from Metal Earth. These are perhaps not entirely to 'scale', as compromises have to be made, but they're certainly worth a mention.

Vac forming, resin, white metal and photo-etch have held sway in more specialised kits and aftermarket accessories for decades. The latter three are still widely used, and even vac forming can still occasionally be found.

Blow moulding

Mention should also be made of blow moulding. This almost always uses vinyl as a material and is equally almost exclusively used for models of figures. The mould is similar to that being used for resin kits, but instead of pouring resin, vinyl is injected (in a similar manner to a styrene injection kit) and air is then blown in to push the vinyl to the edges of the mould.

There are some limitations with this method. The vinyl is somewhat soft, hence its use for figures, though the parts can be made quite large. The short-run company Screamin' used it for its large horror and fantasy figures, most made to 1:4 scale. These were usually in a small number of large parts that needed superglue to hold them together. Because of this 'soft' nature, blow-moulded vinyl has rarely been used to make models of craft – in fact, there seem to be only two recorded instances of its use. The use of vinyl has also only recently come in with the introduction of acrylic paints. It couldn't be used before then as you couldn't paint it with enamel paints – they would never dry on the surface.

Another material that can be blow moulded, and has been for some kits, is polystyrene itself. This has been used by such companies as Dragon to make large models of rockets, where main rocket bodies have not been standard injection-moulded styrene parts, but have been blow moulded in styrene. (It is actually an extension to flying model rockets, where blow

LEFT **An example of a vinyl moulded kit – this is The Cryptkeeper (from *Tales from the Crypt*), made by Screamin' Products.**

moulded parts are often used as they are far lighter. Weight is the prime consideration for a model rocket that actually flies, so this became a good moulding method for detailed parts.) Rather in the manner of a vac form kit, they do require some trimming of parts, but being styrene, they will then glue to other styrene parts with standard cement.

BELOW **Example of a blow-moulded kit: the body of Space Monkey's V-2 rocket. The moulding plug (right) has been sawn off and will be replaced with the actual injection-moulded nose cone (centre).**

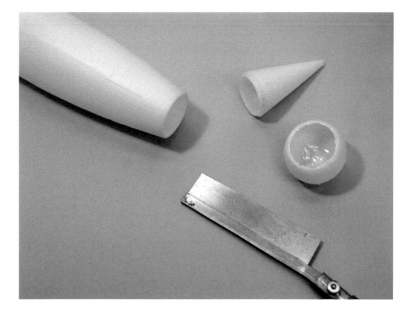

RIGHT There is an increasing use of computers for reference when model building. Here a tablet is part of the work bench set up.

The HaMeX Model Shows

Computers – and the future

BELOW A commercial 3D printer at Gulliver's Gate in New York City, used to turn out parts that will eventually be incorporated into the model layouts on display. A miniature Empire State Building is being made.

As with most things in recent years, computers have found their way even into the initially and seemingly unelectronic world of model making, from using CAD-CAM designs to create the tooling in the first place to digital systems that run model railways and slot car racing to allow more than one vehicle to run on a track.

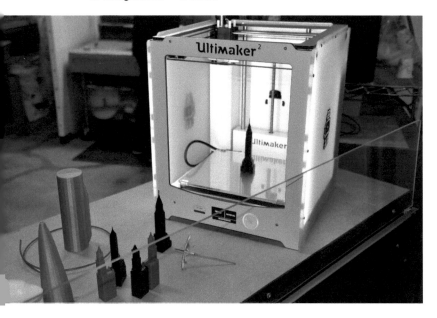

Ultimaker²

Research

Research using a computer search engine is now commonplace, and if a suitable plan or image is found it can be downloaded and printed out. The computer, maybe in the form of a tablet or even a smart phone, can even sit alongside the workbench, so references can immediately be accessed.

3D printing

The one area that could have the greatest impact on model making in the future – and arguably on the world in general – could come from 3D printing. Now termed 'additive manufacturing', it was previously known as 'rapid prototyping', though here the term is more about the speed an object can be produced from when the first plans are drawn up rather than the speed at which it's actually produced by the 3D printer, which in most cases is still irritatingly slow.

Most importantly, this isn't just model making, as virtually anything can be 3D printed including metals and even food and medical parts. Consequently, if there is any world changer in the way items are produced, this is going to be it.

It is a little difficult to say who 'invented the 3D printer', but it is certainly – in the general

sense of the term – detailed in science and science-fiction writer, Sir Arthur C. Clarke's seminal book of 1961, Profiles of the Future. In the chapter 'Aladdin's Lamp', he goes through the idea of in effect a '3D photocopier', or what he termed a 'Replicator' (and remember, this was long before *Star Trek*'s similarly termed gizmo). Here Arthur lists what such a Replicator would need to operate: 'It would consist of three basic parts – a store, a memory and an organiser.' So a store of raw materials, a memory – or computer program – and an organiser, or the machine to do the work. Or, in other words, a 3D printer. (And you would only need one, as the first task of the first Replicator would be to make a second Replicator….)

Putting aside the somewhat mind-boggling notion that it could someday generate *all* material objects (Arthur has his Replicator coming into full use in the year 2090), staying within the slightly more focused field of model making, how is it going to change things?

3D-generated kits

3D printing is already making model kits. Write a computer program, save as a .stl file, feed into a 3D printer, select a source of materials and then watch while it builds the part in front of your eyes. Though, at this stage in 3D printing development, it should be pointed out that if you want to watch you will almost certainly have to bring sandwiches and a comfy chair. So far it is a very slow and laborious, albeit automated, process.

It was probably first used in a very basic way in the early 1980s in Japan and (intriguingly) to make a model kit built up from layers. Later that decade, patents started to be taken out for more commercial forms of 3D printing that would become the first developments in rapid

prototyping. This is when the original 3D printing file format was written – stereolithography (STL) files, still used today.

Very (very) simply, it can be thought of in comparison to a standard printer or photocopier that works in two dimensions: the x and y axis. The 3D printer adds the 'z' axis and prints by layering the material, hence being known as 'additive manufacturing'. (This is in comparison with traditional manufacturing, which has now taken on the title 'subtractive manufacturing', where materials are usually removed during the process.)

Again very simply, the material – ABS (see page 14) is used a lot – is melted and fed into the 3D printer and the computer controls the printer head movement and the feed of the material. One layer is built up, then the next, then the next, until the final shape emerges. And that (and this is put extremely simply) is all there is to it!

For 3D printing to catch on in a big way, firstly the printers will have to come down in cost. Although you can already buy one for a few hundred pounds, dollars or euros that can (slowly) turn off very useful parts for modellers, printers that can do any meaningful work are up in the several thousands, if not tens of thousands of anyone's money. Secondly, the computer files that run it will have to be simpler and more

readily accessible. Thirdly, and likely the most important factor, the printers will have to work much, much faster. But this is only the same as any other piece of modern technology. The first cell phones cost several thousand in most currencies, and just made phone calls. Now they are, in effect, handheld computers capable of doing a multitude of tasks (even making phone calls) and cheap 'burner phones' cost just tens of any monetary value. The first widescreen televisions were tens of thousands, now you can buy them for less than one hundred. The same will almost certainly happen to 3D printers once their significance is realised to the general public.

For now we are at the very early beginning, so 3D printer kit parts – or whole kits – are a slow process done by only a few companies. You can buy a home 3D printer, but they are even slower, are limited in their scope and may be fine for experimentation or to produce a few single parts.

Most model-making 3D printing is currently done by commercial companies such as Shapeways. You generate a digital file – or use one of the existing ones – and send it off. Then wait. You will have to specify the degree of details you require; rougher shapes can be built more quickly (and are consequently cheaper) but will then require a lot of sanding to get a smooth surface and remove the 'steps' that occur in the printing process. You could pay for finer detail, where the layers can be made thinner, meaning less work at your end. But this is more expensive and takes longer, so you will have to balance the cost and time factor.

There is also still a limitation as to how 'thin' these layers can be. The highest quality printable with such a material as ABS at the moment is 0.1mm. Although very thin, this will still show up as a discernible 'step' on the surface of the part, which will need removing. This can be done by sanding: a somewhat slow process, especially if the part is very detailed, and for very complex parts may not be practical anyway. Parts can be dipped in liquids such as acetone that will 'melt' the steps into a smoother surface, but this requires care in handling and constant checking to make sure the liquid is not dissolving too much of the part! But one advantage 3D printing has, or rather the plans have, is that they are scalable. You want a part in 1:72, that can be done, but the same program can also reduce it down to 1:144, or up to 1:48 or 1:32 scale.

So how does this affect the modeller? Currently, it is still down to 'watch this space'. For overall general usage, the 3D printer may take far, far longer to become the norm – if it does at all. Arthur Clarke's 'timescale' is now less than a century away, but this could be something that remains relatively niche. We break a cup and it still may be far easier to go out and buy a new one (or more likely order one online) than to 3D print one. So Captain Picard's order for, 'Tea, earl grey, hot!' may very well produce a cup of tea to his liking, but it might not be manufactured from a Replicator. Instead it might just be courtesy of an Alexa-activated teapot!

ABOVE Test shot of the latest Moebius Models Batmobile – this is 3D printed.

LEFT Example of 3D printing, for an aircraft drag-chute.

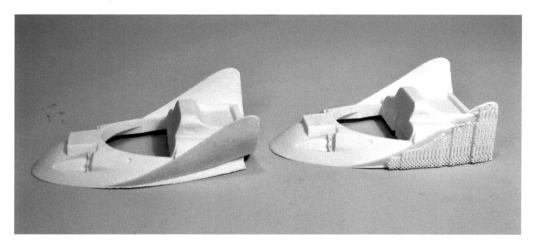

LEFT 3D printed test shot for a potential kit of the Whomobile. Note the one on the right hasn't printed the 'wing' correctly, the left is correct.

Chapter Eleven

Collecting vs. building

There is a strange phenomenon that has developed over some time, where the object was to purely 'collect' the kit, not to actually build it! Admittedly, 'collecting things' is in the human psyche, but usually any collecting didn't prevent the object still fulfilling its task, and most of the time any 'collecting' didn't stop the use of the object in question.

Record collectors could still play that LP without really reducing its value, as long as it was played on a good deck, didn't get scratched and any bonus with the LP – the Beatle cutouts from *Sergeant Pepper* or the UFO from ELO's *Out of the Blue* – remained intact. First editions of Harry Potter could be read, as long as you didn't scribble notes in the margins; jigsaws could be assembled, as long as you didn't lose any parts and die-cast toy cars could be played with as long as – heaven forbid – you didn't throw away the box.

But model construction kits? Wasn't their whole reason for existence, to be, well, constructed? If a model remains forever unbuilt in its box, what is the point of it? To many collectors, however, that was the whole point. In some ways it was equivalent to a vintage bottle of wine, which was only worth anything while it remained with the cork in place. Uncork it and quaff it (assuming it was drinkable anyway) and that was it. Open the kit box and build the kit, and any value that had been (fairly arbitrarily) assigned to the kit was reduced, at the very least by 90%. (This, though, does put it slightly above the wine collectors, where the value sank to zero. Though there is almost certainly a collectors market for open and empty 'vintage wine bottles that used to hold wine...'!)

The model kit collector was also in a slightly better position as – assuming the box was not shrink-wrapped, and most old boxes were not – at least you could open it, gaze at the runners and parts, look through the instructions and even inhale the smell! (Intriguingly, different manufacturers' kits had unique smells.)

The collectable market really only applies to older kits where the box art and even the style of the box, to general opinion, was better than many of the new kits. Admittedly, very much of this – like any collecting – is heavily linked to nostalgia! This nostalgia could also be coupled with the goodies supplied with the kit. In the early days, kit companies were very keen to promote the educational aspect of their products and besides the parts themselves, you usually got an explanatory booklet that gave all the technical details.

OPPOSITE Some people amass large collections. From the Mark Mattei Collection.

ABOVE The Rev. John Burns in his office with his amazing collection of kits. Here he's selected one of Revell's early military sets.

The KCC

A great deal of work for 'collectors' was down to the Rev. John Burns, who ran The Kit Collector's Clearinghouse for many years and produced several volumes of guides, called CVG – *Collectors Value Guides*, which aimed to list all 'collectable kits' and their possible values. John was the first to admit it was an impossible task, though they became The Bible for anyone interested in the history of model kits – appropriate as John's main calling was as a Baptist minister.

All of this has led to a growing trend where people associated with model kits have to seemingly declare if they are a 'builder' or a

LEFT John Burns's *Collectors Value Guide, Seventh Edition*. This was the last produced.

'collector' – as if you could never be both? Most model builders are also 'collectors' by default, as model collections grow because, frankly, the builder will never find time to build everything. There was even a saying from some years ago where you have to buy three new kits – one to build, one to convert and one to save intact (and, these days, then sell on eBay). With the rise of kit prices, buying three of everything isn't so practical these days, but the sentiment is still there.

Something old, something new

Originally kit manufacturers were forever aiming to give their customers something new. Even in the 1950s and 1960s when costs were still (relatively) low, when a model kit had run its course, the kit would be abandoned, removed from the lists and the tooling could be reused. Aurora was one company famous for this. It would scrap the steel tool itself (there was, and still is, money in the high-quality steel used for tooling), then reuse the frame that held the tool, and if, as was often the case with Aurora, the models had been cast from a beryllium mould, this could be melted down and reused. In Aurora's case, even the reference number was recycled, so much so that there is at least one example of the same number referring to three completely different kits!

Many manufacturers updated the subject of

RIGHT Airfix reissued its first Spitfire kit for its fiftieth anniversary. The header was the same but the kit was far newer, though it was moulded in approximately the same blue coloured plastic.

a kit with a much more detailed and accurate offering, so the original kit fell out of the catalogues and the tooling may very well have been scrapped. But that kit may very well have been historic. The first aircraft kit from Airfix was the Spitfire, one of the most well-known and best-loved of all aircraft designs. But this first Airfix kit was actually based on the Aurora 1:48 scale kit, reduced to 1:72. The Aurora kit wasn't exactly accurate, so the faults were translated to the smaller Airfix copy. Airfix soon updated this first fairly crude model and replaced it with a more detailed kit, itself now long surpassed, and replaced with more recent and even more accurate offerings. For the Airfix fiftieth anniversary in 1999, the company reintroduced this original 'Aurora-based' kit – except that it didn't.

The original had come packed in the classic Airfix polythene bag with a header card, so Airfix followed this style in its repackaging. But the kit wasn't the original (likely the tooling no longer survived, even if it had been desirable to reissue such an inaccurate kit), instead it used a much more modern kit of the Spitfire in a far larger poly bag. It was moulded in approximately the same original light blue colour, so collectors got a taste of what the original would have been like, but it was hardly 100% original.

A history of models

The company that possibly did the most to aid collectors so they could to a certain extent become builders was Revell Monogram. Even before the two names came under the same banner (when both were acquired by Odyssey Partners of New York in 1986), Revell had introduced its new series: The History Makers, and Monogram: The Heritage Edition.

The History Makers was started by Revell in 1982, with a second series in 1983. Here the idea was to provide builders with models from early times that had long been out of the catalogues, either because they were the type of model that wasn't to an accepted traditional scale for the subject (they were box scale, or the model was old and had been surpassed by newer, more detailed, and more conventionally scaled, versions). They also included subjects that were frankly 'odd' and didn't really fit any current classifications. Even if it was only the 1980s, the hobby was well over 20 years old, so models perhaps built 'as a kid' and long ago thrown in the dustbin or garbage can could now be built again by the modeller who would now be in their late twenties, early thirties in some vague attempt at regaining some element of youth.

One thing neither The History Makers nor The Heritage Edition did was to recreate the original boxes. Instead, both series had their own distinct box designs, which, of course, have now become collectable in their own right.

Series 1 of Revell's The History Makers was ambitious in that it was advertised as consisting of 28 kits. These were split between aircraft, amour, missiles, space, ships and – as initially advertised – two cars. The aircraft featured such kits as the Douglas X-3 Stiletto in 1:65 scale, Martin SeaMaster in 1:136, Martin Mariner in 1:112 and North American X-15 in 1:64. All these are 'box scales', though it did also include newer kits – well, newer than these – such as the Hawker Typhoon Mk 1B and Messerschmitt Bf 110C-4B, both in 1:32. For armour came the Self-Propelled Howitzer in 1:32, and Armoured Vehicle and Scissor Bridge in 1:40. Missiles, which Revell specialised in during the very early years, included Nike Hercules, Northrop Snark, Bomarc IM-99, Northrop Hawk, and Teracruzer and Mace Missile. There was even the German V-2 missile from the Second World War. Ships included: Arctic Explorer, USS Burton Island, USS Olympia and even the world's first (and only) nuclear-powered cargo vessel, the N. S. Savannah. Finally, add two aircraft engine kits, the Allison Turbo-Prop and Wasp Radial Aircraft Engine.

All were in 'Revell' logo boxes, but three were not Revell originals. In 1977, Revell had acquired one of the other original model company names and its tooling. This was Renwal, perhaps most famous for producing the 'Visible' range of kits, particularly the Visible Man and Visible Women kits from the late 1950s. Notable for not being a plane or a car or a ship, they also had educational value and found their way into schools. (The Visible Woman, in particular, was of special interest to boys in their formative years). But Renwal also made a range of military kits all to 1:32 scale (and not 1:35) and a range of ships and submarines. For History Makers Series 1, the

ABOVE Some of Revell's first History Makers range.

Teracruzer and Mace Missile, Self-Propelled Gun and Wasp Engine were all Renwal originals.

Not what it seemed

These 'History Makers' all had a 'Revell' name on the box, so the Renwal kits were not issued as such but the kit itself was identical. This meant that anyone who had an original, unbuilt model of a Renwal original, say the Teracruzer and Mace, in its original box; wanted to build it but was aware of the interest already been shown in the value of these 'old unbuilt kits', could instead build the reissue. The plastic was identical and the decals, in many cases, were improved, which helped as old decal sheets could sometimes fall apart if you tried to use them. (See Chapter 8 on restoring decals, pages 118–119). Then if you wanted to display the original box and instructions alongside, well you still had the original box and instruction sheet.

The History Makers Series 1, signified by a dark red themed box, was followed up with Series 2, this time using dark blue so the series could be easily distinguished. Here, the main emphasis

was on missiles (Revell made a lot of missiles) with the Corporal, Nike Ajax, Thor and Jupiter ICBMs, Regulus II and the Jupiter C with America's first successful artificial satellite, Explorer 1. There were some aircraft: the 1:174 Boeing B-52 with X-15,

Douglas D-588 Skyrocket and Messerschmitt M2-262, plus one sole ship, the hospital ship S. S. Hope. Only ten models were announced, but this time all were issued.

History Makers Series 1 actually didn't issue two kits that were proposed. What would be issued depended on what sales were thought could be achieved. Plastics, and consequently the model kit industry is a by-product of crude oil, and although initially very cheap (as it was a by-product in producing such higher-grade products as petroleum) when the oil prices go up, the by-product prices followed them. This particularly hit the kit industry in 1973 during the oil crisis, which led to a 400% increase in the prices of raw materials.

Therefore, the companies had to be careful as to what they decided to issue, and often kits were pre-sold to their distributors, and if they didn't get the promised sales in, the kits were not issued. This happened to two kits in The History Makers Series I, and oddly both were cars: the 1960 Chevrolet Corvette and the Porsche 356 Competition Racer. Both were early multi-piece body Revell kits and is indeed slightly odd, as Revell's main market is the USA and if anywhere is 'car kit crazy' (or just 'car crazy') it is the USA.

The Corvette has admittedly appeared (from AMT and MPC) as a better kit, as has the Porsche and, in fact, several others. The latter were part of Fujimi's exacting Enthusiast Range of kits, notable for the high number of parts in the box and the high prices.

Monogram's approach to The Heritage Edition was similar to The History Makers, though with boxes that didn't perhaps look quite so dark and grim. It only went for one series, though was issued over two years: 1983 and 1984. The range consisted of 15 kits, all of which appeared. These were mostly aircraft, such as the Wright Brothers Kittyhawk, the Ford Trimotor in its Antarctic Expedition guise, and Monogram's own Wright Cyclone, the radial aircraft engine. There was also smattering of space and missiles.

Other reissued kits

Other kit manufacturers would offer old kits again, but usually not within specific series. You would suddenly find an original kit reissued along with other newer models, with no particular fanfare. It was also still an American phenomenon. Non-US model companies also reissued older kits, but until very, very recently, made far less of a fuss about it.

So far these kits were either casual reissues or were part of special series with their own boxes. There was no real attempt to appeal to the old kit collector. It was Revell-Monogram (now one company) that really came up with the idea of reissuing kits 'for collectors' – and maybe the odd builder. This was the Selected Subjects Program (SSP) which began in 1992. Here you really did get a kit that was identical to the original – almost. A reproduction of the original plans, original decals and – what really sold the idea – a reproduction of the original box.

This was around the time when the Internet became a reality and was finding its way into most homes. It was also the beginning of online auction sites. Perhaps it's surprising to realise that eBay began as long ago as 1995, so kit values became 'set', (in a very general sense) and what's more a potential buyer for your model no longer needed to be in the same town as you, where you probably only met up at a local model shop or show, but could be living on the other side of the world. It led to a problem with the very first SSPs, as they were indeed manufactured almost identically to an original, and there were several recorded instances of buyers being duped into buying what they assumed was an original kit from the early 1960s, only to discover when it arrived that it was an SSP reissue from 30 years later.

Careful checking

There could be some clues, especially with box manufacture. In its early years (the 1950s and 1960s) Revell especially had used 'solid' boxes, where the box didn't fold flat but was built up from a pre-assembled thick card base, with the artwork, printed in glossy paper, glued around the box. Even the early SSPs didn't have this; they were 'fold flat' boxes, with the printing directly on the card. But of course you had to a) know this and b) have the box in front of you to examine it. If you were buying at an online auction, that latter was not possible, unless you were extremely good at deciphering any published photo.

Later kits did have more 'clues' on them, prominently in the form of a barcode, which

didn't exist on packaging in the 1960s. Although invented in the early 1950s, they were first only used to track railroad wagons. The first consumer use wasn't until 1974, and they didn't become universally used until a lot later. Close reading of the company address would also now reveal it was Revell Monogram, based in Morton Grove, Illinois.

The original SSP series ran from Phase 1 in late 1992 through to Phase 16 in Fall 1996.

ABOVE **Here many of the boxes were the same size as the original, and from the front look absolutely identical. The original box is actually on the bottom.**

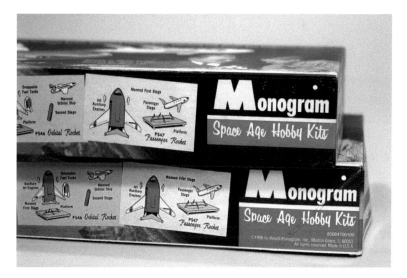

ABOVE **Check the side panel where the new Revell-Monogram address was printed – this was the only real difference.**

LEFT **Old Revell boxes were recognisably 'solid' in nature: a pre-assembled box – top and base – with shiny paper glued to the top. No SSP had this feature.**

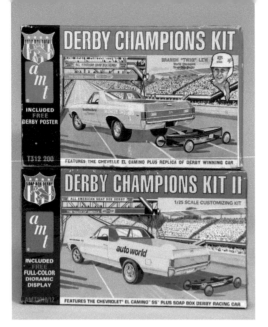

RIGHT When in more recent years, AMT, and MPC started similarly reissuing kits in older boxes, it too had to compromise. The original names (top) had been removed, and in fact the pickup was a different tool. Only the soapbox itself remained as per the original.

Each issue consisted of six kits each from Revell and Monogram, making 12 each 'Phase' and so 192 kits in all – except it wasn't quite. Three kits that were announced but then found that the tooling couldn't be located – or in one case, the McHale's Navy PT Boat, a licence couldn't be obtained, which brings the total down to 189. Then three more were issued twice in different Phases, bringing us down to 186, but that's still a very impressive number.

Not all, however, were original releases – there was a smattering of The History Makers and The Heritage Edition in with these, plus some were from second, even third original issues. But many SSPs went right back to the very beginning.

Later, the two names were combined into one set of issues and the issuing itself became spasmodic; the idea dying out in 1998, when it was reckoned that about everything that could be reissued – i.e. the tooling still existed – had been reissued. However, occasionally kits are today still being issued with 'SSP' on the box.

Staying within the USA, the major model car manufacturers, AMT and MPC, found themselves (like Revell and Monogram), under the same roof when both were acquired by The Ertl Corporation. MPC was first in 1981; AMT in 1983.

What's in a box?

Ertl started its Buyers Choice series, which – as with The History Makers and The Heritage Edition – aimed to bring old kits back to a new market. But in the most part the kits were not issued in original boxes. The boxes were new, though as with the Revell Monogram issues,

they did at least allow builders, who had an original kit, to build it with a clear conscience.

In more recent years, AMT and MPC's current recent owners, The Round 2 Corporation, has mimicked, to a degree, the SSPs with box art that is, if not identical, at least very similar to a kit that was produced 40 years previously. It even went one stage further in that it reintroduced 'solid' boxes – something Revel-Monogram never did. However, there are several instances in which the boxes, particularly for AMT kits, had to be larger as no one could fit the original parts in the original-size boxes. (There was an urban myth – well not so much 'myth', it was fact – that once you had unpacked an original AMT car kit from its box, you could never get the parts back in and the lid back on firmly in place!)

Many of these AMT and MPC reissued kits have retooled parts: parts that could be found in the original kit, but which had been lost, changed or modified over the years. In addition, tyres were retooled to a modern standard and the transparent parts, such as window glass and lights, were supplied in a colour tint as well as clear. Decal sheets were also improved and neat touches, such as a small version of the kit box and a small car display base were added. So you get around 90% original kit and 10% new – enough to satisfy most who wanted to build 'an old kit', but likely enough to pacify collectors who feel their investments could, to quote the advertising slogan, 'go down, as well as up…'.

Scales of collectability

Strangely, some manufacturers are far more collectable than others. In general, Airfix kits are not really 'collectable' in the sense that they can attract really high prices. There are odd exceptions such as the *Southern Cross* (Airfix's first ship) and the Ferguson Tractor (Airfix's very first kit) but these are very much in the minority.

Even other UK-based names don't really find themselves being collectable, in the sense that 'they could be worth something'. The original Frog Penguins are, of course, as they were 'the first'. But these are far more that they are 'Frog Penguins', rather than with any idea they would ever be built. However, the later Frog kits, now of course changing to polystyrene instead of cellulose acetate as a moulding material, do not command that high a price.

The same applies to when Matchbox started model kits, as opposed to die-cast and even older names such as Eaglewall that issue aircraft in 1:96 scale and some small-scale ships. Where you will find higher prices will tend to be with the 'odder' items. Most issues from all these companies are aircraft, but where, say, Frog, branched out into making the Bloodhound Missile, that is one where anyone who had an unbuilt original could expect a very reasonable return if they ever decided to sell it.

Lindberg, given it was one of America's oldest companies as it started in the 1930s, is on the whole not very collectable at all. However, there is, of course, the odd exception. Its five futuristic spaceships from the 1950s are collectable – which includes the first ever 'all-plastic kit of a spaceship' (albeit a flying saucer) dating from 1954. And the combined set of all five kits – Five Spaceships of the Future – are especially so. But the vast majority of kits Lindberg has produced over the decades are only worth face value – if indeed that.

Aurora rises

If any kit company's products were collectable, it was Aurora's. The company lasted from 1950 to 1977, when most of the tooling (that survived and hadn't been reused) was acquired by Monogram. In that time Aurora covered a wide range of model subjects – aircraft, ships, cars, military figures – and the subject it was best known for: figures. And it is figures where the highest prices seem to occur. Again, it is perhaps linked to the fact that once the life of any one kit was deemed to be over, the tooling was scrapped, so there always would be a limited number of kits 'still out there'. (On the face of it, given model kits were designed to be built, it is a wonder that any unbuilt kits are still out there! But there are.)

It is fairly obvious, but for the figures where the original tooling still survives, values tend to be lower down the scale. For example, the Universal Monsters – the horror figures created by Aurora of the 'creatures' from the Universal Studio movies from the 1930s, including Dracula, The Wolfman, The Mummy, The Frankenstein Monster and The Creature from the Black Lagoon – have been reissued a

number of times, first by Monogram and later by Revell, which had been acquired by the holding company, Odyssey Partners, to join Monogram. Then a number of 'individual reissues' of some kits have been made – for example Cine Models reissued its version of Dracula.

However, if you wanted, say, The Witch, The Bride of Frankenstein or *The Munsters*' Living Room you would have had a much harder task. For these kits the moulding had been destroyed by Aurora, with the tooling parts and the kit numbers being reused on new kits. Any unbuilt kits that were still around could command very high prices, especially as, since the mid-1990s, online auction sites gave the seller a world of buyers.

The Lost Aurora companies

When modern moulding techniques were brought in, it led to the growth of 'reproduction

ABOVE Probably the rarest Frog kit – the 1:24 scale Bristol Bloodhound missile.

BELOW Aurora issued many of its kits in several versions, but the original (left) remains the most 'collectable'.

kits'. If an original could be sourced, the parts could be copied, either by remoulding the parts themselves, by pantographing, or these days by laser scanning the parts to produce CAD-CAM programs. Initially, the reproductions were likely only to be available in resin, but then, using the new techniques, traditional injection-moulded styrene versions could be produced.

In even more recent years, new companies – initially and unceremoniously all lumped under 'The Lost Aurora Companies' moniker – came into being. The name came about as they were attempting to produce either reproductions of the 'lost Aurora' kits (such as The Bride) or brand new kits, but in the old Aurora style. Intriguingly this has never happened with any other kit manufacturing name. There were several of these 'Lost Aurora' names but only two made a long-term success of it and still survive. One is Polar Lights – the name obviously a play on 'Aurora' – and the other is Moebius Models. Polar Lights started by using an Aurora-style oval logo, purely replacing the word with its own name. Moebius started with a similar style but in more recent years, moved to its own unique logo in the form of an 'M'. Both have made reproductions of old Aurora kits. Polar Lights retooled Aurora kits where the tooling had long gone, such as *The Munsters'* Family Room and the *Addams' Family* House. Then it followed the latter up with a kit Aurora never made – though could have – the mansion from the movie *Psycho* in a similar H0 scale. (And, yes, you get 'Mother' in the window.)

Moebius followed more along the route of

BELOW Revell Germany's 50th Anniversary saw more reissues, similar to SSPs, in that they were *mostly* in original boxes.

figures, though many, although using the same subject matter, created completely new kits, not reproductions of the Aurora originals. One particular line here is *Batman*, the original TV series, where although Aurora had made several including Batman and Robin, here new kits recreated new poses and added several more. Whether these will ever attain the collectability of the Aurora originals, only time will tell.

Collectables to celebrate
Other 'collectable' series are also arriving as model companies are reaching significant anniversaries. Some years ago, Revell Germany celebrated 50 years with a line of 'Classic Kits'. These mainly used original artwork, though incorporating kits from other companies such as Matchbox that it had bought in the intervening years maybe didn't have quite the same impact?

Heller reached 60 in 2017 and released its own celebratory kits, but as with others, Heller is never really that collectable. The exception, again as with others, tends to be the 'odder' kits and – Heller it is again missiles, with the Parca and Veronique reaching the highest prices.

Oddly it is with some limited-edition resin kits that some of the highest prices in auctions have been achieved. Hardly cheap in the first place, because they are produced in such limited numbers (compared to mainstream injection kits) there never were that many 'out there'. The moulds they are made from have limited lives, so once a short run has been done that is usually it for that subject, unless someone decides to make a new tool. So the numbers really are limited, and if a particular kit catches the eye of at least two bidders – from the seller's point of view, preferably a lot more, but two is usually sufficient – the prices tend to climb.

Catalogue collecting
And it isn't purely the kits themselves that are collectable. Older catalogues are also finding themselves included. Here, of course, the one thing you can do with a catalogue is to copy it – and with the quality of copying these days, you can get results that are almost indistinguishable from the original. But much in the same way as original kit boxes are subtly different to what can be made these days, catalogues are similar, and originals of some

manufacturers can command high prices, even if they are in a slightly tatty condition.

Pre-1960s will tend be to be the most collectable, such as those from Revell or Lindberg, while the 1970s will see similar results from companies such as AMT, who didn't really issue a 'full' catalogue until around that time (up until then it purely had four-page fold out 'catalogues' and individual sell sheets for particular kits). These too can usually get prices in double figures.

Early Airfix catalogues, which were in a smaller horizontal A5 format, can fetch a reasonable sum. The first dates from 1962, with a colour cover and monochrome interior pages, but still listed 137 kits in 10 subject categories. The newer catalogue – although many are considerably larger, perfect-bound and include many other details besides a list of kits – tend to get lower prices. Like kits, this is down to the fact that there are more of them around, but some like the Tamiya catalogues (and here it includes even the newer ones) can command higher prices.

The store display

There's one other modelling collectable that does go back to the beginnings of the hobby and is limited almost exclusively to the US model companies. This is the built-up store display. These were intended purely for hobby shops and consisted of a built model on a card display base. Many of the main US companies issued them – particularly Revell, Monograms and Adams.

The companies made these themselves – they had assembly lines making up the models and some were even slightly modified from the commercial kit. Some car displays for instance, assuming they had a hood, didn't have an engine in place and some even had an extra part manufactured to replace this as an 'oil pan'. The base was printed on strong card, possibly with a clear 'window' to protect the model. The model was fixed onto the base, and the assembly packed in a special box to be mailed to the shops.

LEFT Older catalogues can be collectable. Although they can be colour copied very easily these days, originals are always going to be worth more.

BELOW Shop displays are worth a lot. This is a collection for Monogram's, displayed for its fiftieth anniversary in 1995.

RIGHT **Most American companies did the shop displays, including here a Renwal Nike Ajax, centre right. From the Mark Mattei Collection.**

There is a small but dedicated band of collectors for these shop displays, many of which can command very high prices. Oddly, many can sell for more than for an unbuilt original kit – again as there were so comparatively few of these made. Interestingly, there is also a 'sub-market' for reproductions of these store displays.

Many of the kits themselves are still available, so you have the starting point. Then – and this assumes an original can be located – all that needs to be done is to colour copy the card parts! This is perhaps not quite as straightforward as it could sound, as many of these displays are quite large, so do not fit on a standard copier, so either a commercial one has to be sourced that will print at a larger size, or the copying has to be done in sections. Glue these onto a card backing cut and fold to match the original, and with a built model in place, you have a reasonable representation of the original. In many cases, not all the displays were that large, some bases were only a little

larger than the models, so copies of these can be made more easily.

And in the end?

Will modern kits become collectable? If we knew that, we'd all become millionaires! But these days, unlike in older times, we are faced with the situation that people in general are far more aware of 'collectables'. 'Collectables' are sold as just that – collectables.

There is the usual advice that anything sold 'as a collectable' may do lots of things, but 'collectable' – in that 'retaining its sale value' – almost certainly won't be one of them! 'Collectables' are invariably produced in high numbers, so any value that has been assigned to them will be proportionate to the numbers loose in the market. The overall advice has to be always buy – and build – something that you like, not on the basis it will someday become 'collectable'. That might someday be a bonus, but it is in no way guaranteed.

ABOVE One of the oddities: the only time Revell and AMT combined with these 1:32 car kits. Later issued with just 'Revell' on the box, and although collectable in their own right, not as much as these.

ABOVE Rarest here in this Revell selection of vehicles in 1:48 scale is the Bekins Removal Van (bottom). This is because the tooling was converted into the Honest John transporter (top left).

BELOW One of the few kits of 'lighter than air' craft, the Adams' kit of the *Around the World in 80 Days* La Coquette balloon. Not often seen in its unbuilt state, it's even rarer built.

BELOW One of the few exceptions to 'the oldest is the rarest' with the Revell Westinghouse Atomic Power Plant. This original is indeed rare (and expensive) but the second issue, in a far plainer box, is rarer, so commands higher prices. This, however, is the far better box.

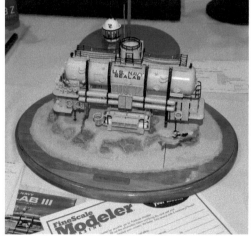

LEFT Another kit hardy ever seen unbuilt, let alone built: the Aurora Sealab. Photographed at a Wonderfest held annually in Louisville, Kentucky, USA.

Chapter Twelve

Clubs, competitions, displays and photography

Model making could be described as a somewhat isolated hobby. Building an individual model is usually done by an individual. Consequently, clubs and organisations were soon started to allow modellers to share their interests and knowledge.

Clubs

Clubs themselves by their very nature can range from a loose association of a few enthusiasts meeting round one of their houses, who possibly don't even think of themselves 'as a club', to the opposite end: the International Plastic Modellers Society (IPMS). This has become the largest modelling organisation worldwide, with Chapters in many countries of the world. It began in the UK in 1963, when it was purely known as the PMS.

Who invented the IPMS?

The Americans invariably assume they invented the IPMS. Arguably they did, as it didn't really become the 'IPMS' until an American modeller applied to start a US Chapter a year later in 1964, so by default it then become 'International'. However, the initial idea certainly did start in the UK.

These days, there are at least 62 countries with an IPMS. Under that are a vast number of local clubs that are affiliated to the IPMS, although there are also a good number that aren't. The IPMS also has Special Interest Groups (SIGs) that deal with, as the name suggests, specific interests. These can range from specific manufacturers – there is an 'Airfix SIG', for example – to a particular subject, such as the 'What If?' SIG for projects, in this case primarily aircraft that were planned but never got built for real.

SIGs tend to range across clubs and even countries, so many, if not most, keep in touch these days electronically by social media. There are SIGs specialising in the following subjects (and this is in no way a full list):

- Aerobatic Display Teams
- Battle of Britain
- Bomber Command
- Classic British Jets
- The DC3/C47 Dakota
- Formula 1 and Motorsports
- The Harrier

OPPOSITE A typical railway club. This is in mid-Texas, but apart from the types of buildings on display, it could likely be anywhere.

- Hot Rod and Custom Cars
- Israeli Defence Forces
- Luftwaffe
- NASA
- Portuguese Military Aviation
- Sci-Fi and Fantasy
- The Spitfire
- US Air Forces of the Second World War
- Vietnam.

ABOVE A high view of one of the UK IPMS Scale Model World Shows, held in November in Telford, UK. This is one hall – there are a total of three of equal size!

ABOVE One of the many IPMS Special Interest Groups (SIGs).

LEFT The 'What If?' SIG.

Competitions and shows

Clubs run shows and competitions, which is the place for individual modellers who may have been slaving away on a creation for most of the year to finally show off their toil. The largest such show worldwide is generally acknowledged to be the IPMS Nationals, called Scale Model World, held each November in Telford in Shropshire, UK. Ironically, this is larger than similar US shows, including America's own Nationals, primarily as it is not just a show for UK modellers. Modellers travel from many other European countries, as well as some further afield, including North America.

The IPMS Nationals run competitions across the whole range of scale models, so anyone who has spent the past year building their pride and joy, could possibly think of entering their creations, and you never know, maybe even get a gold. But if you are going to participate, the model has to be got to the location.

Transportation

One thing most modellers soon discover is that models do not always travel well. The details many modellers put into their creations are fine as long as the model isn't touched or moved. The slight problem if you are taking the model to enter a competition, or even purely putting it on display, is that it is almost certainly going to be touched and moved, both quite a lot.

Some models are easier to deal with than others, and it definitely helps if you are transporting the model yourself – packing it at one end of the journey, travelling with it and unloading it for display at the other end. A military diorama on a solid base with everything firmly fixed down could possibly just need a suitably sized cardboard box that can be placed somewhere secure in a vehicle.

Car models are also reasonably easy, and if you need to move several, they are all roughly the same size. They are also not very tall, so the vegetable boxes from supermarkets are ideal – they are also free and you'll be doing a small bit for recycling. You could add a sheet of bubble wrap in the bottom, then individually wrap each car – being careful of details such as wing mirrors – and position them in the box, with more bubble wrap in-between so they don't move or roll about. These veg boxes also have the advantage for general storage in that they can be stacked, and in fact, as the type of corrugated card used for these boxes is extremely strong, they can be stacked fairly high!

Aircraft models can be more tricky to transport. If they are fixed firmly to a base, that is a start. However, aircraft usually have weak points in the form of undercarriage legs that may hold the model securely enough if it is just standing there but during, say, a car trip, forces such as cornering and braking can put undue stresses on these thin legs. One alternative way to move them is to turn them upside down, so the undercarriage legs are pointing upwards into the air and not bearing the weight of the whole object. But in this scenario, you could now have to deal with propeller blades, or aerials or turrets on the upper surfaces, which are now on the underside.

BELOW

Transportation: using kebab sticks in polystyrene to hold models in place.

BELOW RIGHT Then place the held model in a larger container.

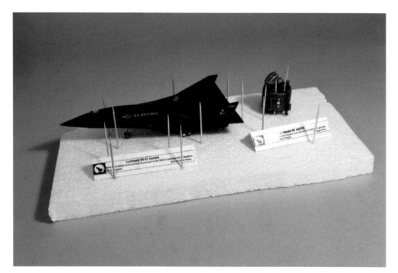

One way to alleviate some stresses is to take a sheet of expanded polystyrene (as mentioned in Chapter 9, see pages 129–131) and push wooden sticks such as kebab sticks, which are already sharpened at one end, into the polystyrene sheet around the model to hold and support it more securely in place. The same method can actually apply to any model, such as an individual military vehicle or a ship. The polystyrene base itself can then go into its own box, such as our veg boxes, which can be found in various heights to take 'taller' models, with maybe room for several models.

Individual figures can be wrapped in bubble wrap and placed in boxes – though, again, be aware of 'sticking out' bits! Those already on bases could be somewhat 'top heavy' – they are taller than wide, but if there are several, stand them all in a suitable box and carefully support them with bubble wrap.

PACKING WITH PEANUTS

There is the alternative packing material of expanded polystyrene beads, also known as 'peanuts', due to their shape. Although, yes, these are very effective for packing as they 'fill gaps' better than just bubble wrap, they are difficult to deal with as they tend to get everywhere! At the start of the process, the packing is fine. Put the model in the box and pour the beads around. But that's just the start, they then have to be unpacked and repacked at the other end. The first part is straightforward – the model can be carefully pulled out of the box of beads, and put on display. But on subsequent repacking, the model can't just go back in a box full of beads and expect the beads to sit conveniently around it as before. You have to pour the beads out of the box – which means another box or similar to put them in – then put the model back in and pour the beads around it again. At this point, beads will almost certainly spill out and you'll be grovelling around on the floor picking them up individually! And if you have to do this several times, it can be a time-consuming and thankless task.

If you intend to move the models more than a few times, it could be worth investing in (or making) special holders and boxes for individual models, though this is a less flexible system and won't necessarily be easy to adapt if the models the case is primarily built for are then replaced with others.

If, for any reason, you can't travel with the model and are intending to move it by post or courier, this is going to be a far trickier situation. Here the model really had to be fixed down tight so that it can't possibly move, and packaged in such a way it will survive in any foreseeable situation (and probably some unforeseeable ones…). The package may not always be in the dry, so the box should be waterproof, and you won't be able to guarantee that labels that state 'Fragile' or 'This Way Up' will be adhered to. If you are shipping internationally, there could be customs to contend with and declaration forms could be required. None of this is impossible to solve, but it certainly needs very careful thought and planning.

You will also have to rely on sympathetic people 'at the other end' to unpack your model for display. However, at least you have the knowledge that they are almost certainly modellers themselves and so should treat your creation with respect. It could be an idea to include with the package any special instructions you feel could help, such as 'Lift only by the base' or 'Model not attached to base'. If the model is being entered in a competition, and some damage does occur in transit, judges are usually aware such traumas

ABOVE The author stores his built kits in supermarket vegetable boxes. They are also very useful for safe transportation of the models.

can happen and will normally treat the entry with sympathy, ignoring any unplanned damage.

Classifications

When entering competitions it helps if you enter the right category or class. This may be an obvious statement, but it's surprising how many times it has been got wrong! Of course, it considerably helps if the setters of the competition get their categories right in the first place, so carefully reading of the R&Rs (rules and regulations) always helps. Some categories are more defined than others: a model of a Formula 1 car is a Formula 1 car, so would fit where categories define: 1) just cars of any type, 2) race cars of any type, or 3) specifically Formula cars.

With a model of a Jeep or Land Rover, though, it may not be so clear. In civilian form – finished in bright red or blue – it would logically fit in with a vehicle classification. But if it's camouflaged in olive drab and has a machine gun on the roof, you will probably be better placing it in the military category. This could alternatively mean it represents some dystopian 'Mad Max' scenario, so a third option could be that it fits better in a science-fiction class!

A model of the V-2 rocket could create similar problems. If it's built as a wartime missile, it would seem fairly obvious to enter it into a 'military AFV' or 'military missile' class. But supposing it is built as a research rocket, designed to be launched from the White Sands Missile Range in New Mexico? It is, in effect, exactly the same 'wartime rocket', but this time it performs a totally different 'civilian' task. If the competition has a research rocket or space rocket category, could it more logically be placed there? Certainly one to check before sending in the entry form!

Dioramas can be one of the most difficult to categorise. Some competitions allow a certain amount of 'diorama' features for a single model, before it is defined as a 'diorama'. As far as aircraft are concerned, many if not all have pilot and crew figures in situ, but supposing they are standing by the access ladder? These may be allowed, but can you then add a figure of an engineer or, muddying the waters even more, a starter truck? One for thoroughly checking the R&Rs and if doubt, contact the competition organisers for clarification. There have been many instances where a good model had failed to win an award, however deserved, as it fell foul of the regulations and was entered in the wrong class. Some competitions allow individual judges to move a model from a 'wrong' category to a 'right' one, allowing the model a far better chance at fair judging, but this isn't always the case.

Any model intended for entry to a competition should ideally include details about how it was built. If a class allows 'a kit built with aftermarket parts', exactly what these parts are could help the judges. If a model is of a very obscure subject, some history could also be useful. Judges are expected to be experts in their own particular field, but even the best and most experienced can't know everything.

Many competitions allow the judges to move models where no one else is (apart from the builder), as it can help to get a full view of the model. If this is the case, ensure they know what can safely be moved and what, say, is not fixed down, so extreme care will be required.

Displays

Even at home you will presumably want to display your model (or models) somewhere. The one main problem models attract (though admittedly this is a factor with anything, anywhere) is that of dust. Models are unique in that, unlike a vase that can be dusted with reasonable ease and even washed, models have 'bits' sticking out and these 'bits' tend to make conventional dusting out of the question as they can break off.

Consequently, models ideally need to be under cover and many model companies also make display cases. These tend to be slightly limited in size. Many are designated specifically for cars, and these all – even comparing a Mini to a Cadillac – roughly tend to be the same sort of size. But these cases would also take small aircraft or ship models. Larger models will need specifically built cases, or a whole display case with doors. Though, be aware – even a supposedly sealed door does not prevent dust getting in! You will be surprised how much seems to get through even doors that are rarely opened. It is, however, going to be less than if the model is sitting out in the open.

You can buy specialist vacuum cleaners that

are supposed to be delicate enough to deal with dust on models, but frankly their usefulness is debatable. Overall, dusting is best done with a large brush, but one that has fine soft bristles. This brush should only be used for this task, don't expect one that has been used for painting to be suitable; even carefully cleaned, the bristles will soon lose their softness.

Photography

Photographing the finished model has always had an appeal. Initially this would have been on film, with the possible intention of sending it in to win a place in the 'readers creations page' in a model magazine. Now it seems that everyone has a digital camera, even if it is purely the one in your phone, and there are a vast amount of outlets in which your photos can be published. You may have your own website or Facebook page, or maybe a Flickr account where you store your images.

Photography can range from a purely casual snap of the finished model, basically showing that 'here's a model I've actually finished', to making it look 'real' using relatively simple setups.

ABOVE On the large size, but this could be the type of cabinet to display your models. But some dust will still get in! From the Dean Milano Collection.

FAR LEFT When photographing a model inside, it will invariably always be 'a model'...

LEFT ... Photographing it outside, against a real sky, gives the model more realism. This is the Real Space Models Soviet N-1 launcher.

Going digital

Putting aside the arguments for and against film versus digital – a complete subject in its own right – most will likely be shooting on digital. Digital photography has the advantage of being able to see immediately what you've shot and being able to immediately shoot again, unlike a roll of film where you were constantly calculating how many more exposures you had left and whether you needed to go and buy another roll. Shooting additional digital images do not cost any more – most memory cards can store hundreds of high-resolution jpegs. However, tips and tricks that were developed during the era of film are still appropriate to digital.

One main potential problem modern digital camera users have is that many aspects on their devices are automatic, and in many cases you have little control over how they operate. Producing an image on any camera – film or digital – is down to two factors: the speed of the shutter and the amount of light allowed in through the lens. The latter is controlled by the iris in the lens and is termed the f-stop. Generally, these run from f-2.8 through to f-32; f-2.8 being in effect wide open and f-32 stopped down to a small pin hole. The larger the maximum aperture the 'faster' the lens, though with a disproportionate increase in price. For example a lens that opens to f-1.8 will probably cost twice the amount of one that only opens to f-2.8.

Whatever this larger figure, the main problem is that the more the lens is in wide open mode, the smaller the depth of field, and when shooting models, depth of field is important, as that is the only factor that keeps it all in focus. In addition, the speed the shutter operates is directly opposite to the aperture. The smaller the f-stop, the slower the shutter speed and more 'handheld' blur could happen. Consequently, most model shoots will have to be done on a tripod.

Many digital cameras work as a default in automatic mode and they balance the speed of the shutter against the aperture. So the speed of the 'click' (whether there is an audible 'click' or not!) is balanced against the amount of light that is allowed in, and the electronics make a compromise. Consequently, the advice is to try and use a camera where you can control

the settings, ideally an SLR, nowadays termed a DSLR or digital single lens reflex. These are the types of cameras that also have separate lenses, so you can select the lens best used for the task. In this case, you can set the f-stop to a small value, such as f-32, and the speed will slow down by a proportional value, so you could be at, say, $\frac{1}{15}$th of a second and you will definitely need the camera on a tripod.

Shooting models effectively

One factor to bear in mind when shooting models is to try to not use the flash, which again can be a problem with some of the 'totally automatic' devices. This particularly applies if you're attempting to make the photo look real. Due to the closeness of such a shot, this will make the whole image look very flat, and you will likely get over-exposures and odd reflections of areas that will overemphasise them. It is possible to use balanced flash setups using more than one flash head (and not the one on the camera itself), but this requires additional specialised equipment. If you can shoot outside using natural light, this usually gives excellent results. A slightly cloudy day will remove odd shadows, and the lighting will be overall very balanced.

Inside, using photofloods – or modern LED equivalents – will work much better than flash, though again this would require extra equipment. There are small light boxes made, designed for shooting small objects, which most hobby models will be, though these again will need to be bought. Using existing lights around the home can work, and any odd colour temperature balances, which can make the image too red or too blue, well that's what photo-manipulating computer programs are there to correct!

There is also a point about the angle at which to shoot the model. If it is purely to image the model 'as a model', a high-ish angle – perhaps a three-quarter front angle will work – showing off the structure of the aircraft to best advantage. However, if you're trying to shoot the model 'for real', you'll need a few tricks employed by the special effects miniatures filming industry. Here, the mantra has always been to keep the shot as low as possible, in effect mimicking the eye of the

beholder. Given that most people are up to six feet, or somewhat under two metres tall, this will mean the height of the camera lens has got to be scaled down to similar scale height, and consequently ends up virtually sitting on the base board of the model, so you are slightly looking up at it. This will also depend on the scale of the model: the larger the scale, the less importance it will have, but most hobby models will be on the smallish size. This is not applicable to every circumstance. A photo of an aircraft in flight will invariably look like a model, however shot, but then many real airliners look 'modelish' in flight – not helped here as

RIGHT And the resulting shot, looking up at the ship.

there is nothing else in shot for comparison. However, the reasoning holds true for most circumstances.

Another advantage of digital is that you can easily 'bracket' shots – that is take a set of exposures which vary in settings to make them darker, through neutral to slightly lighter. This isn't totally restricted to digital – you can do this with film – but you usually had to take each shot separately, changing settings in-between. Some digital cameras at the upper end of the market can be set to do this automatically. This means you can pick which exposure works best, though frankly most photo-manipulating programs can do this as well. Of these programs, Photoshop is the best known and has become the generic term, but there are other such as ACDSee, or camera manufactures' such as Nikon or Canon's own programs. It used to be that the majority of the work taking a photograph had to be done pre-shoot, such as adding filters to get certain effects. These days it is mostly all done, to use the movie term: 'post production', so after the photo has been taken.

A place to meet

Even with the way the World Wide Web has taken over most aspects of life – model making included – competitions and model shows in general are a great way to meet other

RIGHT The type of base with a slope at the front, used for much special effects miniature filming is here demonstrated by the late Ian Scoones, long-time special effects supervisor, variously at Hammer Films, Century 21 and the BBC.

ABOVE **Meeting at model shows: this is the Timeless Hobbies stand at a Scale Model World.**

ABOVE RIGHT **It's easier to buy for your modelling needs if you can talk face-to-face. Here is Paul Fitzmaurice (right) CEO of Modelling Tools at a Milton Keynes Scale Model Club show.**

RIGHT **Airfix shows off new products at a Scale Model World.**

modellers and – to use the modern term – to network.

Dealers are usually at such shows, and in fact these days many only attend model shows as they do not have retail premises. So unless you are content to buy online, which can be tricky unless you are absolutely sure of what you require, face-to-face chats with sellers at shows are an ideal alternative.

Besides the competition element, and dealers, model shows are generally places to meet people with similar interests to yourself. Even with many local clubs, some modellers still do not belong to these clubs, but may attend the larger shows. Perhaps this is the place you can locate your local club (IPMS or not) and talk with them. Maybe it's time to join?

RIGHT **The Revell stand at an earlier iHobby Expo show in Chicago, USA.**

References and model companies

These days when considering research, it's very easy to say that it'll all be found 'on the net'. To a great extent this is true, though with the proviso that sometimes there is too much information on the Internet, and sorting what you want from what you don't is not always straightforward and in many cases can lead to extreme frustration! However, don't forget that good old-fashioned paper references (i.e. books and magazines) still have an important role to play. Plus, even these days, not everyone has a computer, tablet or smartphone with direct access to the Internet, though connections are found everywhere in schools, colleges, community centres, libraries and Internet cafés.

Assuming you do have Internet access, one very important point to remember when searching is that it is only as good as the information or question you are putting in – and even then it doesn't always work. You have to remember computers are dumb, and although *you* may be quite aware that when you key in 'Harrier' you mean the vertical take-off plane, a search engine such as Google or Bing will probably just look for 'Harrier' in its original sense and you'll get loads of images of birds of prey winging their way over the moors! So you would have to specify key words: say, 'Harrier aircraft' or 'Harrier VTOL'. Even what you could think of as very specific wording can sometimes bring up items which makes you wonder exactly what the logic being used is?

Websites for modellers

Regarding websites as general sources for modellers, it's probably wise to point out (if anyone still isn't aware) that the word 'model', as far as the Internet is concerned, can be interpreted in two somewhat different ways (even if the origins of both meanings are the same, well, more or less). You have, at least, been warned!

Note also that most websites also have many links to other related pages.

Here 'mainstream' refers to companies that produce kits in injection styrene, which would normally be found in hobby stores and model shops (assuming, that is, any still exist near you…). 'Specialist' indicates what are usually one-man (apologies, but it is always seems to be one 'man') operations that produce kits in all materials – except injection styrene – and which are normally only available from specialist hobby shops and/or by mail direct from the company's website. These companies are also generally known as 'garage' companies

Mail address and websites are given for the majority, though remember that not all websites begin: www. All those below only require http:// in front to work (although most browsers don't need that to be specific these days) – assuming, that is, that the site is still valid.

MAINSTREAM COMPANIES

These are the majority of the major ones that currently appear to be in production, though it isn't guaranteed to be exclusive. To be listed as 'mainstream', the primary moulding material is polystyrene (though some other materials – resin, photo-etch, white metal, etc. – may be included). If the primary moulding material is resin, these are listed under 'specialist companies'.

ACADEMY

Academy Plastic Model Co Ltd.
521-1, Yonghyeon-dong, Uijeangbu-si, Gyeonggi-du,
South Korea
The major Korean model producer that used to work with Minicraft in the US, though that connection was severed in 1997.
www.academyhobby.com

ACE MODEL

Ace Model, Ukraine
Makes military subjects in 1:72 and 1:35 scale.
www.acemodel.com.ua/en

AFV-CLUB

Hobby Fan Trading Co.
No 7, Alley 7, Lane 225, Mintsu West Road, Taipei, Taiwan
Created in the late 1980s to make kits of subjects not covered by other companies. These were primarily military, but now include aircraft.
www.hobbyfan.com.tw

AIRFIX

Hornby Hobbies Ltd., Margate, Kent CT9 4JX, UK
One of the first model kit companies and still one of the best-known names worldwide. Over the years produced a wide range of subjects, particularly aircraft. Now owned by Hornby, along with Humbrol, Corgi, Scalextric and Hornby Railways.
www.airfix.com

AMODEL

Exclusive distribution: IBG, Benedykta Hertza 2 04 – 603, Warsaw, Poland
Ukraine company, created in 1995 with a wide range of aircraft models in most conventional scales, from 1:32 to 1:144. Uses preformed parts for some of the large fuselage models such as the Myasishchev and Buran space orbiter.
en.ibg.com.pl/en,producent,amodel,7,1,name,asc.html

AMT

Round 2 Models, 4073 Meghan Beeler Drive,
South Bend, IN 46628, USA
One of the original American model companies, best known for its car models. It then introduced the first Star Trek kits, and its famous five-piece 'Man in Space' set. Having been taken over by Lesney, it was then acquired by Ertl, which itself was taken over by RC2 (Racing Champions). Consequently it joined its original rival, MPC, as that had also been bought by Ertl. Both companies were then acquired by the new Round 2 company in 2009.
www.round2models.com/models/amt

AOSHIMA

Aoshima Bunka Kyozai Co Ltd, 12–3 Ryutsu Centre,
Shizuoka City, Japan 420
One of the oldest model companies in the world, with beginnings in the 1920s making wooden kits. Moved to plastic in the early 1960s and is still producing a wide range of models.
www.aoshima-bk.co.jp

ATLANTIS MODELS

Atlantis Toy and Hobby Inc., 435 Brook Avenue Unit-16,
Deer Park, NY 11729, USA
Founded in 2009 by the former owners of Megahobby.com, Peter Vetri and Rick DelFavero. Initially reissued kits from other tooling, though making its own series of 'flying saucers'. In early 2018, acquired much of the Revell-Monogram and Aurora and Renwal, tooling, when the Revell Group stopped trading after the Hobbico collapse.
www.atlantis-models.com

AZ MODEL

AZ Model, Above Calcium 364, Křenice u Říčan 250 84, Prague East, Czech Republic
Created in 1997. Produces aircraft kits in 1:144, 1:72 and 1:48 scales, plus decals.
www.azmodel.cz

BANDAI

Bandai Co., Ltd., 5-4 2-chome, Komagata, Taito-ku,
Tokyo, Japan
Well-known Japanese toy manufacturer that also made kits over the years. Many are classic Japanese anime characters, though it has also made more traditional modelling subjects. Recently has produced new and highly detailed Star Wars craft, some reissued for Europe by Revell-Germany.
www.bandai-hobby.net

BIGMODEL

'Bielwood', 43-332, Pisarzowice Ul. Szkolna 59, Poland
Primarily produces airliners in 1:144 scale. Other aircraft and military are planned in standard scales.
www.bigmodel.eu

BRONCO

Ningbo Weijun (Bronco) Mould & Plastic Co. Ltd., D Building No.688, Ling Feng Shan Road, Beilun, Ningbo, China
One of the newer Chinese companies, established in November 2004. Makes a wide range of aircraft, military and ships in various standard model scales.
www.cn.bronco.com

DAPOL

Dapol Ltd., Gledrid Industrial Park, Chirk, Wrexham
LL14 5DG, UK
Founded by David Boyle in 1983, Dapol primarily deals with UK 00 and N gauge rail items. It acquired the Airfix range of trackside accessories and rolling stock (which included the Kitmaster range) in 1985.
www.dapol.co.uk

DOYUSHA

Doyusha Model Co Ltd., 4-27-21, Arakawa, Arakawa-ku,
Tokyo, Japan
One of the older Japanese names, still in production with a wide range of kits.
www.doyusha-model.com

DRAGON

Dragon Models Ltd., B1, 10/F, Kong Nam Industrial Building, 603–609 Castle Peak Road, Tsuen Wan New Territories, Hong Kong
Producer of aircraft, military and space kits.
www.dragon-models.com

EASTERN EXPRESS

Nizhnyaya Syromyatnicheskaya, 11, Moscow, Russia
Founded in 1992 in Moscow. Primarily makes aircraft and military models, but with some figures and – oddly – the ex-Frog South Goodwin lightship!
www.ee-models.ru

EBBRO

Ebbro, 7- 7 Chiyoda 7-chome, Aoi-ku, Shizuoka City, Japan
Created in 1998. Specialises in 1:20 scale F1 and 1:24 French vehicles. Also a 1:48 scale Honda Jet.
www.ebbro.co.jp

EDUARD

Eduard Model Accessories, Mirova 170, 435 21 Obrnice, Czech Republic
Created in 1989 initially to make accessories, mainly photo-etch, for other manufacturers' kits. The company then moved into highly detailed injection styrene kits of their own, mainly aircraft in the standard scales.
www.eduard.com

EMHAR

Bachmann-Europe PLC, 13 Moat Way, Barwell, Leicester LE9 8EY, UK
A brand initially set up by Toyway, which was taken over by Pocketbond, itself then acquired by Bachmann-Europe. Makes 1:72 scale aircraft and military and a unique range of 1:24 scale Bedford lorries.
www.pocketbond.co.uk

ENCORE MODELS

Squadron, 1115 Crowley Drive, Carrollton, TX 75006-1312, USA
Name used by the model distribution company, Squadron, for kits that it has adapted from other manufacturers. See also 'Squadron' under 'Distributors'.
www.squadron.com

FALLER

Gebr. Faller GmbH, Kreuzstraße 9, 78148 Gütenbach, Germany
Germany's best-known model railway manufacturer. Much is pre-assembled and 'ready-to-roll', but many of the buildings are available in kit form and adaptable to other scenarios. In the past, Faller also made aircraft kits.
www.faller.de

FINEMOLDS

53–2 Matoba, Oitsu, Toyohashi, Aichi 441-3301, Japan
Specialist model kit producer, including Star Wars subjects.
www.finemolds.co.jp

FROG

Hobby Bounties & Morgan Hobbycraft Centre, 865 Mountbatten Road #0291/92 , Katong Shopping Centre, Singapore 437844, Republic of Singapore
The original British model name, now owned by Hobby Bounties, as an Anglo-Singapore company. Issuing some new kits and some Frog originals.
www.hobbybounties.com

FUJIMI

Fujimi Mokei Co. Ltd., 4-21-1 Toro, Shizuoka City, Japan
Founded in 1948 making wooden ship models, Started its plastic range around 1970, with kits across the range; aircraft, cars, ships and military. It is one of the larger of the Japanese model companies.
www.fujimimokei.com

GLENCOE MODELS

Glencoe Models LLC, PO Box 337, Rochdale, MA 01542, USA
Created by Nick Argento in 1987, the company has reissued many classic kits, including those from Strombecker, ITC, Adams and Hawk.
www.glencoemodels.com

GREAT WALL HOBBY / G.W.H.

Shanghai Lion Roar Art Model Co., Ltd., Room 210, No 87 Lane 410, Long Wu Road, Shanghai P.R., China
Model kit division of Lion Roar, making large-scale aircraft and Chinese spacecraft. The Lion Roar name is used for conversion kits.
www.lionroar.net

HASEGAWA

Hasegawa Seisakuso Co Ltd, 3-1-2 Yagusu Yaizu Shizuoka 425-8711, Japan
One of the major Japanese kit companies with a wide range of subjects: military, aircraft, cars, ships and airliners.
www.hasegawa-model.co.jp

HAWK

Round 2 Models, 4073 Meghan Beeler Drive, South Bend, IN 46628, USA
One of the earliest model names in the USA, making a wide range of models. The name and tooling was acquired by Round 2 in 2013. Some Hawk kits have been reissued.
www.round2models.com/models/hawk

HELLER

Heller Joustra S.A, Chemin de la Porte, 61160 Trun, France
Founded in 1957 by Léo Jahiel. Since then the company has been through several ownerships, including being joined to Airfix when both were owned by Humbrol. However, it was not acquired along with Airfix and Humbrol when they were bought by Hornby, and Heller now runs as an independent company. It issues many of its own classic kits and some new, across the range of aircraft, ships and galleons, and cars, using its own (unique) 1:125 scale, for some aerospace subjects. In early 2019, Heller was acquired by the German company, Glow2B.
www.heller.fr

HK MODELS

Hong Kong Models, Flat 12, 12/F, Tak Lee Industries Center, Tsing Yeung Street, Tuen Mun, New Territories, Hong Kong
Created in 2010 to produce large highly-detailed aircraft models in 1:32 scale.
www.hk-models.com

HOBBY BOSS

Yatai Electric Appliances Co, Ltd.,
Nan Long Industrial Park, San Xiang, Zhong Shan,
Guang Dong 528463, China
One of the newer Chinese companies making high-quality aircraft, ship and military kits.
www.hobbyboss.com

HORIZON MODELS

Horizon Models Pty Ltd, PO Box 305, Drummoyne NSW 2047, Australia
A new company started by Tony Radosevic in 2015, with its first kits dealing with early American space subjects. Uses injection styrene and photo-etch.
www.horizon-models.com

IBG MODELS

IBG, Benedykta Hertza 2 04 – 603, Warsaw, Poland
Manufacturer of a wide range of military, ship and aircraft models in traditional scales. Also distributes many other makes and is an exclusive distributor for Amodel.
en.ibg.com.pl/en,producent,ibg-models,170,1,name,
asc.html

ICM

ICM Holding, 9 Borispolskyya str., Building 64,
Kiev 02660, Ukraine
One of the new companies to emerge from Ukraine becoming an independent country. ICM makes aircraft and military items, many from the mid-Wars era, plus figures and civilian vehicles in 1:35 military scale.
Some have been upscaled to 1:24, including Ford Model T kits.
www.icm.com.ua

ITALERI

Italeri S.p.A., via Pradazzo, 6/b, 1-40012 Calderara di Reno, Bologna, Italy
Began in the 1960s and has gone through two name changes: it was originally Artiplast but this was changed to Italereri and then simplified to Italeri. In recent years it taken over former Italian rivals ESCI (acquired from Ertl) and Protar and works in conjunction with Testors in the US and Revell-Germany. Makes a wide range of kit subjects.
www.italeri.com

KAIYODO

Kaiyodo 19-3, Yanagi-machi Kadoma-shi, Osaka, 571-0041 Japan
Produces mostly Japanese-based items, primarily figures. It also makes an even larger 2001 Discovery than the Moebius kit.
www.kaiyodo.co.jp

KP MODELS

Kovozávody Prostějov, Nad vápenkou 364, 250 84, Praha východ, Czech Republic
Producer of 1:144, 1:72 and 1:48 scale aircraft models.
www.kovozavody.cz

LINDBERG

Round 2 Models, 4073 Meghan Beeler Drive, South Bend, IN 46628, USA
One of the earliest American kit names that started as O-Lin in the 1930s. Producer of the first 'all plastic space kit', the Flying Saucer/UFO in 1954. The name and tooling was acquired by Round 2 in 2013, with some kits being reissued as 'New Lindberg'.
www.round2models.com/models/lindberg

MACH-2

17 rue Emile Combs, 78800 Houilles, France
Proprietor: Didier Palix. Mach-2 mostly deals with aircraft and some vehicles. Includes the Lift-Off range of 1:48 scale models based around the Thor-Delta launcher and a 1:72 range of Soviet/Russian A-Type launchers. Moulded in styrene, but uses short-run injection techniques.
www.mach2.fr

MARUI

Tokyo-Marui, A5-17-1 Ayase, Adachi-ku, Tokyo 120, Japan
Founded in 1965, initially making construction kits as well as motorised cars, ships and tools. It then started to produce 1:1 scale guns and arms (variously gas and electric powered) which have become the company's speciality. Besides sporting use, many are also used in the movie industry. The radio control car side is still strong, however the conventional kit side has declined. Marui is often incorrectly referred to as 'Tilt', as the Japanese Katakana letters for 'Marui' look similar to the Roman letters for 'Tilt'!
www.tokyo-marui.co.jp

MASTER BOX

Ukraine
One of the new companies emerging from the Ukraine. Master Box has a range of military vehicles and many figure sets in the same 1:35 scale. It has also introduced a range of highly detailed figures in 1:24 scale, which includes modern truckers and hitch-hikers, US cops & robbers, the Old West, space operas and Greek mythology.
www.mbltd.info

MENG

Rui Ye Century (Shenzhen) Hobby Co. Ltd., Rm. 3016, Blk. A, Galaxy Century Bldg., 3069 Caitian Road, Futian District, Shenzhen, Guangdong, China
Founded in 2011 to produce high-quality models, mostly military, with some ships and cars. There are a number of modern soft-skinned military vehicles in 1:35 and a 1:24 scale Hummer. Intriguingly, most catalogue divisions are named after dinosaurs – some more appropriate than others. For example, ships come under the Plesiosaurus Series!
www.meng-model.com

MINIART

MiniArt Models Ltd., 144 B Kharkivske Highway,
02091 Kiev, Ukraine

Established in 2001, MiniArt was one of the new companies to emerge from the Ukraine. It makes a number of 1:35 military vehicles but also a wide range of diorama buildings, parts and accessories – arguably more than any other company. These are in 1:35, though could be adapted to other scales. Some buildings are made in 1:72 and there is also a range of 1:16 scale figures.

miniart-models.com

MINICRAFT

Minicraft Models (US) Inc, 1501 Commerce Drive,
Elgin IL 60123, USA

Started by Al Trendle in 1970 as a US importer of Japanese kits, Minicraft now designs and issues many of its own kits.

www.minicraftmodels.com

MODELCOLLECT

ModelCollect Ltd., Guangzhou, China

Created in 2012, a Chinese model company, specialising in military in 1:72 and 1:35, and large aircraft models in 1:72. The catalogue includes a slightly surreal mix of both real and 'what if?' subjects.

www.modelcollect.com

MOEBIUS MODELS

Pegasus Hobbies, 5515 Moreno St., Montclair,
CA 91763, USA

Created by Frank Winspur in 2006. First recreating some of Aurora's old SF and fantasy figures, then producing new tooling for similar subjects before branching out into 1:25 scale American cars and trucks. Acquired by Pegasus Hobbies in 2018, but continues to run as an independent name.

www.moebiusmodels.com

MONOGRAM

See: **REVELL – MONOGRAM**

MPC

Round 2 Models, 4073 Meghan Beeler Drive,
South Bend, IN 46628, USA

Similar to AMT, MPC was created in the 1960s to make model car kits. It became famous for producing the first Star Wars kits. It was acquired by Round 2 in 2009.

www.round2models.com/models/mpc

MRC

Model Rectifier Corp, 80 Newfield Aveue,
Eldon, NJ 08837, USA

An importer of kits for the US market, including many from Academy and Italeri.

www.modelrectifier.com

PEGASUS HOBBIES

Pegasus Hobbies, 5515 Moreno St., Montclair,
CA 91763, USA

Created by Larry Thompson and Tom Macomber in 1987. The company runs a large model store in Montclair, billed as 'Largest in SoCal' (Southern California). It initially produced aftermarket parts for model cars and then moved into wargaming buildings, then science fiction and fantasy models and some aircraft. These are moulded, unusually, not in standard styrene but in ABS. In 2018 it took over Moebius Models, though that continues to run as an independent name.

www.pegasushobbies.com

PLATZ

Platz Hobby Ltd., 3-1-1 Kusanagi Shimizuku, Shizuokashi,
Shizuoka 424-0882, Japan

Founded in 2000, Platz makes a range of aircraft kits and some military. Some of these are also tied into the very Japanese anime series Girls und Panzer. Platz also produces modelling tools and is a distributor and retailer.

www.platz-hobby.com

POLAR LIGHTS

Round 2 Models, 4073 Meghan Beeler Drive,
South Bend, IN 46628, USA

Originally set up as the kit name for the Playing Mantis section of RC2, and an obvious play on the 'Aurora' name, the first kits from Polar Lights were recreations of old Aurora kits. New kits then started to be made, including a series from Star Trek. Polar Lights was acquired by Round 2 in 2009.

www.round2models.com/models/polar-lights

PST

PST (PromSnabTorg, JSC, Minsk, Belarus

Producer of mainly military subjects in 1:72.

www.pstmodel.com

RENWAL

See: **REVELL – MONOGRAM**

REVELL – MONOGRAM

Revell USA LLC, 728, Northwest Highway, Ste 302,
Fox River Grove, IL 60021, USA

Two of the best-known names in modelling, combined since 1986. Both companies have issued many model kits across the subject range, and in the past Revell had acquired the Renwal name and tooling, and Monogram much of the Aurora tooling. R-M was acquired by the large model and hobby distribution company, Hobbico, in 2007. Hobbico, however, went into liquidation in early 2018. When Revell-Germany was taken over by Blitz in mid-2018 this holding company also acquired the Revell-Monogram US name and much – though not all – of the tooling. The remainder went to Atlantis Hobbies, though the NASCAR tooling was sold to the new company, Salvinos JR Models.

www.revell.com

REVELL – GERMANY

Revell GmbH & Co. KG, Henschelstrasse 20-30,
D-32257, Bünde, Germany
Although part of the overall Revell Group, it ran very much as an independent company and although it was eventually acquired by Hobbico, this wasn't until 2011, four years later than R-M. It was consequently in a better position than Revell-Monogram when Hobbico went into liquidation in early 2018. Revell-Germany was taken over by the German company Quantum Capital Partners, under the name Blitz, in mid-2018. This included the American name and stock, though not the staff or premises.
www.revell.de

RODEN

Roden Ltd., 7a Nevska Str., OF.35, Kiev, Ukraine
Manufacturer of military vehicle and aircraft kits in various scales. Part of a larger company that does more general injection moulding, engineering and CAD-CAM.
www.roden.eu

ROUND-2

Round 2 Models, 4073 Meghan Beeler Drive,
South Bend, IN 46628, USA
Overall company that owns, AMT, MPC, Polar Lights, Lindberg and Hawk model kit names.
www.round2models.com

SALVINOS JR MODELS

Salvino JR Models,
1240 E Ontario Ave #102 PMB 327, Corona, CA 92881, USA
A new company, purely dealing with American race cars, using new tooling. It also acquired the NASCAR tooling from Revell-Monogram in 2018.
salvinosjrmodels.com

SMĚR

Směr Production Team,
Bellova 124, 109 00 Praha 10 - Petrovice, Czech Republic
Czech company founded in 1952. Manufactures a wide range of products and toys – kits are only a part of this. The majority are from existing tooling.
www.smer.cz

SPECIAL HOBBY

Special Hobby, s.r.o., Mezilesí 718/78, 193 00 Prague, Czech Republic
Part of the MPM range of companies. Borders between being a 'mainstream' and a 'garage' company. Produces a wide range of aircraft and military items.
www.specialhobby.eu

TAKOM

Takom (HK) International Co. Ltd.,
Dong Guan, China
Founded in 2013 in Hong Kong, Takom mainly specialises in military kits in 1:72, 1:35 and 1:16 scales, including many unusual subjects.
www.takom-world.com

TAMIYA

Tamiya inc., 307 Ondawara, Suruga-Ku,
Shizuoka 422-8610, Japan
One of the major Japanese model companies and arguably the best known. Created in 1948 by Shunska Tamiya, initially making wooden ship kits and only later moving to plastic. Tamiya's ranges encompass most modelling subjects and it has large radio control, robotic and educational model divisions.
www.tamiya.com

TRUMPETER

Wasan Plastic Model Co,
Nang Long Industrial Area, San Xiang, Zhong Shan,
Guang Dong, China
The largest and best known of all the new Chinese model companies, Trumpeter makes a wide range of aircraft, military and ship kits and some American cars
www.trumpeter-china.com

VALOM

Zlešická 1808/10, Praha 4 – Chodov, 148 00, Czech Republic
Founded in 2002. Produces aircraft, including many unusual subjects, in 1:48, 1:72 and 1:144 scales.
www.valom.net

WALTHERS

Wm. K. Walthers, Inc., 5601 West Florist Avenue,
Milwaukee, WI 53218, USA
America's major model railroad manufacturer. Much is pre-assembled, but many of the layout buildings and accessories are available as kits and adaptable to other subject matter.
www.walthers.com

WAVE

Wave Corporation,
1-10-1 Kiboshida Higashi-machi, Musashino-shi,
Tokyo, 180-0002, Japan
Founded in 1987, Wave produces model kits, accessories and tools. The vast majority of kits are of classic Japanese anime subjects.
www.hobby-wave.com

WINGNUT WINGS

Wingnut Wings Ltd,
PO Box 15–319, Miramar, Wellington 6022,
New Zealand
Specialist in 1:32 scale Second World War aircraft kits and decal sets.
www.wingnutwings.com

ZEBRANO

Zebrano, Minsk, Belarus
Created in 2009 by Vladimir Kiselev. Initially working with such as PST. Makes unusual subjects of mainly Soviet armour and figures in 1:72, 1:43 and 1:35 scale. Kits in injection styrene, accessories in resin.
www.zebrano-model.com

ZOUKEI MURA

Zoukei-mura Inc., Kyoto, Japan

One of the newer Japanese companies, created by Akihiro Nakatani and specialising in highly detailed aircraft models, primarily in 1:32 scale.

www.zoukeimura.co.jp/en/

ZVEZDA

Zvezda LLC, Promyshlenna str.2,
Moscow Region, Russia

A new-style Russian kit company, created in the early 1990s on the break-up of the Soviet Union. Uses modern techniques and primarily makes military and aircraft models. Also make a wide range of figure sets in 1:72 scale, and some modern and old-time ships. Some production is in conjunction with Revell – Germany.

https://zvezda.org.ru/

SPECIALIST COMPANIES

ANIGRAND CRAFTSWORK

Flat F, 23 Floor, Block 4, Waterside Plaza, Wing Shun Street, Tune Wan, NT, Hong Kong

Specialist producer of resin kits, featuring a number of aircraft, space and X-plane subjects.

www.anigrand.com

ATOMIC CITY

Atomic City Engineering,
Hanford, CA 93230, USA

Proprietor: Scott Alexander. Atomic City makes short runs of SF subjects plus the 1:12 scale injection styrene kit of the Mercury Capsule; distributed by MRC. See also MRC in the 'mainstream' listing.

www.atomiccitymodels.com

FANTASTIC PLASTIC

Fantastic Plastic Models,
LLC, 25501 Willow Wood Street, Lake Forest,
CA 92630, USA

Proprietor: Allen B. Ury. Manufacturer of a wide variety of multi-material, mainly resin-based aerospace models.

www.fantastic-plastic.com

KORA MODELS

J. Wolkera 74, 756 61 Roznov pod Radhostem,
Czech Republic

Proprietor: Robert Koraba. Kora produces many resin armoured vehicle kits and, with NewWare, a series of V-2 conversions based on the Condor kit.

www.lfmodels.cz

LVM STUDIOS

Goudplevier 106, 5348 ZG Oss,
The Netherlands

Proprietor: Leon van Munster. Producer of complete multi-material kits of such space subjects as Soyuz, plus photo-etch sets for detailing existing kits, including the Hasegawa Voyager space probe and complex launch gantries for the Soyuz and Mercury Atlas launch pads.

https://b-m.facebook.com/lvmstudiosnl/

NEW WARE

Zelazneho 6, 71200 Ostava 2,
Czech Republic

Proprietors: Tomas Kladiva, Peter Cigan and Andi Wuestner. Producer of many specialist accessory sets for space modellers to update such kits as Revell's International Space Station and Mir kit, plus complete kits of Soviet/Russian craft such as Soyuz and Vostok.

mek.kosmo.cz/newware

REALSPACE MODELS

813 Watt Drive, Tallahassee, FL 32303, USA

Proprietor: Glenn Johnson. RealSpace Models has the largest range of specialist material spacecraft kits in the USA, making everything from a 1:200 Skylab adaptor for the AMT Saturn 5 kit, to Voyager, Viking and Magellan space probes in 1:24 scale. Also makes detailing sets and decal sheets. The company distributes the detailed plans of David Weeks.

www.realspacemodels.com

SHARKITS

9 rue de la Picardiere, 78200 Perdreauville,
France

Proprietor: Renaud Mangallon. Founded by Franck 'Sharky' Wagner to make specialist aerospace subjects, mostly in resin. The range includes several missiles and some SF subjects.

www.sharkit.com

STRATOSPHERE MODELS

Proprietor: Stéphane Cochin. Specialist manufacturers of limited-edition kits of science fiction subjects, plus some real craft, including the DC-X. Now also does 3D design.

www.picturetrail.com/stratospheremodels

UNICRAFT

Ukraine

Proprietor: Igor Shestakov. Specialist producer of resin kits, featuring a number of aircraft, space and X-plane subjects.

www.unicraft.biz

WELSH MODELS

93, Fonmon Park Road, Rhoose, Vale of Glargan,
CF62 3BG, UK

Uses vac-form and resin to make, mainly, transport aircraft.

www.welshmodels.co.uk

3D PRINTING

This has a separate heading as 3D printing companies tend to work in a completely different way to conventional model companies. Most of the many 3D/adaptive manufacturing companies that now exist around the world deal directly with commercial applications, designing and producing industrial items but using 3D printing as opposed to more traditional methods. Although in theory they could produce a part of a model kit, they may not be set up to deal with individual requests.

Consequently, this listing has to be limited to those companies that either deal specifically for the modeller or can accept small printing runs. Even then, this may only be part of an overall business. (After all, Airfix started off by making toys and household appliances that were injection moulded, as well as model kits.)

This can only be a representative list. More seem to be coming online every day, so this list is likely to be quickly out of date.

BOYCE AEROSPACE HOBBIES

Boyce Aerospace Hobbies, San Diego, California, USA
Started originally by Alex and Sheree Boyce in 1995, making tradition flying rocket parts. Revamped in 2015, now exclusively using 3D printing to make similar parts.
www.boyceaerospacehobbies.com

BUILDPARTS

C.Ideas, 125 Erick Street, Suite# A115,
Crystal Lake, IL 60014, USA
Founded in 1998, C.Ideas can produce a variety of subjects from a wide range of materials.
www.buildparts.com

GIBLETS CREATIONS

Giblets Creations, Oxford, UK
Started by James Gilbert in 2016 to primarily make parts for modellers. Most subjects are SF in nature, though anything can be printed.
www.gibletscreations.co.uk

MODDLER

Moddler, 2325 Third St. Suite 224 San Francisco, CA 94107, USA
Started by special effects veteran John Vegher to produce 3D printed parts mainly for the FX industry, but can deal with any type of part.
www.moddler.com

MODELU

3 Tyny Sarn, Llanwnog, Powys, SY17 5JF, UK
Created in 2016, mainly to make life-capture of people to reproduce as figures for railway layouts, but includes many other subjects.
www.modelu3d.co.uk

PART2PRINT

Part2Print, U Krcske vodarny 1134/63, 140 00 Prague 4, Czech Republic
Created in 2003. Dealing with all types of 3D printing, including that for model making.
www.part2print.cz

SCULPTEO

Sculpteo, 10 Rue Auguste Perret,
94800 Villejuif, France
Sculpteo, 169, 11th Street, San Francisco, CA 94103, USA
Created by Eric Carreel and Clément Moreau in 2009. Can deal with large commercial orders or smaller personal work. Able to print using a wide variety of materials.
www.sculpteo.com

SHAPEWAYS

Shapeways, Long Island City, NY, USA
Shapeways, Eindhoven, The Netherlands
Currently the best-known name in 3D printer parts for the modeller. It works via 'communities' that supply designs and printing facilities. Using the online service, you can order pre-listed items to your required scale and quality, or upload your own designs to be printed.
www.shapeways.com

GENERAL SUPPLIES

AK INTERACTIVE

AK Interactive, S.L., Logroño, La Rioja, Spain
Started by Fernando Vallejo in 2009 to manufacture a very wide range of paints and weathering materials for modellers.
www.ak-interactive.com

ALCLAD II

Alclad II Lacquers
Created in 1991 in the UK, with US branch in 2001. Produces a wide range of airbrush-ready paints
www.alclad2.com

ARCKIT

MBM Building Systems Ltd. 17 Clyde Road, Ballsbridge, Dublin 4, Ireland
Architectural building system in kit form
uk.arckit.com

BARE-METAL FOIL

Bare Metal Foil Co,
PO Box 82, Farmington, MI 48332, USA
Producer of Bare-Metal Foil and other modelling accessories.
www.bare-metal.com

EMA and PLASTRUCT

Engineering Model Associates,
1020 S. Wallace Place, City of Industry,
CA 91748, USA
EMA Model Supplies Ltd.,
14 Beadman Street, London SE27 0DN, UK
EMA is the major producer of specialist model parts made initially for professional modellers of chemical plant models and the like. It can, however, be adapted to a wide range of modelling projects from the special effects industry to the hobbyist. For the last, the division 'Plastruct' was introduced to supply the smaller ranges of EMA parts.
www.ema-models.co.uk
www.plastruct.com

EVERGREEN

Evergreen Scale Models, Woodinville,
WA 98072, USA
Major manufacturer of styrene strips, shapes and accessories.
evergreenscalemodels.com

HUMBROL

Hornby Hobbies Ltd., Margate, Kent CT9 4JX, UK
The UK's major model paint manufacturer, founded in 1919 in Kingston upon Hull as the Humber Oil Company. It moved into modelling paints, then other accessories from the 1950s, and became Humbrol. In 1976 it was acquired by Borden, which also at the time owned Heller. In 2006 it was then acquired by Hornby.
www.humbrol.com

MIG-AMMO

Ammo of MIG Jimenez, S.L.,Avd. Villatuerta 31,
31132 Villatuerta, Navarra, Spain
Paints, washes, textures. Publishes the Weathering Magazine
www.migjimenez.com

MR HOBBY

GSI Creos Corporation, 2-3-1, Kudan Minami, Chiyoda-ku, Tokyo,102-0074, Japan
Major Japanese producer of hobby paints and accessories. The overall company was initially created in 1931 and became Gunze Sangyo in 1971. Changed to GSI Creos in 2001. Has used the Gunze Sangyo name in the past for both paints and model kits. Now uses the 'Mr Hobby' name for all hobby-related items.
www.mr-hobby.com

SLATERS PLASTIKARD

Slaters Plastikard Ltd., Old Rd, Darley Dale, Matlock
DE4 2ER, UK
Producers of wide range of plastic rod and strip, embossed sheet and railway items
www.slatersplastikard.com

TESTORS

The Testor Corporation, 440 Blackhawk Park Avenue, Rockford, IL 61104, USA
America's main model paint and accessory supplier, Testors also issued kits from companies it has acquired over the years, including Hawk and IMC. It also produced a series of UFO kits of its own. Most kit names and tooling have now been acquired by Round 2.
www.testors.com

TREEMENDUS

Ashton-on-Mersey, Sale, UK
Producer of many landscaping materials
www.treemendus-scenics.co.uk

VALLEJO

A.P. 337 – 08800 Vilanova i la Geltrú,
Barcelona, Spain
Created in 1965 by Amadeo Vallejo, in New Jersey, USA. Moved to Spain in 1969. Manufactures model paints, as well as paint for the fine-art market
acrylicosvallejo.com

WOODLAND SCENICS

PO Box 98, Linn Creek, Missouri 65052, USA
Major supplier for all scenic modelling materials
woodlandscenics.woodlandscenics.com

Distributors

Even with the demise of many model shops and hobby stores around the world, some do, fortunately, remain and many have moved over to online and mail order. It is impossible to list all distributors here – check your local Yellow Pages or try an online search – but below are some with which the author has had personal experience or that have been recommended.

CREATIVE MODELS

Creative Models Ltd, Units E3 & E4,, Ronald House, Fenton Way, Chatteris, Cambridege, PE16 6UP, UK
Importer and distributor of a wide variety of model-related items
www.creativemodels.co.uk

CULT TV MAN SHOP

CultTVMan, 248 E. Crogan St., Suite 202, Lawrenceville, GA 30046, USA
Proprietor: Steve Iverson. Very wide section of all types of science fiction, fantasy and factual space kits, plus accessories.
www.culttvmanshop.com

FEDERATION MODELS

P.O. Box 110796, Palm Bay, FL 32911-0796, USA
Supplier of many multi-material science fiction kits.
www.federationmodels.com

HANNANTS

H.G.Hannant Ltd, Harbour Road, Oulton Broad, Lowestoft, Suffolk NR32 3LR, UK
Proprietor: Nigel Hannant. The UK's largest model kit distributor, specialising primarily in aircraft and military. Sells many decals and accessory sets as well as its own paint ranges.
www.hannants.co.uk

HOBBY BOUNTIES

Hobby Bounties & Morgan Hobbycraft Centre, 865 Mountbatten Road #0291/92 , Katong Shopping Centre, Singapore 437844, Republic of Singapore
Proprietor: Peter Chiang. Large general hobby supply shop. Also owner of the FROG name.
www.hobbybounties.com

HOBBY LINK JAPAN

Hobby Link Japan Ltd., Tatebayashi-shi, Nishitakane-cho 43-6, Gunma 374-0075, Japan
Proprietor: Scott T. Hards. Excellent source for Japanese kits, tools and accessories. Offers mail order worldwide.
www.hlj.com

MEGAHOBBY

MegaHobby.com,110 Hurlock Avenue, Magnolia, NJ 08049, USA
Proprietor : Alan Bass. Created in 1999 as a distributor of all types of model items.
www.megahobby.com

MODELLING TOOLS (was LITTLECARS.COM)

Uncle Jacks, Lavendon Road, Olney, Bucks, MK46 4HH, UK
Proprietors: Paul and Jackie Fitzmaurice. Very wide range of modelling tools, paints and accessories. Available online and mail order, and has stands at many UK model shows.
www.modellingtools.co.uk

MODELSFORSALE.COM

Unit 3, Dean Close, Raunds, Northants, NN9 6BD, UK
Proprietor: Vince Brown. Specialist kit supplier, including paints. Mail order and some UK model shows.
www.modelsforsale.com

SPOTLIGHT HOBBIES (formerly HOBBY HEAVEN)

PO Box 141424, Grand Rapids MI 49514, USA
Proprietor: Tom Carter. Primarily model car kits. Also runs the Spotlight Hobbies Message Board.
www.spotlighthobbies.com

SQUADRON

Squadron, 1115 Crowley Drive, Carrollton, TX 75006-1313, USA
Originally created in 1968 in Detroit, Squadron is one of America's major model distribution companies, dealing with hobby products from around the world, including kits, accessories and tools. It uses the ENCORE MODELS name for its own kits.
www.squadron.com

STARSHIP MODELER

P.O.Box 549, Lake Villa, IL 60046, USA
Proprietor: John Lester. Mainly SF, plus paint, tools, books and magazines
www.starshipmodeler.com

TIMELESS HOBBIES (was COMET MINIATURES)

Timeless Hobbies Ltd., Unit 6, Leys Farm, Chelmsford Road, High Ongar, Essex, CM5 9NW, UK
Proprietor: Tony James. The UK's largest specialist science fiction model, toy and 'collectable' supplier.
www.timeless-hobbies.com

And finally, if even after all these you still cannot locate something you need, you may just have to resort to eBay: **www.ebay.com/www.ebay.co.uk**, or whatever is your own country domain.

OTHER USEFUL SITES

INTERNATIONAL PLASTIC MODELLERS' SOCIETY

Various International Plastic Modellers' Society websites from around the world. Most other countries follow a similar syntax, or use a search engine.
UK: **www.ipmsuk.org**
US: **www.ipmsusa.org**
Canada: **www.ipmscanada.com**
Australia: **www.ipmsaustralia.com.au**
New Zealand: **ipmsnz.hobbyvista.com**

SCALE MODEL NEWS

www.scalemodelnews.com

MILANO MODEL AND TOY MUSEUM

www.toys-n-cars.com

MODEL STORIES

modelstories.free.fr (en français)

THE AUTHOR'S WEBSITE

www.matirvine.com

Index